New York City
with Kids

NEW YORK
CITY
with Kids

2ND EDITION

ELLEN R. SHAPIRO

Published by Prima Publishing, Roseville, California. Member of the Crown Publishing Group, a division of Random House, Inc., New York.

PRIMA PUBLISHING and colophon are trademarks of Random House, Inc., registered with the United States Patent and Trademark Office.

ISBN: 0-7615-1598-4
ISSN on file

03 04 05 06 DD 10 9 8 7 6 5 4 3 2 1
Printed in the United States of America

Second Edition

Visit us online at www.primapublishing.com

Contents

Chapter 6 Dining   283

Chapter 7 Shopping   353

List of Maps

List of Quick Guides

List of Indexes

Abbreviations and Icons

BR	Brooklyn	MTE	Midtown East
BX	Bronx	MTW	Midtown West
CH	Chelsea	Q	Queens
CT	Chinatown	SH	SoHo
EV	East Village	SI	Staten Island
FD	Financial District	TBC	TriBeCa
GD	Garment District	TD	Theater District
GP	Gramercy Park/Flatiron	TS	Times Square
GV	Greenwich Village	UES	Upper East Side
LES	Lower East Side	US	Union Square
LI	Little Italy	UWS	Upper West Side
MT	Midtown	WV	West Village

City Fact

Helpful Hint

Money-Saving Tip

Learning Tip

Insider's Tip

For Steven,
who always sits beside me

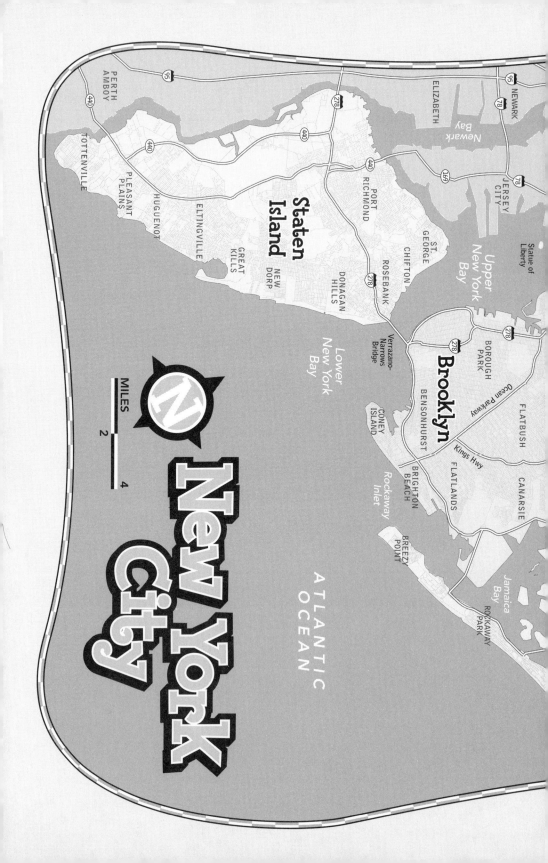

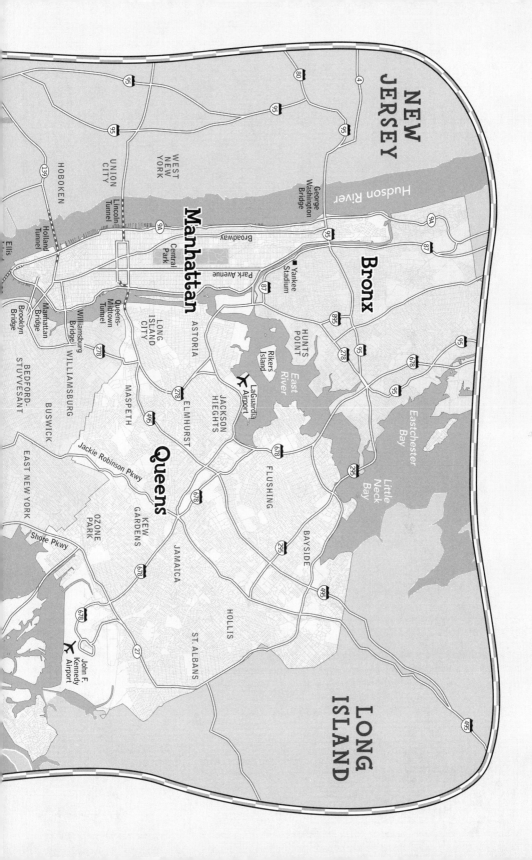

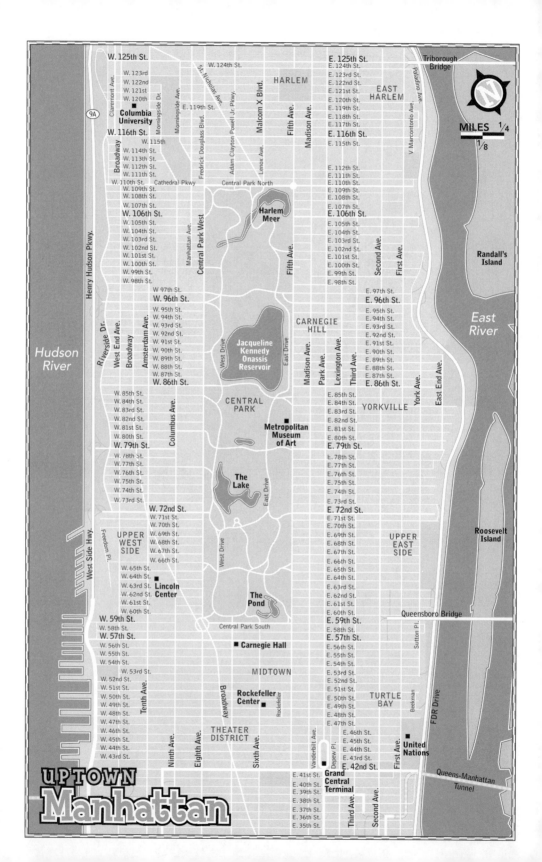

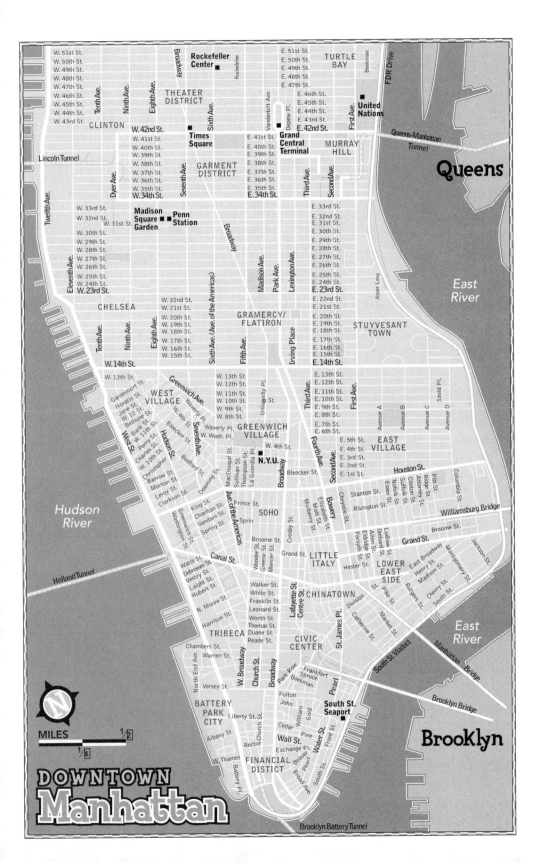

Acknowledgments

New Yorkers can be the most generous people in the world, and I was the grateful beneficiary of that generosity when I researched and wrote the first edition of this book. In creating this second edition, I witnessed yet another avalanche of generosity. I'd like to thank all the people who were so giving of their time, expertise, and support:

Liz Tober, for her insightful teenage advice into shopping and dining. The many hotel reservationists and front-desk clerks who took time out from selling rooms (and making money) to help me when I needed a fact or crucial hotel tidbit. The hotel managers (especially Victoria Barr and Marcel Fohlinger), for the hours spent taking me around to see every aspect of their hotels' facilities and answering my endless stream of questions—all on short notice. The many helpful museum employees and public-relations representatives, especially Mary Record, Helen Lazzaro, Sari Becker, Ned Kulakowski, Curtis Stallworth, and Michael Norris. Professor Richard Sugarman, for his sense of humor and continued moral support. Everyone, friends and strangers, who contributed advice for the Insider Tips. The team at Prima, especially Jamie Miller and Tara Joffe, for having the vision to turn my manuscript into this beautiful, soon-to-be new bestseller. Few people would be up to the task of keeping current on all that is going on in the ever-changing city of New York, but Paige Marino, my fact-checker extraordinaire, relentlessly pursued the latest and most accurate information right up until the last second before we went to press. Robert and Mazi, the art geniuses, for their insight on museums and knowledge of galleries and peaceful public spaces. Andrew and Addie for their excellent strategies for crowd-avoidance with kids. My neighbors Ken and Jane for always having the answer. My cousin Jane, for her moral support and watchful eye regarding city shopping trends and fashion. My mother, Sue, for her clippings, brochure collecting, and generous sharing of her excellent and extensive early childhood insights. My brother Jonathan, because he's an idea guy. My father, Jack, and brother, Michael, for their love and low-key support. My mother-in-law, Penny, for sharing her city wisdom. Momo, our bulldog, for snuggling with me when I needed a break.

And most of all, to my husband and editorial assistant, Steven Shaw, for his critical eye and his never-ending support and for putting up with me when I spin myself into a whirling dervish of stress. Truly, I could not do it without you, nor would I ever want to.

Introduction

This is the best time in history to be a kid in New York City. Today's New York is a shining, clean, safe metropolis and one of the most family-friendly cities on the planet. The Gotham of the twenty-first century is eminently walkable, loaded with history, culturally enriching, endlessly diverse, and teeming with arts, activities, entertainment, and food for every taste and budget. And New Yorkers are the nicest people on Earth, a secret that was well kept for ages but that became public knowledge in the aftermath of the September 11 tragedy.

This book will help you and your family get the most out of New York. My goal in writing was to make it the clearest, most comprehensive, and most current guide to New York City for families with children in every age group. I built this book from the ground up, relying only on up-to-the-minute sources, interviews with dozens of parents and children, and thousands of hours of research—not to mention a lifetime of living in and around New York City. Paying special attention to the needs of all kinds of children—from toddlers to teens, as well as the adults who travel with them—I've included hundreds of activities, shops, restaurants, hotels, events, and resources for children of all ages. In revising the manuscript for this second edition, I've added scores of new entries, and even whole sections. I spent months checking and rechecking, updating and correcting, in order to keep the content of this book on the cutting edge.

Before we start our journey, let's take a look at New York City, present, past, future, and throughout the year.

New York City Today: The Greatest Show on Earth

In four centuries, there has never been a better time to visit New York. The city is in the midst of its greatest revitalization in history, tourism is on the rise, construction is growing (up, of course!), the indomitable spirit of New Yorkers can be felt everywhere, and every nook and cranny of the City is blossoming as a result.

- By far the most significant news for vacationing families is New York's amazingly quick recovery from the September 11 tragedy. Not only has the city picked up the pieces and kept its spirits high, but it has also gone ahead and moved forward with a never-before-seen degree of pride, patriotism, and enthusiasm. Even in the midst of a national economic slowdown, New York feels like a boomtown.

- New York's major drop in crime became common knowledge during the 1990s. Safety in New York City has been improving by leaps and bounds over the past decade, and things continue to get better. All major categories of crime—including murder, rape, robbery, and auto theft—are at their lowest points in three decades, and New York is now by far the safest large city in America.

- Moving into the twenty-first century, New York City remains the national capital of the arts, banking, publishing, finance, accounting, advertising, fashion, and law. It's home to the United Nations, and many major overseas corporations choose New York as their base of U.S. operations. More Fortune 1000 companies are headquartered in New York than anywhere else in the country.

@ Most of the action happens on a tiny island, Manhattan, which is only 22.7 miles square—probably smaller than your hometown. The total area of all five boroughs of New York City (Manhattan, Brooklyn, Queens, the Bronx, and Staten Island) is just 301 square miles. Yet the City has 6,374.6 miles of streets and had nearly 36.7 million tourists from across the country and around the globe visited last year. They spent more than $21 billion during their stays.

@ The revitalization of Times Square and the Theater District continues on a grand scale with new office buildings, hotels, shops, and the restoration of the historic Biltmore Theater (212-399-3000, www.manhattantheatreclub.org), which was closed for fourteen years and is scheduled to reopen for the 2002–2003 Broadway season.

@ With 714 miles of track, 469 stations, and 6,089 subway cars, New York's subway system is the world's largest. The subways run twenty-four hours a day and carry 1.2 billion passengers a year, while the City's public bus system consists of 300 routes and carries 600 million people a year (by far the most in the nation) on 4,200 buses.

@ The Port Authority of New York and New Jersey is investing almost $2.7 billion to provide direct rail connections at both John F. Kennedy and Newark International Airports. AirTrain Newark began operation in October 2001, and has averaged more than 1,800 passengers a day—greatly exceeding expectations. AirTrain JFK is expected to begin service to and from the Howard Beach AirTrain Terminal late 2002/early 2003, followed by the opening of Jamaica AirTrain service by June, 2003.

@ The checkered cab-like catamaran shuttle boats by New York Water Taxi (212-742-1969, www.newyorkwatertaxi .com), which launched its initial service during the summer of 2002, promises to be a new favorite connecting neighbor-hoods, parks, and cultural attractions along the West Side, Lower Manhattan, and Downtown Brooklyn waterfronts.

❧ New York is sporting two new, minor-league baseball teams: The Staten Island Yankees (718-720-9200, www.siyanks.com), playing in a new stadium that seats 6,886 and boasts a stunning view of the Manhattan skyline and the Statue of Liberty; and the New York Mets-affiliated Brooklyn Cyclones (718-449-8497, www.brooklyncyclones.net), playing in a state-of-the-art facility at historic Coney Island.

❧ The American Folk Art Museum (45 W. 53rd St. at Sixth Avenue, 212/265-1040, www.folkartmuseum.org) cele-brated the opening of an all new $18-million structure de-signed by award-winning New York architects Tod Williams and Billy Tsien and Associates in December 2001. Encompassing a 30,000-square-foot exhibit floor, featuring enhanced facilities and four times the former exhibition space, the stunning new structure is the first entirely new museum building in New York since 1966. The building joins neighbors the Museum of Modern Art, the American Craft Museum, and the New York Public Library's Donnell Library Center on the 53rd Street block between Fifth and Sixth Avenues.

❧ In late 2002, The Skyscraper Museum (212-968-1961, www.skyscraper.org) opened its permanent home at the southern tip of Battery Park City. The museum delves into the city's architectural history, commemorates those who created it, and celebrates the world's most "vertical" skyline.

❧ With immigrants continuing to pour in, the City boasts a plethora of ethnic neighborhoods, plus more than 100 eth-nic newspapers, including 25 catering to the Russian community alone. The languages spoken in the streets and on the subways range from Spanish, Arabic, Urdu, and Korean to Chinese, Hindi, Hebrew, and Russian.

@ A major boost to the City's image, economy, and celebrity status, the film industry plays an important role in the New York economy. Some sixty to ninety productions are filmed daily, with a total of 22,851 aggregate shooting days. Just walk around the City any day of the week, and you're bound to bump into a film crew, walk onto a set, or spy a star.

@ In cultural terms, you can't do better than 150 museums, thirty-eight Broadway playhouses, scores of off-Broadway and off-off-Broadway productions, more galleries than museums, and thousands of concerts, performances, and special events—and that's just the beginning.

Timeline of New York City History

New York is the economic capital of the world today, but that's nothing new. For almost as long as European settlers have been in North America, New York has been the center of the action.

9000 B.C.–A.D. 1524: The area now known as New York City was occupied by Native Americans.

1524: Giovanni da Verrazano, a Florentine explorer hired by the French to chart the northeastern coast of North America, was the first European to visit New York.

1609: English explorer Henry Hudson rediscovered New York on a mission to find the Northwest Passage. He claimed the area for his employer, the Dutch East India Company. When Hudson reported back on the beauty of Manhattan and its ample natural treasures (furs, birds, and fruits), New York made an indelible impression on Europe.

1626: The area was established as a Dutch fur-trading post, eventually called New Amsterdam. Peter Minuit, the director of the Dutch East India Company, purchased the island from local tribes for goods worth sixty guilders (about $24, though some historians dispute this account).

1653: New Amsterdam became a city with a population of 800.

1664: New Amsterdam became the British colony of New York. Under British rule, Manhattan (then known as New York) gained prominence because of the shipping industry— it had an excellent natural harbor, extensive riverfront property for building piers, and easy access to the open ocean. The entire city occupied only the area that today runs from Wall Street (named because it was the site of a wall built to protect against invasion) to the southern tip of Manhattan.

1775: The first bloodshed in the struggle for independence occurred in New York, when the Sons of Liberty, a local patriotic group, clashed with British soldiers. One of the Sons of Liberty was killed, and several were wounded.

1783: The British surrendered to the revolutionary colonists. George Washington said farewell to his generals in his historic speech at Fraunces Tavern (which you can still visit today).

1789: George Washington was sworn in as president of the United States of America on the balcony of Federal Hall on Wall Street. New York's population was 33,000. New York remained the nation's capital until 1790.

1792: The stock exchange was founded.

1811: John Randel Jr., an engineer, headed up a commission that mapped out all the streets from Houston Street to 155th Street, before most of them were even built. With minor modifications (like the addition of Central Park), this is the rectilinear grid we see in New York today. Below

Houston Street, the streets still run on the old meandering Dutch plan, which is why it's so hard to find your way around down there!

1820: New York's population grew to 250,000.

1825: The Erie Canal opened, connecting New York City, via Albany, with Buffalo, the Great Lakes, and the Western territories, and guaranteed New York's commercial preeminence for years to come.

1863: During the Civil War, Irish immigrants began the "draft riots," in response to a provision that allowed wealthy men to pay $300 to avoid military service. The rioters soon turned against the City's black citizens, who they blamed for the war and also for taking many jobs. More than ten black men were lynched in the streets, and a black orphanage was burned to the ground.

1870: The American Museum of Natural History was founded.

1880: New York's population reached 1.1 million. The Metropolitan Museum of Art opened.

1883: The Brooklyn Bridge was completed.

1892: The Ellis Island Immigration station first started registering immigrants on Friday, 1 January 1892. Famous immigrants to pass through its doors included Bob Hope, Marcus Garvey, Irving Berlin, and the von Trapp family.

1898: The five boroughs—Manhattan, Queens, the Bronx, Brooklyn, and Staten Island—voted to become incorporated into the entity of Greater New York.

1912: Scheduled to dock in New York at the end of her maiden voyage, the *Titanic* instead met with the tragedy that prevented her from ever reaching the City's shores. Of the 2,200 passengers aboard the ship, 675 were rescued by a

Cunard liner, which delivered the passengers to the very same dock at which the *Titanic* was supposed to arrive.

1923: Babe Ruth hit his first home run in Yankee Stadium in the first game ever played there.

1930: The population reached seven million, thanks in large part to immigration.

1939: The World's Fair was held in Flushing Meadows, Queens.

1969: The Jets and the Mets won the Superbowl and the World Series, respectively.

1970s: After years of mismanagement, New York City plunged into financial crisis.

1973: The World Trade Center opened.

1993: Rudolph Giuliani was elected mayor. He is widely credited with being the impetus for New York's current economic boom and improved public safety.

2001: The World Trade Towers, a symbol of New York and America, were destroyed in a terrorist attack. New Yorkers, with the support of friends across the country and around the globe, held their heads high in the face of adversity and continue to rebuild their city with grace and courage.

Looking Forward

The City That Never Sleeps is also the city that never rests on its laurels. Never still or silent, the City is always changing and evolving. New York is looking ahead with grand ambition. From expanding and updating the classics, like the Museum of Modern Art and Radio City Music Hall, to revitalizing long-neglected neighborhoods, like Harlem, the City's growth and booming economy promise to preserve New York's position as a world leader among cities.

@ New York's largest subway expansion in recent history is underway. The Metropolitan Transportation Authority's (www.mta.nyc.ny.us) five-year, $17.2-billion plan includes new trains, buses and two new subway lines, including a rail link to LaGuardia Airport.

@ The first new construction begins in Lower Manhattan since September 11. The Museum of Jewish Heritage: A Living Memorial to the Holocaust is expanding to triple its space (to be completed in fall, 2003). The new 70,000-square-foot East Wing will include a theater and performance space, a memorial garden, a family history center, additional gallery space, a library and resource center, and a café.

@ The Guggenheim Foundation (a Frank Gehry-designed project) will create a new architectural landmark on Piers 9, 11, 13, and 14, near the South Street Seaport. The new museum is expected to create more than 2,500 jobs, attract two to three million visitors per year, and generate an additional $280 million in annual economic activity.

@ Randall's Island Pavilion is the first major new live stage venue to be built in New York City in more than thirty years. It is scheduled to open in May of 2003, and the plans for this 19,200 seat facility include forty to fifty annual concerts, festivals, and events throughout the summer.

@ A new Jewish Children's Museum (718-467-0600, www .jcmonline.org) in Crown Heights, Brooklyn, is scheduled for completion in 2003. The interactive, hands-on exhibits aim to teach children of all races and ethnicities about Jewish history, heritage, and culture.

@ Sharing the 168th Street Armory with one of the great indoor tracks in the country, The National Track and Field Hall of Fame (212-923-1803, trackhall.com) celebrates great athletes like Jesse Owens, Jim Ryun, and Florence Griffith-Joyner. The museum, with three floors of exhibits and an interactive learning center, is scheduled to open in early 2003.

🕑 Harlem, a thriving cultural center during the 1920s and 1930s, is now on the up and up. New shopping centers and suburban-sized grocery stores have been built and even more is underway, along with scheduled face-lifts for famous favorites like the Apollo Theater, Minton's Playhouse, the Art Deco Lenox Lounge, and the Renaissance Ballroom. Residents are sprucing up many of the beautiful, aging brownstones that line the streets.

Note: Every effort has been made to ensure that the information in this book is current and accurate. New York is a rapidly changing city, however, especially in the aftermath of September 11. Please, before you set out to visit an attraction, use public transportation, or commit your valuable time in any way, take the simple step of making a phone call to confirm your data.

I welcome your comments, corrections, and thoughts. Feel free to e-mail me at ellen@nycwithkids.com and visit the Web site at www.nycwithkids.com.

CHAPTER 1

Planning the Journey

When to Go

Everybody has a favorite time of year in New York, but it's highly debatable whether there's a best time to go. If you asked me, I'd say it depends primarily on your priorities.

- ℮ I'm very sensitive to the weather, which can be a major concern when traveling with small children. My personal favorite seasons in New York are spring and fall, when it's delightfully cool but sunny, and your choice of activities is virtually unlimited. Then again, New York has a relatively moderate, temperate climate year-round. Even the worst days of summer and winter are quite bearable compared with equatorial and arctic extremes.

- ℮ If you want to enjoy the outdoors, winter may not be your best bet; at the same time, winter is the best season for sales, to see the Christmas windows, and to take in all of New York's holiday spectacles. There's nothing like Christmas or New Year's in New York, but these are also the most expensive times to be in the City.

@ If you're looking to avoid the crowds, there's no better time than summer, when the theaters, museums, and restaurants are emptiest (though it's all relative—most out-of-towners, no matter what time of year they visit, would be astonished to hear locals remark that "the City is so empty"). Summer is also great for taking advantage of New York's multitude of free outdoor concerts, performances, and activities at the parks and museums. Your chance of getting a great discounted package air-and-hotel deal is typically best in summer.

@ If you have special interests, check the calendar of events on the following pages, research your desired activities and events (see chapter 5), and plan your trip accordingly.

The Year in New York City

Here's a look at the major recurring events that happen year-in, year-out in New York City. Tens of thousands of other activities and events are going on all the time there (see chapter 5), but most don't adhere to such a strict calendar—you'll have to re-search them close to the time you'll be visiting. Not all of the events listed here are specifically for kids, though many are. This is more to give you an idea of the rhythm of the City, to help you plan as well as possible, and to think about your trip.

January

The big post-holiday sales get going at the major department stores and also at many smaller shops.

The ten-day New York National Boat Show at the Javits Center exhibits the latest in boats, related equipment, and sea-worthy toys (212-216-2000).

Leading dealers in the field of so-called visionary art—also sometimes called naïve art or art of the self-taught—exhibit their wares at the Outsider Art Fair, at the Puck Building in SoHo (212-777-5218).

February

The New York Yankees Fan Festival celebrates both the team and the fans. Meet team players, past and present, test your swing, or participate in a memorabilia auction (718-293-4300).

Chinese New Year celebrations, which are spread over the course of two weeks, include lots of noisy fireworks, banquets, and the historic paper-dragon dance that winds through Chinatown (212-484-1222).

During the Westminster Kennel Club Dog Show, as many as 3,000 dogs strut their stuff at the annual event at Madison Square Garden (800-455-3647). It is the second-longest-running animal event in the country (after the Kentucky Derby).

14 February: The Empire State Building is the site of the Valentine's Day Marriage Marathon, when couples marry on the observation deck (212-736-3100).

The Annual Empire State Building Run-Up is an invitational event wherein 150 runners run, push, scramble, and wheeze up the 1,576 stairs to the eighty-sixth-floor observation deck.

March

The St. Patrick's Day parade is one of the longest running (and recently most controversial) events in New York City. The parade starts at 11:30 A.M. at 44th Street, goes up Fifth Avenue, and turns on 86th Street for the finish.

The International Asian Art Fair is held, with dealers from around the world showing art and artifacts from the Middle East, Southeast Asia, and the Far East (212-642-8572).

Late March–Early April

The Ringling Bros. and Barnum & Bailey Circus arrives in New York each spring, and, upon its arrival, the animals are walked (at about midnight) from Penn Station to Madison Square Garden, where the circus takes place.

Favorite Spring Activities and Attractions

1. Going to a Yankees or Mets baseball game (p. 273)

2. Walking over the Brooklyn Bridge (p. 172)

3. Watching the arrival of the Ringling Bros. circus animals (p. 264)

4. Renting and rowing a boat in Central Park (p. 245)

5. Taking a Circle Line cruise around Manhattan (p. 65)

6. Sitting at an outdoor café (ch. 6)

7. Visiting the Bronx and Brooklyn botanical gardens (pp. 236, 240)

8. Going to the Central Park Easter Egg Hunt (p. 241)

9. Watching the St. Patrick's Day parade (p. 4)

10. Stopping by Macy's Flower Show at Rockefeller Center (pp. 5, 179)

The Triple Pier Expo (Piers 88, 90, and 92) is a big antique event, but if you miss it in the spring, there's a showing in November as well (212-255-0020).

April

The Macy's Flower Show takes place each year in Rockefeller Center the week before Easter.

The Easter Parade goes up Fifth Avenue and ends at St. Patrick's Cathedral, at 51st Street and Fifth Avenue.

Antiquarian Book Fair is held at the Seventh Regiment Armory (featuring first editions, rare volumes, manuscripts, autographs, letters, atlases, drawings, prints, and maps, with prices ranging from low double digits well into five digits and beyond).

*Pausing for the
National Anthem
at Yankee Stadium*

The Major League
baseball season kicks
off (running through
September or October,
if we're lucky): New York
Yankees in the Bronx (718-293-6000); New York Mets at Shea
Stadium in Queens (718-507-8499).

During the first week of April, approximately 7,500 pipers
and drummers descend en masse on Fifth Avenue to celebrate
National Tartan Day. ScottishPower Tunes of Glory (917-305-
1200, ext. 232; www.pipefest.com) will build on the success of
the Millennium Piping Festival, where 8,500 pipers and drummers from all over the world visited Edinburgh, Scotland, to
help raise funds for people with cancer (donations are made to
Marie Curie Cancer Care and Gilda's Club).

May

The Cherry Blossom Festival blooms at the Brooklyn Botanic
Garden (718-623-7200).

Bike New York is the The Great Five Borough Bike Tour, a
42-mile ride that begins in Battery Park and ends with a ride
across the Verrazano-Narrows Bridge (212-932-0778).

The International Fine Art Fair includes works from the
Renaissance to the twentieth century.

Congregation Shearith Israel (the Spanish and Portuguese Synagogue, the oldest congregation in America) sponsors a Sephardic Fair (212-873-0300).

Tap Dance Extravaganza events are held around Manhattan (718-597-4613).

Memorial Day Weekend
(and following three weekends)
Washington Square Outdoor Art Exhibit is an arts-and-crafts fair with hundreds of exhibitors in and around the park (212-982-6255).

In May 2002, the first annual Tribeca Film Festival (212-941-3977, www.tribecafilm.com), founded by Robert De Niro and Jane Rosenthal, celebrated the spirit of New York City and the international independent film community in lower Manhattan. The Festival showcases world premiere and independent films and has a special family-friendly Children's Film program.

June

The Texaco New York Jazz Festival (212-219-3006) sponsors 350 performances of classic, acid, Latin, and avant-garde jazz at clubs and public spaces around town.

Lesbian and Gay Pride Week features the world's biggest annual gay pride parade, a film festival, and countless other events.

National Puerto Rican Day Parade is the largest of its kind in the United States.

JVC Jazz Festival New York is a huge jazz event featuring jazz greats and unknowns all around town.

Late June–Early July
The Washington Square Music Festival features free outdoor concerts on Tuesday evenings with classical, jazz, and big-band sounds (212-252-3621).

Favorite Summer Activities and Attractions

1. Riding the carousel in Central Park (p. 244)

2. Watching the Fourth of July fireworks on the East River (p. 9)

3. Strolling through, shopping, browsing, and snacking at neighborhood street fairs (ch. 4–7)

4. Stopping for ice cream at Serendipity or the Chinatown Ice Cream Factory (pp. 320, 322)

5. Going to free summer concerts in Central Park (p. 246)

6. Strolling along the boardwalk, visiting the beach, and riding on the Ferris wheel at Coney Island (and don't miss a hot dog from Nathan's and a visit to Philip's Candy next door) (p. 88)

7. August sales—shopping at the big department stores (and the small stores, too) (ch. 7)

8. Checking out the tall ships during Fleet Week (leading up to the Fourth of July) (p. 9)

9. Taking in free Monday night movies in Bryant Park (p. 8)

10. Attending the U.S. Open tennis tournament (p. 276)

June–August

Midsummer Night Swing, a fabulous outdoor dance event at Lincoln Center's Fountain Plaza, offers open dance and nightly lessons (212-875-5766).

Bryant Park Film Festival. Monday night movies in Bryant Park are a huge social scene and happening event—and there are free, mostly classic, movies.

Central Park SummerStage features free events on weekday evenings and blues, Latin, pop, African, country, dance performances, opera, and readings on weekends (212-360-2777).

Shakespeare in the Park (212-539-8500; 212-539-8750 seasonal phone at the Delacorte Theater), sponsored by the Joseph Papp Public Theater at Central Park's Delacorte Theater, tackles the Bard and other classics, often with a star performer or two from the big or small screen.

The New York Philharmonic gives free concerts around the City's parks (212-875-5656).

Celebrate Brooklyn features pop, jazz, rock, classical, klezmer, African, Latin, and Caribbean music and theatrical performances, at the band shell in Prospect Park in Brooklyn (718-855-7882). And it's all free.

Early July–Mid-August

The Museum of Modern Art. Classical music, performed by students of the Julliard School, is presented in the Summergarden on Friday and Saturday evenings (212-708-9400).

July

Independence Day

Great Fourth of July Festival's downtown festivities include live entertainment, arts and crafts, and a parade from Bowling Green to City Hall.

South Street Seaport Fourth of July festival.

East River Fireworks Fourth of July fireworks. The best you're likely to see—ever!

Tall Ships on the Hudson River, Fourth of July

Vantage points are best from 14th to 41st Streets along the FDR Drive (which is closed to cars for the event) and the Brooklyn Heights Promenade.

Lincoln Center Festival features classical and contemporary music concerts, dance, stageworks, and non-Western arts.

August

Along with January, this is the big time for clearance sales in New York City. Clothing, electronics, and everything else get marked down all over town.

Lincoln Center Out-of-Doors (212-875-5108) is a series of music, dance, and family-oriented events lasting almost the entire month.

Harlem Week is the world's largest African American and Hispanic festival, where events include concerts, gospel performances, the Black Film Festival, and Taste of Harlem Food Festival (212-862-7200).

Mostly Mozart Music festival at Lincoln Center includes free afternoon concerts, and evening concerts for a fee (212-721-6500).

Brooklyn County Fair is just like fairs in the country.

Late August–Early September
U.S. Open Tennis Tournament is held at Flushing Meadows-Corona Park in Queens (800-524-8440).

Labor Day Weekend
West Indian American Day Parade is New York's largest parade (held in Brooklyn) and only one of the many events that occur on this day. Festivities begin Friday night with salsa, reggae, and calypso music at the Brooklyn Museum and end Monday afternoon with a huge parade—floats, costumed dancers, stilt walkers—nothing is missing. And don't forget about the West Indian food and music (212-484-1222).

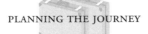
September

Feast of San Gennaro honors the patron saint of Naples with this fabulously colorful event on Mulberry Street in New York's Little Italy.

Broadway on Broadway is a free two-hour outdoor concert in Times Square.

New York Is Book Country is an event held along Fifth Avenue, between 48th and 57th Streets, during which publishers set up shop so you can see their upcoming wares, meet authors, play games, and sometimes even get free stuff (646-557-6626).

Late September–Early October

The New York Film Festival is the City's most prestigious annual film event (212-875-5610).

October

The International Fine Art and Antique Dealers Show is one of the world's finest shows (212-642-8572).

Greenwich Village Halloween Parade is a must-do event, at least once (www.halloween-nyc.com).

October–April

New York Rangers hockey is at home at Madison Square Garden.

New York Knicks basketball is at home at Madison Square Garden.

November

The New York City Marathon is a citywide event for runners and spectators alike that draws competitors from all over the world. Participants run through all five boroughs before finishing in Central Park.

Veteran's Day Parade heads down Fifth Avenue to the United War Veterans Council of New York County.

Favorite Autumn Activities and Attractions

1. Cheering the New York City Marathon (first Sunday of November) (p. 11)

2. Viewing the Thanksgiving Day Parade (p. 12)

3. Checking out the changing leaves in Central Park from the top of the Empire State Building (p. 174)

4. Going to Old Home Day at Historic Richmond Town (third Sunday in October, on Staten Island)

5. Observing the Halloween Parade in Greenwich Village (p. 11)

6. Taking a trip to the Union Square Greenmarket (to buy fresh cider, apples, and donuts) (p. 344)

7. Seeing the new fall fashions at the City's trendiest boutiques (ch. 7)

8. Checking out the San Gennaro Festival in Little Italy (September) (p. 84)

9. Going to KidAround Downtown (special programs for kids ages 3 to 12)

10. Celebrating at the New York Is Book Country Fair (September) (p. 11)

Thanksgiving Day

The Macy's Thanksgiving Day Parade is a favorite New York event (as is now the "balloon stroll" the night before, where city folk gather to watch the balloons being inflated before the big event). Gigantic balloons coast down Central Park West, starting at 77th Street and finishing at Macy's at Herald Square.

November–January

The Radio City Christmas Spectacular features the fabulous Rockettes at home at Radio City Music Hall (212-247-4777).

Thanksgiving Weekend Through New Year

Christmas windows are a New York City tradition. The best decorations are usually seen at:

- Saks Fifth Avenue (611 Fifth Ave. at 49th St.)
- Lord & Taylor (424 Fifth Ave. at 38th St.)
- Bloomingdale's (Lexington Ave. at 59th St.)
- FAO Schwarz (767 Fifth Ave. at 58th St.)
- Barneys (660 Madison Ave., between 60th and 61st Sts.)
- Macy's (Broadway at 34th St.)

It's best to start at 58th Street and stroll down Fifth Avenue until you hit Saks (stopping at Rockefeller Center, St. Patrick's Cathedral, etc.), stroll up the other side of Fifth to 57th, and then walk over to Madison to see Barney's windows and the other shops along Madison Avenue (like the Polo stores at 72nd St.). Macy's requires a special detour further downtown.

December

Kwanzaa Fest is the world's largest celebration of African American culture and includes entertainers, cultural exhibits, and attractions for children (718-585-3530).

Handel's *Messiah* usually begins at 7:30 P.M., at the Cathedral of St. John

Radio City Music Hall

Favorite Winter Activities and Attractions

1. Ice-skating in Rockefeller Center (p. 179)

2. Viewing the Christmas windows along Fifth Avenue (p. 13)

3. Watching the Radio City Christmas Spectacular Show (p. 261)

4. Attending *The Nutcracker* ballet at Lincoln Center (p. 261)

5. Drinking hot chocolate at Serendipity (p. 322)

6. Visiting the Living Nativity at St. Stephen's Church and the giant Menorah lighting (p. 15)

7. Exploring Grand Central Station, indoors, where it's warm (p. 176)

8. Seeing the Christmas tree at Rockefeller Center (p. 179)

9. Going to a hockey or basketball game at Madison Square Garden (pp. 274–275)

10. Buying (and eating) roasted chestnuts, hot pretzels, and honey-roasted peanuts from street vendors

the Divine (212-316-7540; 212-662-2133), and runs for several performances; call for dates.

Midnight Mass on Christmas Eve, Cathedral of St. John the Divine, has music for choir, brass, and organ; a sermon; and candle lighting. The service usually begins at 10:30 P.M.; call for details (212-662-2133).

Midnight Mass is also held on Christmas Eve at St. Patrick's Cathedral; plan far in advance because you will need to mail in for tickets (212-753-2261).

The giant Chanukah Menorah lighting is at Fifth Avenue and 59th Street.

The Rockefeller Center Christmas tree, one of the tallest in the country, makes headlines annually when it is first lit—it's an event that draws thousands of spectators each year.

New Year's Eve
The ball drops in Times Square.

Midnight Run is a five-mile fun run sponsored by the New York Road Runners Club (212-860-4455; www.nyrrc.org).

Fireworks.

And at least a hundred other New Year's Eve events.

New York Weather

The following table shows 70-year average temperature and precipitation ranges for New York City.

Month	Low (°F)	High (°F)	Rain (in.)	Snow (in.)
January	26	38	3.11	7
February	26	42	3.08	8
March	38	51	4.1	5
April	40	65	3.76	1
May	49	74	3.46	0
June	59	82	3.15	0
July	67	84	3.67	0
August	66	84	4.32	0
September	56	79	3.48	0
October	46	70	3.24	0
November	37	48	3.77	1
December	30	46	3.68	5

Source: The Weather Channel (www.weather.com)

Research and Resources

Throughout this book, in the relevant chapters, I've listed Web sites, newspapers, magazines, and specialty publications that will help you plan specific activities and events, such as sports, arts, shopping, and transportation. In addition, here are some general resources that can help you plan your trip and learn a little bit about New York before you visit:

- New York City has three major newspapers: *The New York Times* (www.nytimes.com), *New York Post* (www.nypost .com), and *New York Daily News* (www.nydailynews.com). Of these, the *Times* is the best for activity and event listings. In particular, the Friday *New York Times* "Weekend" section has extensive arts and entertainment listings, as well as a special "Family Fare" section listing kid-appropriate events. The *Post* and *News*, although not as valuable for trip planning, are excellent introductions to the local attitudes and issues of New York City, as is the *New York Observer* (www.observer.com).

- Two free newspapers, the *Village Voice* (www.villagevoice .com) and *New York Press* (www.nypress.com), also offer extensive local event listings as well as in-your-face New York opinions. They are available on many street corners, from clearly marked dispensers.

- *New York Magazine* (www.nymetro.com) and *Time Out New York* (www.timeoutny.com) are the best weekly magazines for local listings, although in my opinion, *Time Out* is slightly better. Both are often available in Barnes & Noble and Borders bookstores across the country. *Where Magazine* (www.wheremagazine.com) also has excellent listings, and you'll probably find a free copy waiting in your hotel room.

The New Yorker magazine has less comprehensive listings but is the most literary of the local weeklies. If you have a teen who's interested in reading what some of New York's most articulate voices have to say about a variety of issues, you should grab a copy.

- Families may want to take a look at some of the local publications geared toward New Yorkers with kids: *New York Family* (www.parenthoodweb.com), *Big Apple Parent* (www .parentsknow.com), and *ParentGuide* (www.parentguide news.com).

- On the Web, the most extensive general New York information comes from www.newyork.citysearch.com, which lists all manner of events, shops, theaters, restaurants, and more. The www.nytoday.com site, which is an outgrowth of *The New York Times*, also has good information, especially on restaurants.

- Two other important Web sites are those of the New York City's official tourism marketing agency, NYC & Company (www.nycvisit.com), and the New York City Government (www.ci.nyc.ny.us). Both contain a wealth of information— practical and educational—for visitors. Or, if you prefer, you can stop by or call New York City's official Visitor Information Center at 810 Seventh Avenue (at 53rd Street), 212-397-8222.

- For local television and radio news, check out NY1 News (www.ny1.com, Channel 1 on most New York City cable TV systems) and 1010 WINS AM radio (www.1010wins .com).

- The above resources could keep you busy for months, but if you have special interests, you can also pursue thousands of New York City Web sites listed online at Yahoo.com.

Top Ten NYC Titles for Early Readers

1. *Amy Elizabeth Explores Bloomingdale's*, by E. L. Konigsburg

2. *Tar Beach*, by Faith Ringgold

3. *Abuela*, by Arthur Dorros

4. *Nothing Ever Happens on 90th Street*, by Roni Schotter

5. *Music Over Manhattan*, by Mark Karlins

6. *Journey to Ellis Island*, by Carol Bierman

7. *The Brooklyn Bridge*, by Elizabeth Mann

8. *The Little Red Lighthouse and the Great Gray Bridge*, by Hildegarde H. Swift, illustrated by Lynd Ward

9. *The Adventures of Taxi Dog*, by Debra Barracca (see also *Maxi, The Star* and *Maxi, The Hero*)

10. *Eloise*, by Kay Thompson

And a few extra for good measure . . .

You Can't Take a Balloon into the Metropolitan Museum, by Jacquiline Preiss Weitzman and Robin Preiss Glasser

The House on 88th Street, by Bernard Waber

My New York, by Kathy Jakobson

Next Stop, Grand Central, by Maira Kalman

Getting the Best Deals

To get good deals for New York City, you've got to be savvy. Following is a list of hotel and airline discounters (many of whom discount both). But remember, just because you get an air or

Fountains at the Metropolitan Museum of Art

hotel quote from a Web site or a discounter, it doesn't mean it's the best price going, so be sure to learn your prices and shop around.

Airline Ticket Discounters

Travelocity
www.travelocity.com
Best for airline discounts, but you can book hotels here, too.

Microsoft Expedia
www.expedia.com
Air and hotel discounts.

Cheap Tickets
800-377-1000
www.cheaptickets.com

Fly Cheap
800-FLY-CHEAP
www.flycheap.com

Orbitz
www.orbitz.com

Hotwire
www.hotwire.com

Hotel Discounters

Accommodations Express
800-444-7666
www.accommodationsexpress.com

Helpful Hint

The best thing to do is plan your vacation far ahead—book plane tickets and hotel reservations and call it quits. You're sure to get the best advance-purchase plane ticket fares available (the only way you'd do better would be by last-minute booking; not only is that a gamble, it's also highly inadvisable for families). Because hotel rates are often based on availability, you'll get reasonable rates, if not rock bottom. After you book, call the hotel once every month and inquire about room rates. Don't tell them you already have a reservation; just ask about rates to find out if you can re-book if rates have dropped. (See chapter 4 for more advice.)

Central Reservations Service
800-950-0232
www.reservation-service.com

Express Reservations
800-356-1123
www.express-res.com

Hotres.com
www.hotres.com

Hotel.com
800-964-6835
www.180096hotel.com

Quikbook
800-789-9887
www.quikbook.com

Turbo Trip
800-473-7829
www.turbotrip.com

800-USA-HOTEL
800-872-4683
www.1800usahotels.com

Money-Saving Tip

Read the travel section in your local paper, pick up a copy of the Sunday *New York Times*, and check other big city papers for travel deals (usually in the Sunday papers). Air–hotel travel packages are often a great way to save money, and, if the timing works out, you can save hundreds of dollars. Find out as much as you can about the hotel because the last thing you need is for you and your family to have sleepless nights.

What to Pack

Packing for a vacation to New York City shouldn't be that much different from packing for a vacation anywhere else, and the one reassuring thing is that if you forget it—whatever it might be—you can always find it in the City, maybe even for less. A few important things to remember:

New York City is a walking town, so bring comfortable shoes. Sneakers (or whatever shoes your kids find comfortable, although open shoes like sandals aren't advisable on account of the traffic dangers and the dirt) are acceptable attire for everyone in all but the dressy restaurants and perhaps the opera and symphony. Even if your transportation is primarily by taxi, inevitably, you'll find that it will end up being easier to get to certain destinations by bus or subway, which also means at least a short walk on either end. And the best way (if at all possible) to see New York is really on foot, so why not be comfortable? At the same time, New York City can also be a formal city (in this town, you can *never* be overdressed), and it's nice, on occasion, to dress up. Therefore, it's good to throw in a pair of slacks and a button-down shirt for boys and a skirt or dress for girls. You'll be sure to impress the locals with your spiffy family.

For carting things around, you and the kids will each be best off with a backpack. Moms can pack something a little more stylish for going out on the town, but for general city exploration, with all that you'll probably end up carrying (snacks, extra clothes, water, sightseeing materials, etc.), it's the most efficient and painless (literally) way of carting the load. And by the way, carry the backpack as it was intended—on your back. Tourists who insist on carrying their backpacks on their fronts are a dead giveaway—it's like wearing a sign.

Infant strollers are a mixed blessing in New York City. It's generally easy to navigate the streets with them, but things get tricky on public transportation and in taxis. The bothersome part is getting into and out of and onto and off of whatever. Subways are worst of all because of all the stairs (virtually no elevator access). If you're traveling as a couple, at least you have enough hands to get the job done, but it's also difficult to keep your eyes on the children. Bus travel is a bit easier; you only have to navigate a couple of stairs. No matter what, it's best to avoid rush hour—especially on the subway. With taxis, you're best off with a quick-folding stroller that's easily tossed into the trunk. Consider a soft carrier like a Snugli for infants, and a backpack carrier for toddlers, as alternatives to a stroller. That way, everyone will need naps at the same time!

Winter in New York can be cold and windy, so it's best to pack a good coat, hats, gloves, and scarves. If you forget any of these items, all but the coats can be bought on the street for about $5. It's also good to have a pair of boots—if it snows; even though the plowing is extremely efficient, New York gets pretty messy.

Summer, especially during July and August, is often hot and, worst of all, humid. As everyone is always saying, "It's not the heat, it's the humidity." Unfortunately, New York often gets hit with both, so keep that in mind if you're visiting during this time of year. Neat shorts and tee shirts are acceptable virtually everywhere, and hats (and sunglasses) are advisable for all. Do keep in mind that all commercial enterprises (including public transportation, restaurants, and hotels) are well air conditioned, so it's a good idea to keep a sweatshirt or long-sleeved shirt handy for each of the kids.

Spring and fall in New York are magnificent, but the seasons are often fraught with variable weather—snow or rain in April and Indian summer in November. Usually, things start to warm up in mid-April, with temperatures climbing toward the end of the month and into early May. September and October usually promise sunny and similar temperatures to May, with the mornings and evenings crisp and cool—perfect autumnal weather to go with the changing leaves. It's best to have a range of clothes for these seasons. Layering is an efficient way to keep warm—and cool—and it's also a good strategy for avoiding overpacking.

Information for International Travelers

National Holidays

Even on national holidays, you'll find that many shops and restaurants in New York City remain open, and public transportation functions 365 days a year, 24 hours a day. However, most banks, government offices, and many other businesses will be closed on most holidays.

New Year's Day: January 1

Martin Luther King Jr. Day: third Monday in January

Presidents' Day: third Monday in February

Memorial Day: Last Monday in May

Independence Day: July 4

Labor Day: first Monday in September

Columbus Day: second Monday in October

Veterans Day: November 11

Thanksgiving: fourth Thursday in November

Christmas: December 25

New Year's Eve: December 31

Smoking and Drinking Laws

International travelers may be unfamiliar with various laws—nothing that will get you into extreme trouble, but it's good to be aware. New York City has very strict smoking laws, and if you break them, countless people will be quick to tell you. For the most part, smoking is not allowed in any indoor area, including restaurants, and virtually all establishments abide by this rule (although a few don't). Fortunately for smokers, most bars do allow smoking. Which brings us to alcohol. The national legal drinking age is 21 (though in restaurants, if you're looking to give a taste of wine to a teen, it isn't strictly enforced).

Health Insurance

It is absolutely crucial to purchase a travel insurance plan that includes health insurance. The United States does not have a nationalized medical program, and so anyone needing medical

Top Ten NYC Titles for Pre-Teens

1. *From the Mixed-Up Files of Mrs. Basil E. Frankweiler,* by E. L. Konigsburg

2. *The Cricket in Times Square,* by George Selden

3. *Stuart Little,* by E. B. White

4. *Harriet the Spy,* by Louise Fitzhugh

5. *The Pushcart War,* by Jean Merrill

6. *Brooklyn Doesn't Rhyme,* by Joan W. Blos

7. *All-of-a-Kind Family,* by Sydney Taylor

8. *The Adventures of Ali Baba Bernstein,* by Johanna Hurwitz

9. *Maria Tallchief, American Ballerina,* by Adele De Leeuw

10. *The Chosen,* by Chaim Potok

attention is responsible for any medical expenses incurred. Obviously, we hope you'll never need it, but health care in this country, and especially New York City, is *extremely* expensive for the uninsured, so I urge you to purchase a reliable plan before you depart from home.

Visas, Passports, Immigration, and Customs

Currently the United States has a reciprocity entry arrangement called the Visa Waiver Pilot Program (VWPP). This enables citizens of the following countries to enter for a period of ninety days or fewer without obtaining a U.S. visa: Andorra, Argentina, Australia, Austria, Belgium, Brunei, Denmark, Finland, France, Germany, Iceland, Ireland, Italy, Japan, Liechtenstein, Luxembourg,

Monaco, the Netherlands, New Zealand, Norway, San Marino, Slovenia, Spain, Sweden, Switzerland, and the United Kingdom. The only requirements are: Travelers cannot extend the visa, they must have a nonrefundable round-trip ticket, and passports must be valid for six months from the return date.

For those traveling from countries not included on the VWPP list (or those needing extensions), you must obtain a visa from the U.S. embassy or consulate in your country (or from a nearby country if there isn't one in yours) by filling out the required paperwork and providing a 1½-by-1½ inch passport photo (37-by-37 mm). There is no charge for the visa.

Because laws do change, to avoid any problems or confusion, it's best to check online for the most up-to-date information. Go to www.travel.state.gov and click on VISAS at the U.S. State Department Web site. For information on Immigration and Naturalization Services (INS), go to www.ins.usdoj.gov.

Customs allotments entitle each person over the age of 21 to enter the country with 1 liter of alcohol and 200 cigarettes (one carton), 50 cigars (non-Cuban), or 1 kilogram (4.4 pounds) of chewing tobacco. You may carry up to $10,000 undeclared in cash, traveler's checks, money orders, and so on. If you carry more than that, you must declare it.

Embassies and Consulates

Embassies are located in Washington, D.C., though most countries have consulates and/or missions in New York (because the United Nations is here). If your country isn't listed below, check the phone book for local listings or go to www.embassy.org/embassies.

Consulate Contact Information for New York City:

Australia
150 East 42nd Street, 34th floor
212-351-6500
www.australianyc.org

Canada
1251 Avenue of the Americas
212-596-1600
www.canada-ny.org

Ireland
345 Park Avenue
212-319-2555

New Zealand
780 Third Avenue
212-832-4938

United Kingdom
845 Third Avenue
212-745-0202
www.britain.com

Banking

You're best off using credit cards (you'll not only get favorable exchange rates, but you'll also have an itemized list of your purchases upon your return home, and you won't have to carry so much cash) and ATM machines (you draw your cash in U.S. dollars [USD] to avoid the hassles of banks and costly surcharges, though many ATMs do charge a $1 to $4 service fee, depending on your bank at home). Visa, American Express, MasterCard, Discover Card, and Diners Club are all widely accepted. You should probably have at least one credit card with you for big-ticket items, such as hotel bills and any unexpected expenses.

Banks are open Monday through Friday, usually from 9 A.M.– 4 P.M. Many banks are also open half-days on Saturday (9 A.M.–1 P.M.). In Chinatown, both Chase Manhattan and Citibank have branches that are open seven days a week (with limited hours on Saturday and Sunday). The Chase Manhattan Bank at Liberty and William Streets does not charge a commission fee for changing international currencies into USD.

Currency

U.S. currency is pretty straightforward. Bills come in $1, $5, $10, $20, $50, and $100. $50s and $100s will be nearly impossible to use in taxis (cabbies don't carry much cash). If you need change for big bills, it's best to break them at your hotel or at any bank.

Coins come in one-cent (a penny, $0.01), five-cent (a nickel, $0.05), ten-cent (a dime, $0.10), twenty-five-cent (a quarter, $0.25), and $1 pieces (though the $1.00 coins aren't very popular).

Postage

International postage for postcards is fifty cents (forty cents to Canada). A letter of up to ½ ounce to an international destination is sixty cents (forty-six cents to Canada). Aerogrammes (single-sheet foldover lettergrams) are fifty cents each.

Electricity

U.S. electricity runs on 110 volts to 120 volts (sixty cycles). So if you're coming from abroad with anything that runs on 220V–240V (like a baby monitor), you'll need an adapter—something that's easiest to bring from home (though you can find one at any Radio Shack or at J&R downtown).

Phoning Home

To call home, dial 011, the country code, and the telephone number. To find the country code, check the front of the phone book in

Money-Saving Tip

To save on international phone calls, purchase a prepaid international calling card and place calls to home from a pay phone in the hotel lobby. You'll save big bucks by avoiding the hotel's significant surcharges and inflated phone charges. Read the fine print on the card carefully before buying, because many advertise low per-minute rates but actually levy a big surcharge on each call, effectively raising the price.

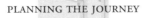
your hotel room, ask the concierge, or dial 00 for the international operator (but don't allow the operator to put the call through because there is a hefty surcharge for any call placed by an operator).

Arrival and Departure

There are countless ways to get into and around New York City, some of which cost no more than a ride on public transportation ($1.50). Others cost hundreds of dollars (helicopter), but, for the most part, taxis are your best bet, at least upon arrival, when you'll be laden with bags and tired (and possibly cranky) kids. Taxis and car services in New York City aren't as costly as you might think, and when you're traveling in a group, sometimes it's actually cheaper to travel in comfort than on a shuttle or private bus (because you pay one fee for the whole taxi, as opposed to paying per person for a shuttle). So before you run yourself through the wringer trying to save a few bucks, do the math. You may find that you're saving no money at all, and you're actually paying more—and suffering the inconvenience.

Airports

There are three major international airports that service the New York metropolitan area. In New York City, they are La Guardia Airport (LGA) and JFK International Airport (both are in Queens), and, in Newark, New Jersey, Newark International Airport (EWR).

Each airport has multiple transportation options to get into Manhattan: taxi, bus, shuttle, car service, helicopter, ferry, and even a bus/subway combo. But for ease and comfort (especially for those traveling with young children), I would strongly advise a taxi or car service or, to save a little money, a shuttle.

By Taxi

La Guardia: Taxi fares will vary depending upon your destination within New York (uptown Manhattan will be substantially less than downtown). For to/from destinations within Manhattan, fares will run around $15 to $29 plus tolls ($3.50) and tip and take fifteen to forty minutes (with light traffic).

JFK: From JFK there is a $30 flat rate to any destination within Manhattan (plus tolls, $3.50, and tip). From Manhattan the fare is $2 for the first ⅕ mile and thirty cents each additional ⅕ mile (plus tolls and tip). There is a fifty-cent surcharge after 8 P.M. Expect the trip to be thirty to sixty minutes (with light traffic), depending upon your final destination.

Newark: The taxi fare to/from Newark airport is the most expensive at about $34 to $38 plus tolls ($10) and tip. Expect the trip to take anywhere from twenty-five to forty-five minutes (with light traffic).

By Bus/Shuttle

Olympia Trails Airport Express	212-964-6233

Olympia offers roundtrip bus service for Newark airport. It takes approximately thirty-five to fifty minutes (more during rush hours) to get into the City, depending upon which drop-off destination you select (Grand Central Station, Penn Station, Port Authority, or the Financial District). The cost is $11 one way or $20 round trip.

Gray Line Air Shuttle	800-451-0455
(Express Shuttle USA)	212-315-3006
www.graylinenewyork.com	

Gray Line offers service for La Guardia, JFK, and Newark airports. It takes approximately thirty-five to forty-five minutes to get into Manhattan from La Guardia, and forty-five to sixty minutes from JFK and Newark (more during rush hours and for travel below Midtown). The cost (one way) from La Guardia is

$16; from JFK and Newark it's $19. Roundtrip tickets purchased at the airport are $26 from/to La Guardia and $28 from/to JFK and Newark. Children under 5 years old ride free. The best thing about Gray Line is that it will drop you off and pick you up at your hotel—door-to-door service in New York City without a full taxi fare is rare!

Super Shuttle	212-BLUE-VAN (258-3826)
www.supershuttle.com	800-BLUE-VAN
	(for out-of-town reservations)

Super Shuttle services La Guardia, JFK, and Newark airports. They say the cost is variable from different points within the City to each of the airports, but as far as I can tell, travel from all airports to any neighborhood within Manhattan costs the same: $19 each way to a residence and $17 to a hotel. Sounds expensive, but each additional person (after the initial cost) costs only $9, and children under 3 ride free. Once again, the driver will pick you up or drop you off anywhere within the City at no extra charge. It's best to book at least twenty-four hours in advance when you are returning to the airport.

By Car Service

There are dozens of car service companies in the City, and using one is a great way to get a little peace of mind. The fare is predetermined (most companies charge $22 to La Guardia, $32 to JFK, and $29 to Newark, plus tolls and tip), so you don't have to worry about meters, directions, or hailing a cab. Call a day or more in advance for a reservation, and a car will pick you up at the terminal (or upon departure, at your hotel). *Note:* If you're calling for an airport pickup and you have a lot of stuff, you can request that your driver meet you near the luggage area—but usually you just meet outside so the driver doesn't have to park.

Accord Car & Limo Service
212-321-1212
800-801-3330

Carmel Car and Limousine Service
212-666-6666
www.carmelcarservice.com

London Towncars
212-988-9700
800-221-4009
www.londontowncars.com

Tristate Luxury Limo
212-777-7171
800-722-7122

Skyline
212-741-3711
800-533-6325

Tel Aviv Car and Limousine Service
212-777-7777
800-222-9888
www.telavivlimo.com

By Ferry

Delta Water Shuttle	**800-533-3779**

The Delta Water Shuttle runs between the Marine Air Terminal
(part of La Guardia) and 34th Street, 62nd Street (both on the
East Side), and Wall Street (Pier 11). The fare one way is $15,
and the trip takes approximately twenty-five to thirty-five minutes. It's fun, if not entirely efficient, and advisable only if you're
traveling *extremely light* and you know the kids will love it (you
can always ride the Staten Island Ferry for free later in your

visit—after you've settled in). You'll most likely have to catch a taxi from the ferry to your hotel.

By Helicopter

Helicopter Flight Services Inc.	**888-WE FLY NY** **212-355-0801**

Helicopter Flight Services can get you between all area airports and your choice of heliports within Manhattan. The fare is a flat rate of $850 per helicopter, and each helicopter carries up to six people (fewer if there is luggage involved). You'll need a taxi from the heliport to your hotel, and unless you're traveling light, you might want to save the helicopter ride for a special treat after you're all settled in.

Public Transportation

There is no direct route from any of the airports into the City on public transportation. But it can be done—if you're up for the challenge. **But I'd strongly advise you, especially if you're carrying lots of luggage and you have young kids in tow, to spring for a cab or car service.** Still, if you're determined to give public transportation a whirl, here are the details.

From/to La Guardia: For the shockingly low fare of $1.50 (with a MetroCard, you get a free bus-to-subway transfer, but not with a token or coins), you can take the M-60 bus to 116th Street and Broadway (Columbia University) and transfer to the 1 or 9 subway for locations on the West Side. You can also take the Q33 bus to the Roosevelt Avenue station (in Jackson Heights) and transfer to the E or F train (subway), or take the Q33 to 74th Street/Broadway station and transfer to the 7 train, which will bring you into Grand Central, where you can transfer to the 4, 5, or 6 trains (East Side). To go to La Guardia, follow the directions in reverse. Expect ninety minutes of travel time for the trip.

From/to JFK: Catch the Long-Term Parking Lot Bus (free) to the A train (subway) station. Take the A train into Manhattan and transfer within the City to get to your specific destination (in reverse, it's the A train marked for "Far Rockaway" and then the shuttle bus).

For further New York City bus and subway information, contact:

New York City Transit (MTA)
718-330-1234
www.mta.nyc.ny.us

From/to Newark Airport: Take New Jersey Transit's Airlink bus #302 ($4) to Penn Station *in Newark* (there are, confusingly, Penn Stations in both New York and New Jersey). From there, you take the PATH train to Manhattan ($1) stopping at Christopher Street, 9th Street, 14th Street, 23rd Street, and 33rd Street (the station at the former World Trade Center site will be closed until at least 2004). To go to Newark, follow the directions in reverse.

For more information on New Jersey public transportation, contact:

New Jersey Transit (NJT)
973-762-5100

Bus

Long-distance buses (Greyhound, Trailways, Peter Pan, Vermont Transit, etc.) arrive into the City at the Port Authority Bus Terminal, which is located between 40th and 42nd Streets from Eighth Avenue to Ninth Avenue. Catch a taxi to your hotel. It's by far the easiest and, with three or more people, will hardly cost any more than the subway or bus (unless you're going to one of the boroughs).

Train

Amtrak trains arrive at Penn Station (31st St. to 33rd St., between Seventh Ave. and Eighth Ave.).

Top Ten NYC Titles for Teens

1. *Time and Again*, by Jack Finney

2. *Old New York*, by Edith Wharton

3. *A Tree Grows in Brooklyn*, by Betty Smith

4. *The Blacker the Berry*, by Wallace Thurman

5. *The Age of Innocence*, by Edith Wharton

6. *Babe Ruth Slept Here: The Baseball Landmarks of New York City*, by Jim Reisler (for baseball fans of all ages)

7. *My Name is Asher Lev*, by Chaim Potok

8. *Bodega Dreams*, by Ernesto Quiñonez

9. *The Great Bridge*, by David McCullough

10. *Here Is New York*, by E. B. White

And a few extra for good measure . . .

New York City Ghost Stories, by Charles J. Adams III

722 Miles, The Building of the Subways and How They Transformed New York, by Clifton Hood

It Happened in New York, by Fran Capo and Frank Borzellieri

Life at the Dakota, by Stephen Birmingham

Car

It could take you a decade and a Ph.D. to learn all of the different ways to drive into Manhattan—the best routes are a frequent source of discussion and debate, particularly among suburban commuters. What you need to know, at the most basic level, is that I-95 from the north and south and I-80 from the west will all lead you to Manhattan. If you're a member of AAA, get a trip-tik tailored to your exact itinerary; if not, see the map of New York City provided at the front of this book or get online and check out one of the following (or a few to cross-reference) Web sites for directions that will be best suited to your travel plans.

Yahoo
www.yahoo.com
Go to the MAPS section

Excite
www.excite.com
Go to MAPS and DIRECTIONS section

Mapblast
www.mapblast.com

Mapquest
www.mapquest.com

CHAPTER

2

Taking Charge
of NYC

Contingency Plans

To ensure that you'll have a wonderful New York vacation, take a cue from the Boy Scouts: Be prepared. Here are a few tips to help keep your trip on track.

Emergencies

It's every parent's nightmare to become separated from a child, but in New York City, because of the sheer magnitude and population, the mere thought of it is overwhelming and devastating. Take the following steps to avoid this scenario altogether:

- Talk to your children before you arrive and again upon settling into the hotel to emphasize the importance of sticking close to either parent. Tell young children to hold onto the stroller of a younger sibling, a parent's hand, or the hand of an older sibling.

- Be sure that each child has the name, address, and telephone number of the hotel in his or her pocket or backpack every day before setting out for your adventures, as

38

well as your cellular phone number (but we'll get to that later).

@ With older children, if you are separating in a museum, zoo, or other attraction, pick a meeting place and time and confirm both before setting off in different directions.

@ Have a plan and discuss it with your children in the event that you do get separated.

@ Consider bringing a cellular phone. Having one along (or even two, one with the older kids and one with the parents, or one for each parent if you plan to separate at all) can raise your level of comfort and security. And if anyone gets separated, you can always be in touch for an easy reunion. Because cellular phone service is currently so reasonably priced (and most plans even include nationwide coverage), I strongly suggest that you consider it for the trip.

@ In closed areas, such as museums, pick a place to meet "just in case," like the information booth. As soon as anyone re-alizes that someone is missing, go to the designated place. As a backup, tell children to find the nearest security guard (easily recognizable by the uniform), who will help the fam-ily reunite (this happens all the time).

@ Outside of the hotel, be sure that the cellular phone is on as soon as you realize that someone is missing (or charge the phone each night and keep it on all day). Advise the kids to call you or, if they're the keepers of the phone, call them. Call the hotel and advise the kids to do the same. If the children are older, you can have a plan (write it down for them in case they're not quite old enough): After a given amount of time has passed, hail a taxi (show the driver the paper with the name and address), and go to the hotel (be sure each child has a small stash of emergency money, $10 or so—enough for a cab to the hotel). Also, tell children to ask a grownup for help (you can discuss who might be an appropriate person to ask—police, other people with children, well-dressed adults in business suits, etc.).

@ In case of a medical emergency, call 911. No money is needed to make this call from public pay phones. Often, though, if the emergency is not life-threatening, you're best off hailing a cab and telling the cabbie to take you to the nearest hospital emergency room.

Avoiding Crime

It's no secret that in the past New York City had its share of crime, but the City gets safer every year—in fact, it's now the safest large city in America. But it's still a major metropolitan area, which means that you must take steps to be sure your family is as safe as possible.

@ Listen to your gut instincts—if you feel unsafe or uncomfortable, you're likely right, and the worst that can happen is that you've erred on the side of caution.

@ Do not enter Central Park (or any other park, for that matter) after dark unless you're going to an event that hundreds or thousands of other people are also attending.

@ Keep a watchful eye on your belongings, though there's no need to be paranoid. On subways and buses, keep bags in front of you or on your lap.

@ Keep your money in front pockets and split the wealth and credit cards between the adults so that no one person has everything.

@ Be unobtrusive with your money, jewelry, and belongings. It's okay to pay cash, but don't walk down the street with your wallet open or bills in your hand. Leave your best jewelry at home if you can, but if you can't live without it, tuck

fancy necklaces and gemstones out of view if you're in a questionable area.

@ In restaurants and theaters, *do not drape your bags across the back of your chair*—hold your belongings in your lap or on the floor in front of you where you can see them. You may even want to hook the strap of your purse or bag around your ankle.

@ Don't be afraid to ask for directions. If you're lost, just stop someone who's "safe looking" and ask for help. New Yorkers might appear rushed and harried (we are), but only a scant few wouldn't stop to help out—even if they're late for a very important meeting.

@ Use common sense. New York is a city like any other, so follow the same rules you would anywhere else to avoid being a crime target.

Common Scams to Avoid

Ah, yes. The old shell game. It looks so simple and yet you can *never* win. Familiar with the saying, "There's a sucker born every minute"? Well, don't be the one to prove it true—here are some common scams to avoid.

@ As a general rule, never give *anyone* any money unless you're paying for something. Plenty of people will ask you for money during your visit to New York City, and, though it may sound cold, you're best off giving none of yours to anyone. Panhandling is against the law in New York. If you want to give money to the homeless, make it a family project, and write a check to a reputable organization that you've researched (or learned about while in town) after you get home.

@ Don't fall for the well-dressed person with the sob story—"I lost my wallet and I need money for the train ticket to

Westchester" or the "I found this wallet with lots of money in it, and if you give me $50 to pay a lawyer to put it in escrow, we can split it" scam. Just because the person is well dressed, it doesn't mean he or she isn't trying to rip you off. Don't let anyone talk you into going to an ATM or lending money ("I promise I'll pay you back! What's your address, I'll mail you a check") or anything else. Just say no and walk away.

@ Avoid the shell game scam (a guy on the street set up with a cardboard box–like table, three shells, and the little red ball—if you pick the shell with the ball under it, you win). Same goes for three-card Monte (similar setup only you're looking for the jack, king, or whatever). You can *never* win—because it's a scam.

@ Avoid riding in unlicensed cabs (livery-service cars). They'll pull over or honk. Most are sedans. Stick to taxis, licensed car services, and public transportation. Be sure the taxi driver uses the meter.

@ When buying things on the street, always agree to a price in advance—before you take out your money. Don't falter on the agreement. If the seller doesn't have change, get your money back and buy the item elsewhere or get change yourself and pay the agreed-upon amount.

Weather

If your plan for the day was to be outside and you wake up to find that it's raining cats and dogs, head for one of the many indoor attractions (theater, museum, stock exchange, etc.) to keep everyone happy and engaged. Even in the snow, the buses continue to run, as do the subways—usually without a hitch (though it's best to avoid taxis in the snow because the drivers are usually unaccustomed to driving in such conditions).

*The Statue
of Liberty*

If it does snow, be sure to head for Central Park. It's a magical place when blanketed in white, and it's one of the few places where the pristine snow stays white for more than a few hours.

Important Telephone Contacts

- Police and Fire Departments: Dial 911 (*Note:* For non-emergency police calls, dial 212-374-5000.)

- Animal Bites: 212-566-2068

- Doctors on Call: 718-745-5900

- Poison Control Center: 212-764-7667

For Animal Emergencies

Animal Medical Center
510 East 62nd Street
212-838-8100

> *Emergency animal hospital, twenty-four hours, seven days a week.*

For Emergency Prescriptions (24-Hour Pharmacies)

Duane Reade
224 West 57th Street (at Broadway)
212-541-9708

Duane Reade
2465 Broadway (at 91st St.)
212-799-3172

Duane Reade
1279 Third Avenue (at 74th St.)
212-744-2668

> For a complete listing of Duane Reade locations and store hours, go to www.duanereade.com.

Rite Aid
303 West 50th Street (at Eighth Ave.)
212-247-8384
212-247-8736

Rite Aid
542 Second Avenue (at 30th St.)
212-213-5284 (main number)
212-213-9887 (pharmacy number)

> For a complete listing of Rite Aid locations and store hours, go to www.riteaid.com.

Passport Information

212-399-5290

General Information

New York Convention and Visitors Bureau
810 Seventh Avenue (at 53rd St.)
New York, NY 10019
212-484-1200
www.nycvb.com

Money-Saving Tip

Bring all basic supplies with you. New York City is a bar-gain-hunter's paradise, but it's also very expensive to buy bulky staples like diapers and formula—especially at the mini-marts in the major hotel neighborhoods. If you're driving and have the luxury of a trunk, you wouldn't be crazy to bring cans of soda, bottles of water, and non-perishable snacks—each item you bring could save you a dollar or more.

Visitor Information Center

The new Times Square Visitors Center in the beautifully restored landmark Embassy Movie Theatre is a great addition to the New York City tourism landscape. It provides one-stop shopping for the most common needs. Some of the services include:

- Free citywide information from multilingual tourist counselors

- Free brochures, including the Times Square Business Improvement District Map, Entertainment Guide, and Restaurant Guide

- The Broadway Ticket Center, where you can purchase tickets to Broadway and Off-Broadway shows

- ATM machines from HSBC Bank USA

- Gray Line/Circle Line bus and boat tour bookings

- A transit booth selling MTA MetroCards (including the $4 one-day unlimited travel Fun Pass) and NYC Transit memorabilia

- A post office booth selling stamps and souvenirs

@ Free Yahoo!-sponsored Internet access so you can check your e-mail

The Center is located at 1560 Broadway, between 46th and 47th Streets, and is open every day from 8 A.M. to 8 P.M.

What Things Cost

New York can be one of the most expensive cities on earth, but it's also home to many of the world's best bargains. Though the basics, like a can of soda or a package of Pampers, are often more expensive than they would be in the rest of the country, prices for many other items may be just the opposite—you'll find substantial discounts on clothes, cameras, and all manner of consumer electronics.

Here's a rough idea of what everyday things typically cost in New York City:

@ Can of soda from a street vendor or mini-mart: $1.00

@ McDonald's Happy Meal: $2.99 with hamburger; $3.09 with cheeseburger; $3.59 with McNuggets; Big Mac Extra Value Meal: $4.69

@ Slice of pizza at a typical pizzeria: $1.75

@ Bagel (plain): $0.75; $1.25 with a "schmear" (cream cheese)

@ Bus or subway ride anywhere in the system: $1.50

@ Roll of Kodak Gold 24-exposure 35-mm color-print film: $2.09 at a discount camera-and-electronics store; $6.00 in a neighborhood mini-mart

@ Taxi from the Upper East Side to the Theater District: $8.00; from Midtown hotels to Greenwich Village: $7.00; from Times Square to the Financial District: $14.00

@ Local call from a payphone: $0.25

- Movie ticket: $6.00 child; $9.50 adult

- Bayer Aspirin: $3.39 (24 tablets); generic aspirin: $3.99 (250 tablets)

- Tylenol pain reliever: $3.99 (24 tablets); generic acetaminophen: $3.99 (100 tablets)

- Digital thermometer: $9.99

- Spill-proof cup: $5.09

- Huggies diapers: $7.49 (24 count)

- AA batteries: $4.49 (4-pack)

- Enfamil infant formula: $3.15 (13 ounces)

- Similac ready-to-feed infant formula: $4.50 (1 quart)

Helpful Hint

Always carry enough cash—about $100—to pay for a meal or get you back to your hotel in a taxi, but never carry too much. New York has ATMs by the thousands, and most establishments accept credit cards (the best way to pay for anything, in case there's a dispute later). Traveler's checks can be useful (and are widely accepted), but they often slow things down. If you have an account at a major bank, you're much better off just getting your cash at ATMs. Most hotels cash personal checks (for guests) for up to a few hundred dollars.

Tipping

Tipping in New York tends to be a little more generous than the national average, but not by much. Of course, the size of the tip is a personal decision and should be influenced by the quality of service rendered, but please remember that many service-industry people make nearly their entire incomes from tips, and you should only withhold a tip under extraordinary circumstances. The following are basic customary guidelines for good service:

- Restaurants: 16.5 percent of the bill (just double the tax, which is 8.25 percent) in a standard restaurant and 18–20 percent in a luxury restaurant

- Bartenders: 15 percent of the tab

- Taxis: 15–20 percent of the fare on the meter, plus an extra couple of dollars if the driver helps you with luggage or packages

- Car service: Same as for taxis

- Hotel doorman: $1–$2 for helping you in or out of a taxi or car with your luggage or packages

- Hotel bellhop: $1–$2 per bag

- Hotel housekeeper: $1 per day per room

- Coat-check attendants: $1 per item

- Parking-lot attendants: $1

- Hairdressers: 15–20 percent

You are not expected to tip at self-service or fast-food restaurants, nor do theater ushers or gas-station attendants expect tips.

Helpful Hint

Some restaurants have taken to adding an automatic service charge for large parties (five or more), so be sure to read your bill carefully. You're not expected to tip over and above this charge.

Sales Tax

New York sales tax is 8.25 percent. This applies to just about every purchase you make, including restaurant meals, though there are a few exceptions: Certain "necessities" are not taxed, such as most grocery items, shoes, and clothes costing under $110 per item.

Area Codes

Four area codes cover New York City: 212, 718, 917, and 646. Calls within and between these area codes are considered local calls (twenty-five cents from pay phones). Most telephone numbers in Manhattan are 212, but due to a recent shortage of the 212 exchange, new Manhattan telephones are being assigned 646 and 917 numbers. In addition, most New York-based cellular phones and pagers are 917 or 646. The boroughs (other than Manhattan) are 718.

Top Ten Free Activities and Attractions

1. Staten Island Ferry cruise (p. 57)
2. New York Stock Exchange tour (p. 177)
3. Sony World of Wonder (p. 394)
4. Big Apple Greeter tours (p. 60)
5. Stroll over the Brooklyn Bridge (p. 172)
6. Thanksgiving Day Parade (p. 12)
7. Christmas windows at department stores and Christmas tree at Rockefeller Center (p. 13)
8. Visit to FAO Schwarz (p. 416)
9. Pay-what-you-wish days at museums (p. 185)
10. Fourth of July fireworks (p. 9)

Getting Around New York City

The primary modes of transportation for New Yorkers, and the ones I strongly encourage you to use, are walking and public transportation. New York is one of the most walkable cities in the world—walking around New York is an activity in and of it-self—and the best way to plan a day's itinerary is to include as much walking as you and your kids can handle. This means clustering your events together so that you can take, for example, a subway in the morning to cover your long-haul travel (say, the trip from your Midtown hotel to the Financial District) and then walk from nearby place to nearby place (from the Stock Exchange to the former World Trade Center site to the Statue of Liberty ferry) before taking public transportation to the next far-away attraction.

Public Transportation

The New York City transit system is one of the most extensive and complex public transportation systems in the world, operating twenty-four-hour-a-day bus and subway service throughout the five boroughs. New York City Transit has more buses than any other public agency in North America and the largest subway car fleet on the planet. Each day, more that six million people use New York City Transit—almost two billion customers annually.

In the boroughs, some subways are still elevated.

Children under 6 years of age ride for free on the public buses and subways. Otherwise, full fare is $1.50, paid with a MetroCard, transit token, or $1.50 in exact change—coins only, no bills (exact change can be used on buses but not subways). This is the fare no matter how long or short your trip is (you could ride the A train thirty-one miles for that fare!).

MetroCards are available on a pay-per-ride basis (with one free ride for every ten purchased), or as unlimited-ride cards, in one-,

City Fact

New York City's subway system is the world's largest—714 miles of track, 469 stations, 6,089 subway cars. Subways run twenty-four hours a day and carry 1.2 billion passengers a year. If you added the number of stations in all other subway systems in America, it would total only thirty-five more than in New York City alone. The NYC public bus system has 300 routes and carries 600 million people a year (the most in the nation) on 4,200 buses.

seven-, or thirty-day denominations. Current prices are $4 for the unlimited ride, one-day "FunPass"; $17 for the seven-day unlimited pass; and $63 for the thirty-day unlimited pass. Unlimited MetroCards are valid for one person's use on all MTA buses and subways (though not on privately run express buses—you need a special MetroCard for that, which, as a visitor, you're not likely to want).

You can purchase MetroCards and tokens at all subway station booths, and many stations have installed automated MetroCard machines where you can purchase or refill MetroCards using cash, credit cards, or debit cards. There are also more than 3,500 MetroCard merchants (many newsstands, check-cashing centers, and currency-exchange bureaus sell them), so finding one will never be a problem. Note, however, that the one-day fun pass is not available at subway station booths—you can only get it from an outside vendor or from the machines. The pass is activated the first time you use it and is valid until 3 A.M. the next day.

Kids love riding in the first car of the train and looking out the front window as the underground tracks go flying by; if you ride a bus, kids can look out the window at the passing pageant of New York City life. The subways and buses are safe, clean, and graffiti-free. Transfers are free between buses and (only if you use a MetroCard) between buses and subways. Ask for a transfer (you'll get a slip of paper with transfer points listed on the back) *when you get on the bus* if you're planning to switch to another bus en route. No transfer slip is needed (or given) for a transfer if you use a MetroCard; subway stations do not give out transfers.

You can get a free copy of a transit map at any subway station booth or at many hotels or visitor's centers. For further information, visit the Transit Authority on the Web at www .mta.nyc.ny.us/ or call the following numbers:

The Transit Authority's Passenger Information Line:
718-330-1234 for people who speak English
718-330-4847 for people who don't speak English

Long Island Rail Road
718-217-5477

Metro-North Railroad
800-METRO-INFO outside NYC
212-532-4900 in NYC

MTA Long Island Bus
516-766-6722

Taxis

New York's cabs let everyone ride together for one price—the fare is per cab, not per person (up to a maximum of four adult passengers per cab, plus one small child in a lap). Taxis are widely

Learning Tips

The New York City public transportation system is a wonderful topic for a school report. Did you know that:

- The reason New York City buses don't accept paper money is because coins and tokens are removed from fare boxes by giant vacuum hoses. This process would shred bills.

- By tradition New York's bus and subway fares have always been identical, but they strayed apart for two years (between 1948 and 1950) when the bus fare was seven cents and the subway fare was ten.

- The first woman subway-train conductor was I. A. Lilly, who began work on Brooklyn Rapid Transit Company cars on December 28, 1917.

- Coin-operated subway turnstiles were first used on May 10, 1920. Before that, subway customers bought fare tickets. Since turnstiles could not handle two coins, tokens were introduced in 1953 when the fare went from a dime to fifteen cents.

- Bus maintenance involves more than 7,000 separate parts.

- The subway uses enough power annually to light up the city of Buffalo for a year.

- Jackie Gleason played a New York City bus operator on The Honeymooners TV series. In real life, his mother worked as a railroad clerk for fifteen years. The Jackie Gleason Depot was once an elevated railcar inspection shop.

available around Manhattan south of 96th Street (they're harder to come by north of 96th St. on the East Side and north of 118th St.—Columbia University—on the West Side). All you have to do is stick out your hand and hail one (kids love hailing cabs since it gives them a good reason to jump up and down and yell). Outside of Manhattan it's a bit trickier, but you can usually hail a cab on the major thoroughfares in Queens and Brooklyn. Otherwise, north of 96th Street in Manhattan, and around Queens, Brooklyn, and the Bronx, there are other certified taxi services besides the yellow cabs for transportation, and you can usually hail one that is cruising.

How do you tell if a taxi is available for a pickup? If the *light on the roof is illuminated,* the cab is available. If it's dark, the cab is full. If the "off duty" sign is illuminated, it's not available for service.

Taxi fares are regulated, and drivers stick to the meter (rates are posted on the doors and inside every cab). The fare is $2 for the first ⅕ mile and thirty cents each additional ⅕ mile. There is a fifty-cent surcharge after 8 P.M. (until 6 A.M.) and a rate of twenty cents per minute if standing. It is customary to tip 15 to 20 percent of the fare. If for some reason the driver doesn't start the meter, ask him to do so after he begins to drive.

Be sure to buckle up! Everyone—kids and adults— should wear a seatbelt at all times!

Car-for-Hire Services

In the Arrival and Departure section in chapter 1, I listed several private car services. You can use these services not only for airport transportation, but also as an alternative to yellow cabs. Although you lose the convenience of being able to flag down a cab any time you want and the car-service cars are more expensive for short rides, the car-service cars do have their advantages: They tend to be larger and more comfortable than taxis; they will appear at a preset time and location (especially important during rush hour, when taxis are hard to come by); and they can be hired by the hour.

This last benefit is one that I encourage families to explore, especially if they're in New York to do a lot of shopping. You can hire a car from any of the major car services for approximately $25 per hour. Thus, for about $150, you can have the equivalent of a chauffeur for six hours—a full day of shopping or sightseeing. To be sure, this is a significant expense, but it's probably cheaper than the sum of all the taxis you'd have to take between twenty different stores, and you can leave all your packages in the trunk of the car while you shop, or even do a drop at your hotel.

Driving and Parking

Driving around the congested arteries of New York City is difficult enough for a seasoned native, and it's something I strongly recommend that visitors not even try. If you come to New York City by car, I suggest you leave your car in your hotel's parking lot for the duration and rely on public transportation for your local motorized transit needs. Not only is driving around the City a hassle, it's also very difficult to park on the street, very expensive to park in a lot (even for a short time), and very expensive to pay for parking tickets (at least $35 a pop). Many cities have parking lots costing fifty cents an hour; in a New York parking lot you'll likely pay $20 or more for the same privilege.

If you do drive in New York City, remember that *right-turn-on-red is forbidden everywhere*, that you must be on extra careful lookout for pedestrians crossing against the traffic signals, and that failure to keep pace with the flow of traffic can be just as hazardous as driving at the typically fast pace favored by New York City drivers. Most streets, with the exception of a few avenues and major cross streets, are one way. Typically, in Manhattan, odd-numbered streets run west, while even-numbered streets run east, although there are some exceptions.

In most neighborhoods of Manhattan, there are on-street parking meters. Most cost twenty-five cents per fifteen minutes.

It's important, however, that you *read not only the meter instructions but also the posted signs nearby*. It may be that a certain meter is only valid during certain hours, so that the mere acceptance of your quarters is not a guarantee that you're complying with the parking laws.

In addition to parking lots and meters, there is free on-the-street parking in most of New York City's residential neighborhoods. Provided you leave no visible possessions in your car, it will likely be safe (auto theft and burglary are no longer major problems in New York's better neighborhoods). Still, you can't just find a parking space and leave your car there for a week. All of New York City engages in what is called alternate-side-of-the-street parking. To allow street cleaning machines to pass, each side of each block must be vacated at certain hours during the week. A given block might require that the left side be vacated from 8 A.M. until 11 A.M. on Tuesday and Thursday, and the right side during the same hours on Monday and Friday. Thus, you will have to observe and learn the parking signs no matter where you choose to park. And, of course, you may not park in front of a fire hydrant or in any other restricted space (indicated by signs or yellow lines painted on the curb).

Transit Fun (Transportation as Activity)

I'm always amazed, and admittedly somewhat surprised, by how much kids enjoy transportation, something that so many of us adults view as mundane or even dread—a necessary evil of getting from one place to another. But when you think about it, it's really not surprising at all, and perhaps it's the adults who need the attitude adjustment. After all, what isn't great about whooshing through New York's maze of underground tunnels on the subway or riding high above the city streets on the Roosevelt Island Tramway? Listed below are favorites of city kids and visitors from around the globe.

Trams and Ferries

Roosevelt Island Tramway Second Avenue (at 60th St.)	212-832-4543 www.rioc.com

Unobtrusively situated on Second Avenue is the Tramway to Roosevelt Island. You could miss it if you aren't looking up or don't hear the clanking as the tram reaches the Manhattan platform. It's a great ride from one side to the other and well worth the cost of the fare (same as riding the bus or subway). You'll glide above Manhattan briefly before you slide high over the East River (parallel to the 59th Street Bridge) and dock on the other side. The views of the City are great, especially if you catch a clear day. There isn't much to do on the other side. Roosevelt Island is a small residential island that's officially part of Manhattan, though its slow pace and lack of vehicles create an environment that's worlds apart. You may want to take a stroll, but you won't be missing much if you just jump back onto the next tram and ride back to the City. Teens may want to check out the Sylvester Stallone movie *Nighthawks*, in which terrorists highjack the Tramway.

Staten Island Ferry	718-815-BOAT www.siferry.com

It used to be that the ferry to Staten Island ("the boat" as commuters call it) cost twenty-five cents, but it is now free. That's right, it's absolutely free, and it's unequivocally one of the best—and most enjoyable—deals going. You can ride the ferry any time, day or night, and there are merits to both times. A daytime cruise affords views of the Statue of Liberty and Ellis Island, the Manhattan skyline, Governor's Island, the Brooklyn Bridge, the Verrazano-Narrows Bridge, cargo ships, tugboats, sailboats, and even the occasional river kayaker. At night, millions of twinkling

*The Staten Island
Ferry*

stars illuminate the
skyline of Manhattan,
the City That Never
Sleeps. Either way, try to spend at least part of the trip outside on
the deck (deck access is on the older ferries only) and keep careful watch for Lady Liberty on the way out, because that's when
you'll get the best view. The ride takes about thirty minutes, and
although you have to disembark at St. George, you can line up
nearby to get right back onto the return ferry. As long as you've
made the trip, though, you may also want to consider some of
the many wonderful activities that Staten Island has to offer (see
chapter 5).

Subway

The New York City subway system is an intricate maze of 714
miles of track, conveniently connecting the neighborhoods of
Manhattan and the boroughs of Brooklyn, Queens, and the
Bronx to one another (Staten Island has a similar system, called
Staten Island Rapid Transit). Within central Manhattan and
much of the boroughs, the trains run underground, while outside the more high-rise, urban areas of the City (yes, there are
some), the trains run above the street on elevated tracks, as they
do in Chicago.

But beyond being an extremely convenient, efficient, and
economical mode of transportation, the subway is also a great
ride. Get on an express train during off-peak hours to get a feel

for how fast the trains really move. You get the best of all rides at the helm of the train—head for the front car where the kids can stand at the window and watch the train barrel through the subway tunnel. The D, B, and Q trains even go across the East River on the Manhattan Bridge. I've never known a kid (or adult) who does not love this experience, and you may find that it takes more than one ride to exhaust the impulse! Be sure to hold on, though, because when those trains get going, they really move fast.

Tours

Many people don't like the idea of a tour—they associate it with tour buses and large, impersonal groups following around a bored leader. But the fact of the matter is that New York City can be a lot more manageable when you explore with an experienced guide. And I think you'll find, with most of the operators below (I've only listed the best established of the bunch), that your tour is much more informative, distinctive, and interesting than you might have imagined.

Walking Tours

Walking tours are a great way to familiarize yourself with the City. It's important to remember, however, that most walking tours are inappropriate for children under the age of 10 because they last ninety minutes to two hours (and up to four hours). During that time you will either be walking or standing on the street listening to history, stories, and details about the area. So unless you have a real trouper with a very good disposition and hearty attention span, you'll likely be better served by a hop-on, hop-off bus tour, a cruise, or some public transportation fun. In all instances, it's important to call in advance to confirm the schedule and book your spot.

Top Ten New York City Movies

1. *Miracle on 34th Street*
2. *Stuart Little*
3. *Home Alone II*
4. *King Kong*
5. *Big*
6. *Superman*
7. *You've Got Mail*
8. *Splash*
9. *Working Girl*
10. *Crossing Delancey*

Adventure on a Shoestring   212-265-2663

Tours run all year round. Neighborhood and theme tours, mostly in Manhattan but a few in the boroughs too (Astoria, Little Odessa). Ask for the haunted tours and the Lights, Action, Camera tour (go to sites of filming). Guides request that only children 10 years and older participate. "Five dollars for thirty-seven years and will never run any higher," says Howard Goldberg, owner and founder.

Big Apple Greeter   212-669-8159
www.bigapplegreeter.org

Tour New York City with a local. Volunteers, known as "Greeters," introduce you to New York City by taking you on a tour in any of the five boroughs. You're matched up with a

Greeter, who is chosen based on various factors—interests of the group, age group, neighborhood, and the like (it's you and the Greeter; no more than six total, please), and your tour will last two to four hours. These tours are completely free—it's our way of saying, "Welcome to New York!"

Big Onion Walking Tours	212-439-1090 www.bigonion.com

Big Onion tours focus primarily on New York's ethnic neighborhoods and historic districts. All guides hold advanced degrees in American history and are licensed by the City of New York. Call or check the Web site for fees.

Central Park Conservancy *Trolley Tours of Central Park*	212-397-3809

A nice way to get an overview of Central Park before you hoof it, these trolley tours last one-and-a-half hours and are offered end of April through end of October (no weekends or holidays). Free.

Central Park Walking Tours	212-860-1370

Walking tours of Central Park with an emphasis on the historical aspects of the upper and lower regions of the park, flora, and fauna. Call for a schedule and fees.

Joyce Gold History Tours *of New York*	212-242-5762 www.nyctours.com

A variety of walking tours offered all over the City. The fee is $12 per person, and children ages 9 and up are welcome. Check the Web site for the schedule of tours.

Lower East Side Discount Shopping Tour
888-VALUES 4
www.lowereastsideny.com

Every Sunday morning (April–December) at 11 A.M. the LES discount shopping tour departs from Katz's Deli (at the corner of Ludlow and East Houston Sts.). For decades the LES has been a destination for discount shoppers; now you too can get the inside scoop on this free tour. Most appropriate for teens.

Rockefeller Center
30 Rockefeller Center
212-332-6868

Grab a map in the lobby of 30 Rockefeller Center for a self-guided tour around the plaza and, while you're at it, don't forget to stop by the *Today* show, which films weekday mornings and often has special guests, like rock stars, who set up outside in the street.

Small Journeys, Inc.
212-874-7300

Custom tours ranging from four hours to six days. These tours are not for the budget conscious—the four-hour tours start at $240 (walking tour), and the coach tours (small, well-appointed vans) have the added cost of the vehicle (starts at about $260). The guides are all seasoned veterans.

A bicycle built for four, Central Park

Sightseeing Bus Tours

You have many options for sightseeing tours in New York City, and I highly recommend a double-decker bus tour *upon arrival*. It's a good way to familiarize yourself and the family immediately with the City (if you don't do it right away, you'll likely find that you've already covered some of the same ground, and the kids may get bored). At the same time, kids will get a kick out of riding around on the top of a double-decker. Seemingly straight out of London, the buses tour throughout Manhattan, stopping at all of the favorite tourist attractions. You can stay on for the full ride, or hop on and off to see the sights. Be sure to call in advance for reservations and updated schedules.

Gray Line New York Tours	212-397-2600
Port Authority,	**www.graylinenewyork.com**
Eighth Avenue (at 42nd St.)	

Double-decker sightseeing tours feature outside seating on the top deck. Narration is available in different languages—just ask.

Harlem Spirituals	212-391-0900
Gospel and Jazz Tours	**www.harlemspirituals.com**

Tours range from Manhattan City tours (New York, New York) to multicultural tours of the boroughs (the Bronx, Brooklyn, A Full Day City Tour, Triboro Tour) and, perhaps the favorite of all, the Gospel and Jazz tours (Harlem on Sunday with gospel brunch). Call or check the Web site for details and prices.

New York Double Decker Tours/   212-967-6008
Gateway Bus Tours   www.nydecker.com
Empire State Building (at Fifth Ave. and 34th St.)

These buses run a two-hour narrated circuit (starting at the Empire State) and are of the hop-on, hop-off variety. Tickets are $12–$18 (downtown/full-city tour) for kids, $20–$30 for adults.

Flightseeing and Cruises

Flightseeing and cruise tours are a great way to get a feel for the overall-island aspect of New York, and they're also loads of fun. Remember to book in advance and call for an updated schedule.

Circle Line Sightseeing Cruises   212-563-3200
Pier 83 (West 42nd St. at Twelfth Ave.)   www.circleline.com
South Street Seaport Pier 16 (at Water St.)

Cruise the waters around Manhattan with trips lasting thirty minutes to three hours. Live music is offered seasonally on many cruises. Beast Speedboat rides are especially popular, and narration is available in many languages.

Helicopter Flight Services   212-355-0801
Downtown Heliport   www.heliny.com
(at Pier 6 and the East River)

Manhattan flightseeing tours and charters.

                                           212-967-6464
Liberty Helicopters, Inc.
                                    www.libertyhelicopters.com

Flightseeing tours around Manhattan (departing from different locations).

New York Waterway	**800-533-3779** **www.nywaterway.com**

New York harbor sightseeing cruises. Free bus service between terminals and many Manhattan locations.

The Spirit of New York **Pier 61, Chelsea Piers** **(at West 23rd St. and West Side Hwy.)**	**212-727-2789** **www.spiritcruises.com**

Lunch, dinner, and jazz cruises around Manhattan departing from Manhattan and New Jersey. Cruising throughout the year.

Pioneer **Pier 16 (at Fulton and South Sts.)**	**212-748-8786**

Historical sailing cruises around New York harbor (through the South Street Seaport Museum). Cruising daily, May through September.

World Yacht Cruises **Pier 81 (West 41st St. at the** **Hudson River)**	**212-630-8100** **800-498-4270** **www.worldyacht.com**

Dinner and Sunday brunch on year-round cruises.

Making the Trip Educational

Simply setting foot in New York City can be tremendously educational. Throughout this book you'll find highlighted Learning Tips, which are designed to make your children's trip as educational as possible—without the classroom and without the books (hey, learning can be fun!). I've selected subjects that will excite and engage kids of various ages. And if your children are taking time off from school for their trip to New York City, I've included plenty of subject ideas for reports and class presentations. Also, don't overlook the timeline in the introduction and all of the potential for learning in the museums. I guarantee you that New York City will engage your children and get their creative juices flowing.

Babysitting

Just because you're taking a family vacation doesn't mean you can't have a night (or two) out on the town without your kids. After all, New York is a great town for adults, too. So, what's the best way to enjoy an evening out without having to worry that you're leaving your kids in bad company? You have two options: Bring a babysitter along with you, or find one in the City.

Obviously, if you have the means to go with the former, the extra hands will come in handy, not just for nights when you want to go out without the tykes, but also during the day when one child wants to do one thing, another wants to do something completely different, and your third child is in desperate need of a nap. Of course, even if you don't have three kids, the extra help can be a godsend, if only to have an extra pair of eyes to watch wandering kids, wait in line for tickets, help squelch tantrum uprisings—all the same things you deal with at home, only multiplied because you're on vacation, and there's so much stimulation. It's hard to keep up with it all.

But not everyone can or wants to have someone who isn't a family member along on the family vacation, so your other option is to go with the latter: Hire a babysitter in the City. This is surprisingly simple and safe. Countless agencies around town

offer babysitting services. They're happy to send a sitter to your hotel while you enjoy an evening out or to lend an extra pair of hands during the day while you're exploring the town. I've selected the five most reputable companies, many of which have been in business for decades. Each of the following agencies does background checks on the sitters, and most retain their employees for years on end. And if you're feeling a little anxious, rest assured—not only are you selecting from the best of the best with this list, but also no babysitting business would last more than five minutes in New York City if it weren't offering reliable and safe sitters. It's not just tourists who use these services, either— plenty of City residents use them, too (my sister-in-law in Brooklyn included).

A word about cost: Though it may seem like the hourly wage of babysitters in New York is astronomical (it is), surprisingly, these agencies don't charge much above the going rate (which, in Manhattan, would be $10 per hour, even to the high-school kid down the block). In fact, some of them don't charge any more at all. It's also standard procedure to pay for the babysitter's transportation.

A Choice Nanny   212-246-KIDS

A Choice is an excellent resource not only for "grown-up" evenings out but also if you need an extra pair of hands while touring. Or, if you decide that the teens will be bored at the Children's Museum, you can split your group for an afternoon, sending the teens off with a nanny/companion (with or without one parent) while you enjoy the museum with the young ones. All of the personnel are fully screened with a thorough background investigation, and A Choice uses only highly qualified people with whom they are very familiar. Rates are $10 per hour and up.

The Baby Sitters Guild, Inc.   212-682-0227
www.babysittersguild.com

Established in 1940, the Guild has been providing babysitters to New York's high-end hotels (like the Four Seasons and the Carlyle) for years. The staff is made up of professionals, including women with baby-nursing backgrounds, teachers, and history and art specialists, some of whom have been working for the Guild for as many as thirty years. Rates begin at $15.00 per hour, with a minimum of four hours (plus transportation fees of $4.50 before midnight and $7.00 after midnight). The Guild is insured, licensed, and bonded and is a member of the Better Business Bureau, the NY Chamber of Commerce, and NYCVB.

Best Domestic   212-685-0351
www.bestdomestic.com

Recommended by twenty-five major publications (including *The New York Times*, *Daily News*, and *Town & Country*), Best Domestic offers twenty-four-hour babysitting service. Within Manhattan, rates are $12 per hour (including transportation), with a four-hour minimum. Office hours are 9 A.M.–4 P.M., Monday through Friday, so book in advance.

Pinch Sitters   212-260-6005

If you need a weekend sitter, call a week in advance. Pinch Sitters provides service in Manhattan and "Brownstone Brooklyn" (the areas of Brooklyn near Manhattan). Office hours are 7 A.M.–5 P.M., Monday through Friday (summer hours are 9 A.M.–5 P.M.). Rates are $14 per hour with a four-hour minimum, and after 9 P.M. there is an additional charge for transportation.

Town and Country   212-245-8400

Babysitters are available for daytime and evening support. T&C does thorough checks on all babysitters, all of whom must have long-term and recent references. For concerned parents, be assured that most of the nighttime sitters have been with T&C for many years. Rates are $12 and up, with a four-hour minimum (plus transportation, $3 during the day, $8 after 8 P.M.). Office hours are Monday through Friday, 9 A.M.–5 P.M. during the school year (so you have to plan ahead for weekends) and Monday through Thursday 10 A.M.–5 P.M., Friday 10 A.M.–1 P.M. during the summer.

CHAPTER
3

Getting to Know NYC Through Its
Neighborhoods

New York is a city of neigh-
borhoods—fascinating, unique neighborhoods unequaled anywhere in the world for their diversity. Yet sadly, most tourists
spend most of their time in New York's least interesting neighborhood: Midtown.

Yes, Midtown is home to the theaters and the theme restaurants, but nobody actually lives there. It's a place where New
Yorkers go to work, and tourists come to visit, and therefore it
has little to offer beyond the commercial. But if you walk just a
few of blocks out of the Midtown core or, even better, ride the
subway a bit, you'll be where New Yorkers actually live; where
the restaurants are more diverse, the sights are more authentic,
and the mere act of walking around is both educational and fun.

The first part of this chapter is an overview of the major
ethnic neighborhoods in New York City, which are wonderful
instructional and (for the majority of us who descend from immigrants) genealogical tools—if your kids are working on term
papers, here's their topic. The second part is a general discussion
of Manhattan neighborhoods, which will help you navigate the

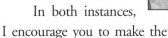

*Street performers
at Union Square*

many wonderful, non-
touristy neighborhoods
of New York City.

In both instances,
I encourage you to make the
exploration of these neighborhoods the core around which you
build your New York vacation. If you use a neighborhood-based
approach to mastering New York City, your kids will come away
from the trip with a coherent set of memories rather than a dis-
jointed set of images. Not to mention that exploring the neighborhoods is free.

Note: Though the bulk of information on attractions (chapter 5), dining (chapter 6), and shopping (chapter 7) is elsewhere
in this book, I have listed points of interest in each neighborhood to enhance the experience of strolling through them. But
please use this chapter with the others because space constraints
allow me to list only highlights here.

Ethnic New York

We're a nation of immigrants. Unless you're a Native American,
your family came here from somewhere else. An amazing 40 percent of people in the United States today can trace their ancestry
to the twelve million immigrants who landed at Ellis Island, in
New York harbor, between 1892 and 1954.

Today, New York remains a major world center of immigration. More than half the City's population was born in another country. This explains why New York's ethnic neighborhoods are such an important part of the City's fabric.

In this section, I've had to strike a balance: Hundreds of ethnicities are represented in New York, and I had to leave many out. I've chosen the neighborhoods that I think are most educational (whether or not you descend from that particular group), accessible, and vibrant. Consider this a starting point. If you come from an interesting background, you may want to hit the library and find your particular enclave—I assure you, it's here somewhere. For example, if you hop on the #7 train (nicknamed "The Orient Express" for the diversity of neighborhoods it serves) in Midtown Manhattan and head out to Queens, you'll pass through neighborhoods populated by Indians, Ecuadorians, Peruvians, Jamaicans, and Chinese—not to mention Shea Stadium, home of the Mets.

Looking at the neighborhood descriptions that follow, you'll discover I've emphasized food. This is because cuisine is the great diplomat—you need no special language skills or historical knowledge to appreciate good food. Children, especially the adventuresome ones, respond wonderfully to the infinite delights of ethnic food markets and restaurants. But remember, feeding your kids on unfamiliar cuisine can be stressful—so it never hurts to pack a few familiar snacks on these journeys.

Chinatown

If you visit only one ethnic neighborhood during your New York vacation, it should be Chinatown. This is by far Manhattan's most vibrant ethnic community. In most others, such as Little Italy and the old Jewish Lower East Side, the immigrants arrived "fresh off the boat." Most started off poor, got jobs, or started businesses and, as they worked their way out of poverty, moved out of the old neighborhood to other parts of the City or to

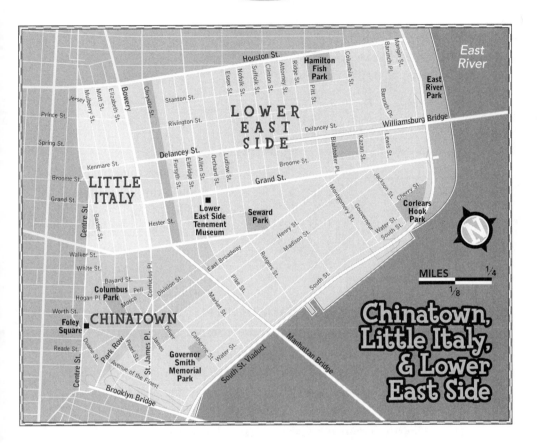

nearby suburbs. As a result, their former neighborhoods—once thriving cultural centers—are today only shadows of their former selves. Not so in Chinatown, where fresh waves of immigrants arrive daily, and the neighborhood's borders keep expanding.

Chinatown is getting cleaner, brighter, and admittedly a bit more westernized. But don't fear; Manhattan's Chinatown still has an excess of character, and the westernization of the establishments in the neighborhood comes from a blend of cultures East and West. For example, the new tea stores and pastry shops that are springing up around the neighborhood are similar to what you would find if you were to visit Singapore and Hong Kong—both with western influence, but the offspring of local Chinese (or Chinese investors from abroad).

Chinatown's very own McDonald's

Take the time to stroll through this neighborhood—you should allocate at least half a day. It's quite large, so don't expect to cover the whole area. I've suggested some places to visit (in the form of directions), but you don't have to do the whole route (especially if you're with small children) and, if you're feeling ambitious or adventuresome, deviate from the directions and strike out down side streets and explore a bit. There's something interesting around every corner.

Starting from the Canal Street subway station (#6 train), walk east along Canal crossing over Centre. On the far right cor-

Helpful Hint

Chinatown is extremely crowded and busy all the time, so keep an eye on your kids and tell them, before you arrive, that it's important to stay close. Pick a meeting place and write down the name and address for each child to keep in his or her pocket. If you do get separated, everyone will know where to meet. A good meeting place is the China-town Ice Cream Factory; it's right in the heart of Chinatown, and everyone will know it. It has a big banner hanging that is visible to anyone who can read (it also has a huge dragon on it for those who can't).

ner of Centre, have a look outside at **Kong Kee Food.** If your children are interested, point out the extensive variety of tofu (fried, pressed, wet, strips), bean sprouts, and wet rice cakes. Are those rice cakes like the ones you see in the supermarket? These items are mainstays of the Chinese diet; an entire store is dedicated to selling them, and yet most westerners don't eat them regularly—unless they're eating in a Chinese restaurant.

As you walk across Canal, you'll see countless little shops, stalls, and outposts. This is a good place to pick up cheap T-shirts (usually three for $10), hats, watches, handbags, umbrellas, traditional Chinese-style clothing, trinkets, and souvenirs. Remember, here every price is negotiable.

Cross over the triangle at Walker Street (staying on Canal) and note the change from dry goods to fish vendors, fruit stalls, apothecaries, and restaurants. Observe the different kinds of fish (some children will enjoy this and will linger, others won't like it at all and will want to move on, but every child seems to be fascinated, one way or another, by the fish vendors).

At 200 Canal, walk into the **Kam Man Food** store (I'll point out another

Learning Tip

Discuss how different cultures incorporate various foods into their diets and rituals. Throughout this chapter, we'll be examining shops where you can observe these distinctive cultural practices yourself.

similar store later if you want to bypass this one). Take some time to wander around. Quite different from the Grand Union, Shop Rite, and Price Club at home, isn't it? How many kinds of dried scallops are there in the big glass jars? How many oysters and shrimp? Look at all of the hot, soy, and hoisin sauces. Imagine if you were Chinese and went to an American grocery store to pick out ketchup, how would you choose?

Just past Kam Man is the **Tai Pan Bakery.** This is a new addition to the Chinatown scene. It's extremely popular with locals and tourists and is a good place to cool down (or warm up) with a drink and a snack if the troops need a break.

Educational note: Have you noticed all of the people selling fruits, vegetables, and foods from carts and stalls? This, again, is a cultural difference and is the way many people sell their wares in China, rather than in stores. Where do people take all of their wares when the day is over? It's a different way of doing things.

Continue along Canal, turning right on Mott Street. This is the main drag in Chinatown. **Ten Ren Tea and Ginseng** (75 Mott St.) is an authentic Chinese tea and herb shop and is definitely worth a browse. Check out the giant teapot (in the corner behind the door) with the dragon etched into its side. How many cups of tea do you think that would hold?

In Chinatown, many of the stores don't have names in English or even street numbers, so it's up to you and your kids to pick and choose and discover great things on your own—you can't look them up in advance.

At Häagen Dazs, go left on Bayard Street. Have a peek at the **Chinatown Ice Cream Factory** (65 Bayard St., 212-608-4170). Look at the flavors. A little different from Baskin-Robbins, isn't it? Lychee, green tea, and red bean are a few of the selections. Those feeling less bold may choose from some of the classics, too.

Continue along Bayard, going right on Bowery (or "the Bowery," as we say here). Check out the Chinese pagodalike **McDonald's**, with Ronald sitting out front on the bench. Everyone seems to love to have a picture taken with Ronald. This is a good place to use the bathroom if anyone needs it. Bathrooms in Chinatown are somewhat hard to come by.

Side step: If everyone is holding up well and doesn't mind a few extra blocks of walking, cross over the Bowery at the crosswalk at Doyers. You have just crossed into what is currently the most authentic part of Chinatown, where the locals shop and live, and where few tourists tread. This section is like an outpost of the neighborhood through which you've just been wandering. As Chinese immigrants flooded into Chinatown over the years, the supply of space could not meet demand, so little by little, the area has expanded to include parts of other shrinking downtown neighborhoods (like Little Italy and the Lower East Side). Take the right fork down Catherine Street, walking on the left. Cross East Broadway. This is a good place to buy fruit for snacks and veggies if you have cooking facilities.

Learning Tip

Look at the different kinds of fruits and vegetables. Chinese eggplant is actually a different shape and color than the kind you're probably used to buying. Do you think it tastes different? Chinese cucumbers are lighter green, have a different texture, and have ridges. Bok choy, Chinese apples, lychees, water chestnuts—look at the different produce. How do you think it tastes? Do you think it's eaten raw or cooked, or perhaps both?

Go right on Henry. Note how peaceful it is here in this residential area, compared with the hustle and bustle of the neighborhood. Turn right on Oliver; can you hear the birds chirping as you walk up the block? Cross over the big expanse of the Bowery to Citibank and turn right onto Mott. You are now at the opposite end of the street from which you started. If you didn't go into Kam Man (or your kids loved it), step into **Kam Kuo Food Corp.** This is where I like to stock up on my Chinese cooking ingredients. Hundreds of items are packed into the space, and if it's imported from the East (other than Japan), you'll likely find it here. Here again, you'll find little shops with souvenirs and trinkets. Kids love to browse through these stores, which are brimming with all sorts of interesting little items.

Take your first left down the hill onto Mosco. If there's no street sign, you'll know it by the long line: This corner is where the **"egg cake lady"** works her magic with two waffle iron–like contraptions. On this corner of Mosco and Mott, if you arrive after hours (whenever the batter runs out), all you'll see is a rust-colored, metal box with an accordionlike metal sheet that covers the "window." This nondescript outpost, which you would otherwise walk by without a second glance, is a hive of activity during business hours. When she's in action, the egg cake lady rolls up the accordion covering, heats up the irons, and ladles scoops of a secret batter into the contraptions. What, you wonder, could be so great that all of these people, from every walk of life, every race, religion, and country from around the globe, line up in the summer heat and the winter cold to get? Are they giving something away? No, what everyone is waiting for is a bag (or ten) of the hot-off-the-press egg cakes made from a secret family recipe. An egg cake is a sweet dessert (probably the only Chinese dessert item that I like—and I like all sweets) that is a cross between a cake, a cookie, and a waffle. Each egg cake is about the size of a quarter, and each order has ten cakes.

If you're with small kids, you might think twice before waiting in a long line. Then again, you could send them down the hill to **Columbus Park** and playground with one parent, while the other stands in line. It's a neat treat and also an interesting chance to talk to the other people—you'll find locals and other tourists alike line up for the unique treat. Would you believe the egg cake lady put several kids through college selling these confections at $1 per bag?

Walk to the bottom of the hill and turn right on Mulberry. If anyone needs a break, the playground across the street is a good place for it. There are plenty of benches, some swings, and lots of room to run around. At the corner of Bayard and Mulberry, in front of the building that houses the **Museum of Chinese in the Americas** (MoCA, 70 Mulberry St.), are a handful of old Chinese fortune-tellers. I've never had my fortune read here (because I've never had it read anywhere), but if your kids are into that sort of thing, this is a great place to do it. Talk about authentic! To visit the tiny museum, step inside the old stone building, climb to the second floor, and go around the corner—there's MoCA. Though it is small, it is the "first full-time, professionally staffed museum dedicated to reclaiming, preserving, and interpreting the history and culture of Chinese and their descendants in the Western Hemisphere." The museum is free to children under 12; there is a $1 charge for students and $3 for adults.

Continue along Mulberry. Along the way, tell the kids to keep their eyes peeled for stacks of food items, such as fifty-pound bags of rice, that are being unloaded and delivered around the neighborhood.

Finish up your walk around Chinatown at the intersection with Canal.

Note: Chinatown has grown so much in recent years that a second Chinatown has emerged in Flushing, Queens. It's also a fascinating neighborhood, but it's far less tourist-friendly than Manhattan's Chinatown (and correspondingly even more authentic). But if you're committed to studying New York Chinese culture to the fullest extent possible, you'll definitely want to check out Flushing's Chinatown, at the end of the #7 subway line.

Little Italy

Italians started immigrating to America as early as the 1700s, but these weren't the Italians who settled in Little Italy—the early arrivals were aristocrats from northern Italy. It wasn't until the late 1800s that the big waves of Italians, mostly peasants from southern Italy, arrived and settled into what we now call Little Italy. Life was hard. The newcomers spoke no English, the area was crowded, and disease was rampant. As with many immigrant enclaves, new arrivals moved in with family members and friends from "the old country," and they worked hard to send money back home to Italy and to bring themselves out of poverty. These later Italian immigrants built, with their physical labor, muscle, and sweat, New York's highways and byways—they are largely responsible for digging the subway tunnels and the streets that we still use today.

As they worked and saved, the Italians of Little Italy wanted what all parents want: a better life for their children. They started to move out of the neighborhood that was like an Italian village to the boroughs and the suburbs. What you see as you walk along Mulberry Street is really a shell of what the community once was. By the way, your kids may be familiar with Mulberry Street from Dr. Seuss's *And to Think I Saw It on Mulberry Street.* You may want to read that book with your family before or while visiting Little Italy. Now, only the elderly still live on these streets. And though some of the old businesses remain, it's mostly the restaurants and cafés that cater to the tourists and to the generations of Italian Americans looking for a weekend outing (from Staten Island, New Jersey, or Long Island) or a little nostalgia (but not nearly as good as Mama used to make).

Starting from the Canal Street subway station (#6), walk east along Canal to Mulberry Street, where you turn left. Or, from the Spring Street subway station (#6), walk east along Spring until you hit Mulberry; turn right onto Mulberry.

From either end of Mulberry Street, make your way up and down the street (or right down the middle on summer weekends, when they close the street to vehicular traffic). Mostly you'll see cafés and restaurants, some of which are more than one hundred years old (although the businesses may no longer be in their original locations). The waiters and maîtres d's will call out to you, inviting you to try their restaurant. There's a friendly air to the whole thing. No one is really being pushy, and it's all sort of like a game—you look at the menu; do you want to eat here or check out the next place? It's great, they'll tell you, and perfect for the kids. You walk on, and they go back to their conversation in Italian until the next group walks by.

All of the restaurants along Mulberry have very good lunch specials, often multiple courses for $5.95–$8.95. They also often offer early bird–type dinners—not fashionable, but perfect for kids (and very economical).

Some of my favorite stops on Mulberry are:

Casa Bella, on the corner of Mulberry and Hester (see chapter 6 for a full description).

Café Roma (385 Broome St.), where the Italians take their coffee. It's especially nice during the summer when the tables overflow out onto the sidewalk, and the atmosphere is so international you could almost swear you were sitting in . . . well, Italy might be a slight stretch, but you'd be surprised how close this comes.

Ferrara's (195 Grand St., follow the signboard) is an old neighborhood favorite. The prices are a bit steep, and the pastry is no better than anywhere else in the neighborhood (but that's still better than most other places—especially once you leave New York), but the people are friendly and eating a cannoli there is sort of like eating a piece of history.

Italian Food Center (186 Grand St.) is by far the best place in the city to get an Italian deli sandwich. If you step in here at lunchtime, you'll find the place packed to the gills. Many of the customers are daily regulars and walk almost half a mile from the courthouses to get a bite of the action. The benches out front are perfect for an impromptu picnic if the weather is good, and the deli also sells drinks so you can make it a one-stop shop.

Alleva Ricotta and Mozzarella (188 Grand St.), established July 1, 1896, is across the street. Stepping into this place is like stepping back in time. The mozzarella here is so good that I've been known to devour large hunks of the stuff shortly after exiting the store. If you have an adventurous bunch, a great meal is some "mozz" from Alleva and some fresh bread from (and a seat out front of) the Food Center. Those not in the mood for something new can always go with a sandwich while the others try the heavenly cheese.

If you're lucky enough to be visiting in September, you can catch the annual **San Gennaro Festival.** People from all over the tri-state area converge on Little Italy; Mulberry Street is closed to traffic, and the neighborhood is alive with lights, colorful decorations, food stands, games, and vendors. It's a real happening scene, but it does get extremely crowded, so if you're with young children, it's best to go before the biggest crowds arrive in the evening—try during the day or late afternoon.

The Old Jewish Lower East Side (LES)

To see the old Jewish Lower East Side as it was back in its heyday will take a strong imagination. A little history will help to set the stage for this neighborhood that was once the heart of Jewish life and activity for poor Jewish immigrants during the second half of the nineteenth century. The first Jews settled en masse in this neighborhood during the 1850s, though interestingly enough, these were not the Jews who imparted their religious and cultural imprint upon this area. These Jews were of German ancestry and shared their tenements with the Irish and other Germans.

It was during the 1880s, when brutal pogroms broke out in Russia and Poland, that the religious Jews of Eastern Europe, fleeing for their lives, settled into life on the LES. This influx eventually established much of what remains of the neighborhood as we know it today. But at the time, the population was swelling by the thousands, and the neighborhood was rife with disease. The streets were strewn with garbage, and large extended families of ten or more people would often share a single room to make their home. It was a difficult life for these newcomers. A few Jewish social aid groups were established by their brethren to help ease them into life in New York. People peddled and sold from pushcarts—everything from vegetables to rags—and made a living working long, backbreaking hours to better their lives. Just after the turn of the century, with more persecution in other countries, immigrant Jews again flooded into the LES. These Jews came from around the globe—more Russian Jews, Turkish Jews, and Greek Jews.

The LES was full of cultural life and activity, not to mention busting at the seams. By the 1920s, as people worked themselves out of poverty and made their fortunes, they looked to move out of the neighborhood to improved lives. The Jewish population has dwindled ever since, but some thriving businesses remain, established by these Jewish immigrants, that are still at the heart and soul of the neighborhood.

Take the F train to Delancey Street. When you exit, you'll be on one of the corners of Essex and Delancey. Walk west (away from the bridge) along Delancey until you reach Orchard Street. Turn right on Orchard.

The main artery of the LES is Orchard Street. This is where the action is and where, on weekends, the street is closed to vehicular traffic (from Delancey to East Houston). At one time, Jews from the neighborhood owned every storefront along this street, but times have changed and now only the most determined remain. What follows are my favorite LES destinations, which can be strung together in a walking tour of sorts—or you can stroll along Orchard Street and pick a few others to throw in, too.

Sosinsky & Sons (143 Orchard St., between Delancey and Rivington) is a secret my husband begged me not to divulge. He always looks as though he's wearing a $100 shirt, but he actually pays $25 at Sosinsky's. This is one of the best places in the world to stock up on men's and teens' dress and casual shirts, bathrobes, and occasionally trousers and even shorts. In Old World fashion, you tell them your size (or they'll measure you) and out come boxes with shirts from which you can choose. The prices are incredible, and the stock often includes shirts from Burberry's,

Gitman Brothers, and other top name brands. The best deals are on factory seconds. Shopping here is a blast—the mother-and-son sales team behind the counter is a great repository of LES oral history.

Katz's Delicatessen (205 East Houston St., corner of Orchard) has what some argue is the best pastrami and corned beef in the world. This is the only place in the City where they still carve the meat by hand. It's a real scene. Don't be intimidated by the shouting or the curt countermen. The hot dogs are also great (they make them themselves), as are the knishes and turkey sandwiches. The sandwich prices might seem steep, but each sandwich is easily big enough for two kids to share. Here you can go with waiter service or counter service. These days, with most of the old-time waiters gone (they used to tell great jokes), you're better off lining up at the counter. Don't be afraid to ask for what you want—nothing shocks them around here, but also don't be surprised if they say no.

Russ & Daughters (179 East Houston St.) is down the block from Katz's and well worth a browse, even if you're not interested in buying. What you'll find here is all of the best culinary representatives from your cousin's (or friend's) bar mitzvah, only done well—whitefish, pickled herring, and so many varieties of smoked salmon that it's actually an education. The dried fruit here is also excellent.

Back along Orchard, turn left onto Rivington to the newly sandblasted and renovated **Shaarey Shimoyim** (89 Rivington St.), the first American Rumanian Jewish Congregation. This building is absolutely exquisite. If you step inside (Saturday is the Sabbath, so don't tour then), the shamis (the guardian of the synagogue) will happily answer your questions and show you around. Donations are welcome, and, as when touring any religious site, it's polite to make at least a token gesture.

Economy Candy (108 Rivington St.) is sure to be a hit with everyone. It is one of my all-time favorites, and I never get out of here without buying something, even if I'm there on the pretext of showing someone around. The candy selection is eye-popping, with standard favorites as well as more exotics both stocked.

Essex Street Market (120 Essex St., entrances at Delancey and just south of Rivington) is an interesting conglomeration of dry goods and foodstuffs. Mayor Fiorello La Guardia created this market in 1939 to keep the neighborhood's pushcart vendors from overwhelming the nearby streets. It's more a place to walk around than to shop in, unless of course you're in the market for a carp. A good children's book (ages 4–7) to read before departure is *The Carp in the Bathtub*. Everyone in the family will get a kick out of the story, and, when you're wandering through the market, you can look for the carp that often are kept in giant rubber "tubs." It always makes my day.

Kossar's Bialys (367 Grand St., just in from Essex) is across Delancey and left at Baskin-Robbins. This place is well worth a peek, even if you don't intend to buy anything, because there's a lot of activity with the dough and the ovens, and it's great to watch the bread come fresh out of the oven on the long wooden sticks (though if you've never had a bialy, it would be a grave mistake to miss the opportunity because they're by far the best in the City, and therefore most likely the best in the country).

People line up and down the block to buy **Guss's Pickles** (35 Essex St.). And if you've ever seen *Crossing Delancey* (a perfect movie for teen girls who are into love stories—with no skin whatsoever and great illustrations of the strains between the traditional and the modern lifestyles), you've seen Guss's. The pickles and other pickled stuff (tomatoes, sauerkraut, etc.) do not get better than this.

Several Judaica stores line Essex Street. At 19 Essex you'll find **Weinfeld's Skull Caps,** where I got the monogrammed yarmulkes for my wedding (they also sell bar mitzvah sets). The **Israel Gift Center** (23 Essex St.) is full of gift items that are expressive of Judaism, with religious items like yarmulkes and talises and adornments like jewelry. At 41 Essex is **Rabbi Eisen-bach,** who carries everything from marriage contracts to eclectic menorahs and antique Judaica.

The **Lower East Side Tenement Museum** (97 Orchard St., tickets at 90 Orchard) is a great place to go to get a really good feel for what life was like on the LES decades ago. The museum is a recreation of tenement life. Special exhibits, tours, and children's programs are also offered.

The **Eldridge Street Synagogue** (12 Eldridge St.), one of many synagogues that used to line the streets of this neighborhood, is a reminder of the rich Jewish life that once characterized these streets. A National Historic Landmark, the synagogue was erected in 1886 and is undergoing a renovation to restore it to its former splendor.

Brighton Beach (Little Odessa) and Coney Island

For Brighton Beach, take the D or Q train to Brighton Beach Avenue (BBA).

For Coney Island, take the D or F train to West 8th Street.

Note: These neighborhoods are in Brooklyn, and take about an hour to reach from Manhattan by subway.

Situated on the Atlantic Ocean, the seaside town of Brighton Beach (named for England's seaside resort of the same name) was, before the turn of the nineteenth century, a high-falutin' resort area for the wealthy. The neighborhood has since changed many times over. In its current incarnation, since the late 1980s, the neighborhood is locally referred to as "Little Odessa" on account of the first wave of Russian immigrants to settle in the area who were from . . . Odessa. Since then, other waves have included Russian immigrants from Kiev, Moscow, and elsewhere.

One of the most noticeable things about stepping down off the elevated train and onto the streets of Little Odessa is that no one is speaking English, and all of the signs are in English and

Cyrillic. It's almost like taking a trip to old Russia, except that here, the food is bountiful and fresh. The main drag is Brighton Beach Avenue—this is where all of the action is: shopping, restaurants, and fruit stands. To get to the boardwalk, pick any side street and walk east, or just ask—everyone knows where it is.

To fill empty stomachs, the best destinations are **Primorski** (282 BBA, near 3rd, 718-891-3111), **Odessa** (1113 BBA, between 13th and 14th, 718-332-3223), and **National Restaurant** (273 BBA, between 2nd and 3rd, 718-646-1225). During the day, these large empty halls seem somewhat drab and tame, but the food is still good, prices are reasonable, and you'll get an authentic Brighton Beach dining experience. At night, they are transformed into nightclub restaurants where the meals are fixed price, the food comes piled on platters, the vodka flows, and the crowd, Russians of all ages and from all walks of life, comes to catch the entertainment and get down on the dance floor. The nightlife scene is great, but best for parents traveling with older teens (and if you do decide to hit one of these places at night, it's a good idea to arrange car service for your ride home).

Caffe Cappuccino (409 BBA, between 4th and 5th Sts., 718-646-6297) is another good lunch spot. Far less cavernous and over-the-top than the aforementioned restaurants, Caffe Cappuccino serves Russian food (the blinis are great) and desserts, while Russian music videos run (at a reasonable, inoffensive volume) nonstop. This is a good place to try the Russian-style tea and sit with the locals (when it's crowded, people share tables).

The best Russian food market is **M & I International** (249 BBA, between 2nd and 3rd). It's always bustling, and you'll find that most of the shoppers are conversing with one another in Russian, but you'll have no problem if you want to order something or ask a question because the counter staff speaks English. All sorts of deli items are stocked in this two-level store, plus prepared takeout foods, breads, candies, kebabs, and canned goods. I like to come here just to browse and people-watch, but there's also plenty to buy if you need some snacks or food for a picnic on the beach.

After you've wandered and window-shopped past the stores selling thigh-high red leather boots and Russian videos, take a stroll on the boardwalk, which on a nice day is one of the most pleasant places to be. At one end (the end you're at in Brighton Beach), you'll find Russian boardwalk cafés, old folks sitting out on benches, and families playing on the beach. On the other end is Coney Island and the New York Aquarium.

The walk down the boardwalk toward Coney Island is an interesting study in the varied cultures of the area. In Brighton Beach, you'll see mostly Russians and people of European descent. As you get farther away from Little Odessa and closer to the activity of Coney Island, you'll see more people of Hispanic descent.

If you're all the way out here anyway, you certainly should check out the **New York Aquarium** (Surf Ave. at 8th St. West, or enter from the boardwalk, 718-265-FISH) and the old **Coney Island Amusement Park.** The amusement park is a bit seedy by modern standards, but it's superauthentic, and your kids will gawk at the now-defunct hulk of the old Cyclone wooden roller coaster. Be sure to grab a frankfurter at the world-famous original **Nathan's** (Surf Ave., corner of Stillwell) and wander over to the wonderful **Philip's Candy** (1237 Surf Ave., next door to Nathan's).

For a break, stop by the huge playground (with foam rubber in appropriate places to avoid injuries) just up from the boardwalk restaurants, where neighborhood children play, basketball and handball games coexist side by side, and the older generation sits on nearby benches and watches the world go by. The beach here gets crowded, but the sand is clean (though I wouldn't recommend swimming in the ocean), and it's a nice place to take a break. There are also a few play areas set up on the beach by the boardwalk, perfect for injury-free play.

Greek Astoria

N train to Ditmars Boulevard.

At the tail end of the 1920s, Greeks started settling in Astoria, Queens, a neighborhood just across the East River from Manhattan that's also known locally as Little Athens. The Greek population in the neighborhood grew as families who were already settled brought relatives to America, and labor bosses would arrange and pay for passage for those willing to work off their ticket. This neighborhood, like the others, has been through ebbs and flows, but unlike many of the others (except Chinatown), Astoria is still growing.

Astoria is full of Greek fish restaurants (the best around), cafés, and pastry shops—the likes of which you've probably never seen anywhere else. Take a stroll through the neighborhood, whose main drags are 31st Street (under the elevated subway) and Ditmars Boulevard. Walking here is like taking a walk through Athens (though a little less polluted and crowded). Don't be surprised if you hear more Greek spoken than English.

As in many ethnic neighborhoods, eating is a favorite pastime here. I've enjoyed many a meal and stroll followed by dessert in this neighborhood—it's truly a lovely way to spend an afternoon or evening. Even better, though, for children who are not up to an extended meal, these same restaurants, where some patrons linger, are extremely welcoming of families and will get the food on the table quickly. Noise and energy are already plentiful, lest you are worried that your crowd might offend anyone.

Elias Corner (24-02 31st St. at 24th Ave., 718-932-1510) is where I send people for fish, and **Telly's Taverna** (28-13 23rd Ave., between 28th and 29th Sts., 718-728-9056) is great for its wide-ranging Greek menu. In summer they have a nice "garden" café out back. **Christos Hasapo-Taverna** (41-08 23rd Ave., at 41st St., 718-726-5195) is the traditional combination of Greek restaurant (steak) and butcher that rivals Manhattan steakhouses—and with better prices to boot. **Lefkos Pyrgos** (22-85 31st St.) and Galaxy (3722 Ditmars Blvd.) are my picks for dessert and coffee.

Along with eating your way through the neighborhood, you should stop to have a look at **Saint Demetrios Church** (31st St. and 31st Dr.). Saint Demetrios has the largest Greek Orthodox congregation outside of Athens. The building itself is an extremely impressive edifice and well worth the visit.

Arthur Avenue— Little Italy in the Bronx

Take the C, D, or #4 subway to Fordham Road, then transfer to the eastbound BX12 bus across the street from the station; get off at the Arthur Avenue stop. Be sure to use a MetroCard, so the transfer will be free.

Manhattanites hate to admit it, but today the most authentic Italian neighborhood in America is up north—in the Bronx, where Arthur Avenue meets East 187th Street. This Italian-American enclave is home to scores of the nation's finest and most authentic Italian shops.

I wouldn't necessarily advocate a pilgrimage to Arthur Avenue on its own merits (it's quite a haul from Manhattan), but the neighborhood happens to be just a hop, skip, and a jump from two of New York's absolute best tourist attractions: The Bronx Zoo and the New York Botanical Gardens (see chapter 5 for details). So if you're planning a day around these two locations, you definitely owe yourself a jaunt to Arthur Avenue.

At **Teitel Brothers Wholesale Grocery** (2372 Arthur Ave., 718-733-9400), you'll find an incredible selection of artisanal Italian food products: gallon jugs of olive oil from Italy's Lucca region (the best in the world), whole wheels of three-year-aged Parmigiano Reggiano cheese (they'll cut you a smaller piece, don't worry), and all the dry goods you'd need to open an Italian restaurant, with discounts that put Balducci's high Manhattan prices to shame.

As you open the door to the tiny **Calabria Pork Store** (2338 Arthur Ave., 718-367-5145), the pungent smell of cured meat and spices smacks you in the face. It's dark inside because the thousands of handmade sausages hanging from the ceiling (each tagged with a code to indicate its age) obscure the light fixtures. Once you've tasted Calabria's silken sopressata, you'll never be satisfied with mass-produced versions.

Like rubbernecking motorists gaping at a wreck, even herbivores can't resist checking out **Biancardi's** (2350 Arthur Ave., 718-733-4058) provocative window display. Poor little bunny, poor little lamb, strung up in the window, fur and all. But this is perhaps the best place in town to purchase impeccably fresh game, beef, lamb, and pork. Call ahead and they can get you just about anything. If you're with young children who might be upset by this display, you might want to walk past quickly—or take this opportunity to explain to them about the food chain.

For a quick pick-me-up, stop by **Madonia Brothers** (2348 Arthur Ave., 718-295-5573) for a hand-filled cannoli. Once you've chosen a hollow pastry shell from the display case, the teenage girl behind the counter will expertly squeeze the sweet ricotta filling into it. This is how cannolis were meant to be. Then wander right across the street to **Enzo's Café** (2239 Arthur Ave., no phone), where the standard for espresso is just as high—it's never bitter and always with a paper-thin layer of foamy *crema* on top.

The first time you visit the **Terranova Bakery** (691 East 187th St., 718-367-6985), Mr. Terranova himself might give you a tour of the enormous coal-fired ovens. On your second visit, you're a regular, and on your third, you'll likely be greeted with kisses. The specialty of the house is a totally addictive, ring-shaped sausage bread. You can get regular Italian loaves, too, and I slightly prefer Terranova's crust to that of the very similar, competing **Addeo Bakers** (Addeo Bakers, 535 East 187th St., no phone) around the corner.

Perhaps the warmest welcome on Arthur Avenue is at **Borgatti's Ravioli and Egg Noodles** (632 East 187th St., 718-367-3799), one of the nation's last remaining manufacturers of fresh, handmade pasta. The salespeople (all family members) cut sheets of pasta to order on the hand-turned press; you can specify whatever width you want for the noodles. Large, fresh ravioli, bursting with excellent ricotta cheese, are the house specialty, and Uncle Larry or one of his nieces will gladly spend all day discussing the finer points of boiling water.

A special treat for wine-aficionado parents: **Mount Carmel Wines & Spirits** (612 East 187th St., 718-367-7833, www.mountcarmelwine.com) is one of America's best-kept wine secrets. This veritable museum of wine has, without question, the best and most comprehensive selection of Italian wines in America. The 1990 Brunello di Montalcinos are all but gone from Manhattan stores, but here you'll find eight of them. The sales help is phenomenal—everybody in the store is fanatical about Italian wine.

After all that shopping and schlepping, your biggest decision of the day remains: Where to have lunch? For something portable, my favorite is **Mike's Deli** (2344 Arthur Ave., 718-295-5033, www.arthuravenue.com) in the Arthur Avenue Retail Market (the retail market is also where you'll find fresh produce and interesting vendors). It's hard to choose between the hot sausage-and-pepper hero and the Big Mike Combo (with mortadella, ham, salami, capicollo, and provolone), so you may as well get both. Another good bet is **Full Moon Pizzeria** (602 East 187th St., 718-584-3451), for a traditional New York slice. But for a sit-down meal, the clear choice is **Dominick's** (2335 Arthur Ave., 718-733-2807), where you'll get a hearty, family-style, no-menu, eat-what-they-cook-that-day, sit-down-at-the-big-long-table-with-strangers feast.

A word to the wise: If at all possible, visit Arthur Avenue midweek, when proprietors are far less harried.

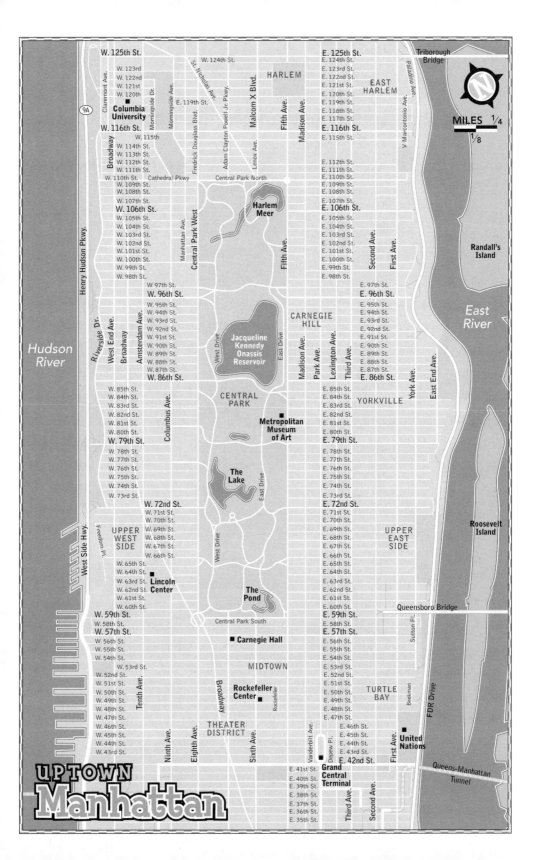

Guide to Manhattan Neighborhoods

The following are brief descriptions of the most important residential areas of Manhattan, which will help orient your family in your travels around the City. For each neighborhood, I've included a list of points of interest that I think characterize the area. Whether you're visiting a neighborhood for a grand tour or just for one specific attraction, store, or restaurant, it's nice to get a general feel for the area before you set out.

Upper East Side

The Upper East Side is one of the two major uptown residential areas of interest to tourists (the other one is the Upper West Side). It's a huge swath of land and contains many subneighborhoods.

I live in Carnegie Hill, a small slice of the Upper East Side that runs from 86th to 96th Streets, and from Fifth to Lexington Avenues. It's an area characterized by sidewalk cafés (you'll see my neighbors Paul Newman and Joanne Woodward, as well as Ralph Lauren, Calvin Klein, and Michael J. Fox, at the nearby restaurants), a family atmosphere, and its proximity to Central Park.

The rest of the Upper East Side is also quiet and houses some of the wealthiest people in America. Moving east from Carnegie Hill, there's Yorkville, which used to be a German neighborhood (you'll still find a few German shops along First Ave., near 86th St.) but is now home to numerous high-rise apartment buildings where a growing number of young professionals live. This is one of the best areas for purchasing kids' clothing and finding an economical family meal.

South of 86th Street lies the Upper East Side proper, where you'll find many of New York's wealthiest families along Park Avenue, Fifth Avenue, and East End Avenue. The Upper East Side is very safe and is therefore perfect for wandering around with your family, even at night.

Finally, across the river from the Upper East Side is the unusual area of Roosevelt Island. An island in the middle of the East River, Roosevelt Island is reached by the famed Roosevelt Island Tramway (a cable car running from Manhattan), which kids absolutely love to ride.

Points of Interest

- @ Madison Avenue Shopping District (Barney's, Polo, and most designer boutiques)

- @ Central Park (Conservatory Garden, Reservoir, Metropolitan Museum, Zoo)

- @ Museum Mile (Metropolitan Museum of Art, Guggenheim, Cooper-Hewitt, Jewish Museum, and others)

- @ Gracie Mansion (Mayor's residence)

- @ Numerous distinguished private clubs (Harmonie Club, Metropolitan Club, Lotus Club)

- @ Temple Emanu-El (largest—bigger than St. Patrick's Cathedral—and oldest Reform Jewish congregation) 1 East 65th Street at Fifth Avenue (212-744-1400)

- @ Asia Society (art collection assembled by John D. Rockefeller), 725 Park Avenue at 70th Street (212-288-6400)

- @ Frank E. Campbell Funeral Chapel (most prestigious in the world; James Cagney, John Lennon, Mae West, and Tennessee Williams were "customers"), 1076 Madison Avenue at 81st Street (212-288-3500)

- @ 92nd Street Y (major Jewish cultural and community center), 1395 Lexington Avenue at 92nd Street (212-427-6000)

- @ Synod of Bishops of the Russian Orthodox Church Outside Russia (dramatic 1917 Georgian mansion, now a cathedral), 75 East 93rd Street, between Park and Madison Avenues (212-534-1601)

@ Islamic Center of New York (New York's first major mosque, designed by Skidmore, Owings & Merrill), 1711 Third Avenue at 96th Street (212-722-5234)

Upper West Side

If you stood at the corner of 68th Street and Columbus Avenue (near where my husband grew up) in 1970 and then traveled via time machine to the same corner in the year 2000, you'd assume your time machine had taken you to the wrong place. What was basically a slum in 1970 is now the site of one of New York's most luxurious new apartment buildings (which also house the exclusive Reebok Sports Club and the Sony IMAX theater). The transformation of the Upper West Side, triggered by the construction of Lincoln Center during the 1960s and bolstered by frantic luxury high-rise construction during the 1980s and 1990s, has made this neighborhood one of the world's great urban reclamation stories.

The Lincoln Square area is the southernmost part of the Upper West Side and has most of the more obvious tourist attractions (Lincoln Center, including the ballet). The rest of the Upper West Side is very residential and, as a result, has wonderful shops, family restaurants, and food markets.

The neighborhood is also home to many young modern Orthodox Jews who are attracted by the Lincoln Square Synagogue, an abundance of kosher restaurants in the West 70s and 90s, and the presence of many other members of their faith.

Points of Interest

@ Central Park (Reservoir, Strawberry Fields, Sheep Meadow, Tavern on the Green)

@ Lincoln Center (New York's major center of the performing arts, including the Metropolitan Opera House, Avery Fisher Hall, and New York State Theater)

@ Christ and St. Stephen's Church (uncharacteristically rural church in the middle of a developed city block), 120 West 69th Street at Columbus Avenue and Broadway (212-787-2755)

@ Lincoln Square Synagogue (1970 Hausman and Rosenberg building, now a leader of the Modern Orthodox movement), 200 Amsterdam Avenue at 69th Street (212-874-6100)

@ Beacon Theater (gorgeous old 2,700-seat theater used for a variety of performances), 2124 Broadway at 75th Street (212-496-7070)

@ New-York Historical Society (spelled with a hyphen, it houses one of the best American collections around), 170 Central Park West at 76th and 77th Streets (212-873-3400)

@ American Museum of Natural History (the premier natural history museum and research institute, now with a dramatic new planetarium), Central Park West at 79th Street (212-769-5000)

West of Midtown: Clinton and Chelsea

Chelsea is in many ways like other young, affluent areas of New York. You'll see attractive couples out for the evening or just walking hand-in-hand down the street. But in Chelsea, the couples are often men.

New York has a very substantial gay population, and the City is historically very tolerant of gays—it would be exceptionally poor form to speak homophobically in Manhattan. And although Chelsea is probably the most visibly gay neighborhood in New York right now, it is also home to many, many happily co-existing people of all stripes and preferences.

Chelsea is near the Garment Center and encompasses the Flower District. The streets feel open, and there are few high-rise

buildings. An array of new stores has opened along Sixth Avenue in recent years; restaurants and shops now line Eighth Avenue, and the western part of Chelsea contains several up-and-coming art galleries. The Chelsea Piers athletic and recreation complex has completed the neighborhood, providing a facility unlike any other in the world.

North of Chelsea is what is now called Clinton—and used to be called Hell's Kitchen. During the early 1990s, a few prestigious corporations and law firms, tired of paying Midtown rents, struck out into Midtown West and relocated their corporate headquarters into this neighborhood, which was formerly made up of porn shops, slums, and some artists' residences (mostly actors and dancers). The presence of these large companies spurred economic growth, and in just the past three or four years this neighborhood has really turned the corner. It's now one of the best places to dine in all New York, especially given its proximity to Midtown and the theaters.

Points of Interest

- Broadway Theater District (most of the major theaters are here)
- Flower district (wholesale and retail), Avenue of the Americas from 27th to 30th Streets
- Antiques (this is a major center of antiques in New York City), Ninth Avenue from 20th to 22nd Streets
- Chelsea Piers (gigantic sports and recreation complex), West Street from 17th to 23rd Streets (212-336-6666)
- Javits Center (New York's largest convention center), 655 West 34th Street at Eleventh and Twelfth Avenues (212-216-2000)
- Port Authority (the main bus terminal for New York), Eighth and Ninth Avenues from 40th to 42nd Streets (212-564-8484)
- Intrepid Sea-Air-Space Museum (beautifully preserved World War II aircraft carrier), 46th Street and Twelfth Avenue (212-245-0072)

East of Midtown: Turtle Bay, Murray Hill, Gramercy

To the east and south of Midtown Manhattan you'll find a mixed bag of neighborhoods, each with its own personality and evocative name like Turtle Bay, Murray Hill, and Gramercy.

Murray Hill and Turtle Bay are genteel and affluent and are very near the United Nations. Thus, many consulates are nearby, and an international flavor is in the air.

The focal point of Gramercy Park is a beautiful private park (the only one in the City) open only to residents of buildings in the neighborhood (and those staying in the Gramercy Park Hotel or lucky enough to have friends living on the park). It's a quiet neighborhood because the park cuts up the streets and prevents most through-traffic. The park is surrounded by nineteenth-century townhouses, and there are many great places to eat in this area.

Points of Interest

- e Union Square Park (including the Union Square Green-market), from 14th to 17th Streets bounded by Union Square East and Union Square West

- e Theodore Roosevelt Birthplace (one of New York's most charming attractions), 28 East 20th Street (212-260-1616)

- e Flatiron Building (called "flatiron" for its shape; this was New York's first self-sufficient skyscraper), 175 Fifth Avenue at 22nd and 23rd Streets

- e Pierpont Morgan Library (America's finest collection of medieval and renaissance manuscripts, and then some), 29 East 36th Street at Park and Madison Avenues (212-685-0610)

Greenwich Village and SoHo

The areas of Greenwich Village (pronounced "greh-nitch") and SoHo (an abbreviation for South of Houston St.) are two of the City's most perpetually hip neighborhoods.

The center of Greenwich Village (called the West Village by some), physically and spiritually, is New York University and nearby Washington Square Park. The residential streets in the center of the Village are elegant and full of attractive old brick townhouses, as well as some apartment buildings. If you're think-

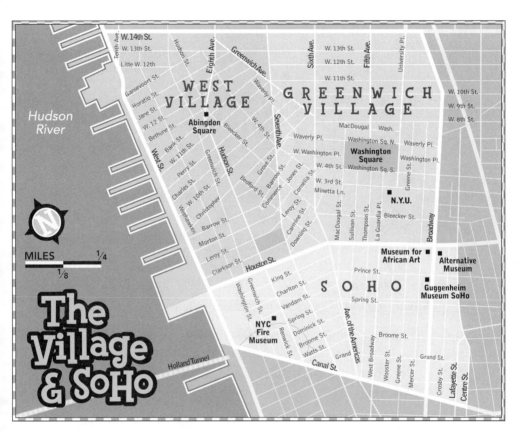

ing funky and unusual, you've got the wrong image—many of the streets in the Village are as dignified as they come.

SoHo, home to the greatest concentration of galleries in the City, is another artists' neighborhood that has undergone extensive gentrification. SoHo is a great and fun area, with incredible restaurants and a bustling nightlife.

The gentrification of SoHo has, as is often the case, caused an outward push. Now, the nearby areas of NoHo (North of Houston), Little Italy (which is no longer home to many Italians), and Nolita (a relatively new designation meaning North of

*Hanging out in
Washington
Square Park*

Little Italy) are fast becoming shopping and
dining destinations as
well.

Points of Interest

@ Numerous playhouses, music venues, galleries, and boutiques

@ Washington Square Park (largest public space downtown,
the focal point being the large Memorial Arch), from West
4th Street to Waverly Place and University Place to Mac-
Dougal Street

@ New York University (major institution of higher learning
and a defining voice in the neighborhood), from West 3rd
Street to Waverly Place and Mercer Street to La Guardia
Place (212-998-4636)

@ Film Forum (New York's premier art house movie theater),
209 West Houston Street at Sixth Avenue and Varick Street
(212-627-2035)

East Village

The designation "East Village" was created to bestow some legiti-
macy on this formerly run-down part of the Lower East Side.
And it worked. The neighborhood is now safe and fun, with bar-

gain stores and restaurants galore and a funky, antiestablishment population. As you walk south from the East Village, you'll enter Chinatown and the Lower East Side—discussed earlier.

Points of Interest

- ℮ Major center of alternative culture, including music and boutiques

- ℮ Saint Mark's Place (the most visible representation of East Village culture), from Avenue A to Third Avenue

- ℮ Cooper Union (famous private college that is the oldest steel-beam building in America), 7 East 7th Street at Fourth Avenue (212-353-4100)

TriBeCa and Lower Manhattan

TriBeCa (an abbreviation for Triangle below Canal Street), with its large-windowed cast-iron buildings, now looks more like SoHo than like the industrial neighborhood it once was. The warehouses and small factories are being reborn as residential apartments—expensive ones. The restaurant situation is excellent, spurred by low rent during the 1980s and now sustained by a desirable clientele despite climbing rents. Not as artsy as SoHo, TriBeCa nonetheless is exceptionally active at all hours, boasts attractive Duane Park, a bike path along the Hudson River, a fair number of clothing and design shops, and great galleries.

South and east of TriBeCa is lower Manhattan, where you'll find Wall Street and all the other downtown and Financial District attractions.

Points of Interest

- ℮ Many artsy and ethnic attractions in TriBeCa

- ℮ Center of the nation's financial markets (New York Stock Exchange)

- Site of many historic landmarks (Brooklyn Bridge, Trinity Church, Woolworth Building)

- Headquarters of government (City Hall, Municipal Building, Federal Building) and courts (state and federal)

- Departure point for ferries to Statue of Liberty and Ellis Island

- Fraunces Tavern (where Washington said farewell to his officers), 54 Pearl Street at Broad Street

- South Street Seaport and Pier 17 (shopping, dining, and outdoor events)

About The World Trade Center and September 11

World Trade Center

Although careful statistical measurements are not yet available, it seems clear that right now "Ground Zero"—the former site of the World Trade towers—is New York's most popular tourist attraction. I've yet to encounter a visitor to New York City who hasn't wanted to visit the site. And of course, New York City residents have mixed feelings about this: On the one hand, the outpouring of support implicit in so many visits to the site is welcome; on the other hand, there is a certain vulgarity in the souvenirs, the spectacle, and the thought that such a place could be an attraction.

If you do decide to visit the site, please do so respectfully—bearing in mind that you and your family are visiting a memorial. Be careful how you act and what you say, because chances are you may be standing near someone who lost a loved one in the tragedy. Remember that those who died in that attack were people with families.

People in and around the city are still grappling with the aftermath of the events of September 11, but at the same time we've all been working to move ahead. This doesn't mean we don't

Still standing. "The Sphere," a symbol of world peace conceived by artist Fritz Koenig, stood in the World Trade Plaza for three decades and survived the attacks of September 11. It currently stands in Battery Park.

think about that day and the months that followed on a regular basis; we just don't talk about it all that much. I've found that people outside of the New York Metro area, when they learn I'm from New York, are eager to discuss the events of September 11 with me—to express their shock, horror, and support—whereas people in the city are pretty quiet on the issue.

To date there are still banners of support, signs to missing loved ones, T-shirts, stuffed animals, flowers, patches, and all manner of other items left by friends, families, and strangers from all over the world in support and love to those who perished in the terrorist attacks. It is likely that these items will eventually be cleared away; though when a memorial to the victims is constructed, many of these items will probably be included. To me, these are the things that are so personal and sad—these are the things that put faces to the list of names.

Take the time to talk with your children (if they are old enough to remember and understand) about the events that transpired in whatever words you deem appropriate for them. Older children will obviously remember the events of September 11 without prompting, and I'm sure they will have already discussed it in some manner with teachers in school and perhaps at home. Children too young to comprehend should be treated with care—parents may wish to split up and take older children to the site and younger children elsewhere. It is very frightening for children to comprehend such senseless disaster, and discretion should be exercised based upon your child's age, personality, and maturity—this is something only you can decide.

Following is a list of helpful Web sites with information from mental healthcare professionals on how to talk to your children about September 11. I suggest you visit some of these Web sites before your trip to New York and perhaps even print out the pages you deem most appropriate for your kids. A ★ indicates a particularly useful or noteworthy entry.

American Academy of Pediatrics
www.aap.org/advocacy/releases/disastercomm.htm

General advice on communicating with children about disasters.

★ *Children's Aid Society*
www.childrensaidsociety.org

General guidelines (for children of any age) on how to speak to your children about the events of September 11.

★ *National Center for PTSD* (Post Traumatic Stress Disorder)
www.ncptsd.org/facts/disasters/fs_children_disaster.html

Advice for children of all ages and guidelines on how to speak with them about the events of September 11.

★ *The Parent Center*
www.parentcenter.com

Especially helpful, the Parent Center offers general advice for children ages 2 through 8 as well as age-specific advice for age groups within that range.

★ *Purdue Extension*
www.ces.purdue.edu/terrorism/children

A good selection of articles with helpful advice on how to talk to children in the aftermath of September 11. Some articles include "Talking to Children about Terrorism and Armed Conflict" and "Parenting in the Wake of Terrorism."

Where to Go and What to Do

The rescue and recovery operation is long since over, and decisions what to do with the space and how to commemorate the tragic event are still in the "talks" phase. Those who are interested can see the "pit"—the hole that was once the lower levels of the Towers. There is currently a pathway along Church Street, and though that may change (to allow greater access and viewing), anyone in the area you ask will know the current access route— even other tourists.

The hole is really just a hole surrounded by a fence. It's the knowledge of what once stood there and what transpired that compels people to go there—that makes the hole a "must visit" destination for people the world over. It is now as much a part of the New York City landscape as the Towers once were—while they were still standing.

Helpful Hint
If you want to help the downtown recovery, don't forget to support the local businesses and restaurants (and that includes Chinatown, too).

Take the time to talk to your kids before you arrive and discuss further while you are standing there what this void represents—why in reality it's so much more than a hole. It's sort of like arriving at the pyramids in Egypt, something you've studied endlessly in school at all different levels, heard about and talked about your entire life, and when you actually see them in person you think, "What's the big deal? They're not so big. My dad's office building is taller." But they were built thousands of years ago, by hand. And that's why they are so much more.

Another worthwhile destination is the Sphere that was located at the center of the World Trade Plaza (there was actually a picture of children playing around the sphere and the fountain it crowned in the first edition of this book). The Sphere is currently located in Battery Park. In front, there is a signboard that details its history, and all around it are the flowers and mementos that people have left. It is battered and burned, but it is not broken— just like, I like to think, the people of the City of New York and the rest of the United States.

CHAPTER
4

Where
to Stay

Hotels

Map shows highlights only. See chapter text for more listings.

The map contains the following labels:

Williamsburg Bridge, Manhattan Bridge, Brooklyn Bridge, East River, Hudson River, Holland Tunnel, Brooklyn Battery Tunnel, South St. Viaduct

STUYVESANT TOWN, EAST VILLAGE, LOWER EAST SIDE, LITTLE ITALY, CHINATOWN, CIVIC CENTER, FINANCIAL DISTRICT, GREENWICH VILLAGE, GRAMERCY/FLATIRON, CHELSEA, WEST VILLAGE, SOHO, TRIBECA, BATTERY PARK CITY

Avenue D, Columbia St., Jackson St., Montgomery St., Cherry St., South St., Avenue C, Pitt St., Broome St., Avenue B, Clinton St., Grand St., Rutgers St., Avenue A, Houston St., Market St., Catherine St., E. 10th St., Rivington St., Allen St., Sou Water St., First Ave., Stanton St., E. 5th St., E. 1st St., Second Ave., Chrystie St., St. James Pl., Broad Ave., E. 25th St., E. 23rd St., E. 20th St., E. 15th St., E. 14th St., Third Ave., Fourth Ave., Bowery, Elizabeth St., Mott St., Mulberry St., Centre St., Wall St., Lexington Ave., Irving Place, Centre St., CIVIC CENTER, Park Ave., Madison Ave., University Pl., SOHO, Grand St., Broadway, Church St., Fifth Ave., Prince St., Spring St., Broome St., W. Broadway, Sixth Ave. (Ave. of the Americas), W. 10th St., Ave. of the Americas, Canal St., Battery Pl., W. 20th St., W. 15th St., Waverly Pl., Seventh Ave., Greenwich St., Washington St., Eighth Ave., Hudson St., W. 14th St., Ninth Ave., W. 25th St., W. 23rd St., Tenth Ave., West St.

MILES 1/2 1/4

N

8 Lyden Gardens (p. 143)

6 The Mark (p. 151)

7 The Milburn Hotel (p. 135)

30 Westin New York at Times Square (p. 159)

32 Marriott Financial Center (p. 146)

31 Ritz-Carlton New York, Battery Park (p. 154)

17 Novotel New York (p. 136)

13 The Peninsula (p. 152)

10 The Pierre (p. 152)

19 Plaza Fifty (p. 147)

25 Millennium U.N. Plaza (p. 151)

9 The Regency (p. 153)

14 St. Regis (p. 157)

3 The Stanhope (p. 156)

5 Surrey Hotel (p. 157)

27 Travel Inn (p. 137)

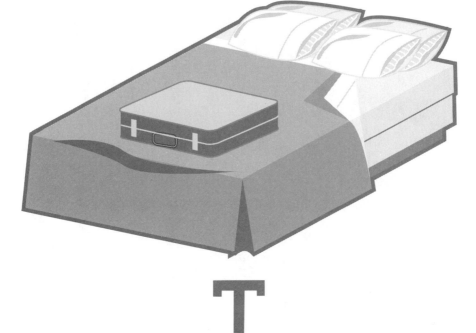

T here's no nice way to say it: Hotels in New York City are expensive.

When visiting New York, your accommodations will most likely consume the bulk of your vacation budget. In most of America, you can expect to find a clean, spacious, modern hotel room for between $50 and $100 per night. In New York, such a room is virtually unheard of—it would constitute the off-season bargain par excellence. The price range for New York hotel rooms begins at expensive (for very basic rooms in out-of-the-way locations, for which you can expect to pay in excess of $100 a night) and climbs to mind-boggling (at the better Midtown hotels, where $400 might buy you the cheapest room on a slow night). What is considered cheap for a hotel room by New York standards might buy you one of the finest rooms in any other city in the country.

New York hotel rooms, like New York apartments, are also often quite small—a particular challenge for families. This should come as no surprise: Manhattan is a tiny island encompassing some of the most expensive real estate in the world, and almost every inch of it is covered either with buildings or

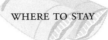

planned parkland. But if you think hotel prices per square foot are bad, you should see what most of us New Yorkers pay per month in rent!

Thankfully, although accommodations in New York City are still outrageously expensive by national standards, recent years have brought a hotel renaissance of sorts. Rising tourism has spurred new construction as well as renovation, thus improving availability of quality hotel rooms across the price spectrum. Since September 11, there has been a mini-boom in new construction, the fruits of which will be ripe by the time this book hits the streets. And with safety rapidly improving all over town, it's now possible for a family to stay worry-free in neighborhoods that, just a few years ago, I wouldn't have been able to recommend with a clear conscience.

In preparing the listings in this chapter, I've inspected literally hundreds of New York City hotels to ferret out the winners in every price category. I've also sought out alternative forms of accommodation, such as short-term apartment stays, which are discussed at the end of this chapter. As with all aspects of city life, there truly is something for everyone.

Getting the Most from New York City's Hotels

If I could offer just one piece of advice to travelers in search of hotel accommodations in New York City it would be: Flexibility is key. Once you've locked yourself in to a particular location or species of accommodation, your options rapidly diminish. Instead, don't be afraid to play outside the box. This is especially true when considering neighborhoods. All too often tourists think they want to stay in Midtown, because that's where the Broadway theaters and theme restaurants are. But it's also where you'll pay the most for a room. Remember, Manhattan is tiny.

Money-Saving Tips

How to get the most out of your New York hotel dollar:

- Look for a room configuration that suits your needs. For example, if you're traveling with one or two kids, you can go with a junior suite (with a double pullout couch) instead of two rooms—a move that could save you hundreds of dollars over the course of a few days.

- Pick places where kids stay free. Many hotels will even add a rollaway bed to your room for a nominal charge.

- Look for included breakfast. The value of a free breakfast cannot be overstated: It saves you not only money but also time. And be sure to fill up before you set out for the day.

- Newer is better. Though old hotels can be charming, your best bets when traveling with kids tend to be hotels that are either new (larger rooms; better floor plans) or newly renovated (bright and clean).

- Look for package deals. Many hotels offer theater packages and other incentives, especially during slow times of year. But be sure you carefully evaluate such packages—there's no point in paying for what you don't want or need.

- Inquire about discounts. Many New York hotels accept AAA, corporate rates, and discounts in connection with professional associations or credit card companies. Be sure you ask when you reserve (don't hesitate to ask outright, "Do you offer any discounts?"), because even a 5 to 10 percent discount can add up.

- Ask lots of questions. Before you book, establish with great specificity what a hotel does and doesn't offer. Don't just take "free breakfast" for an answer—ask what exactly the breakfast includes. If a hotel says it's "kid-friendly," ask what that specifically means. Make sure you get every last bit of information about the hotel's telephone billing procedures—phone calls at outrageous hotel rates can really add up. The more you know, the better your stay will ultimately be.

Even if you stay all the way downtown (perhaps the City's most underutilized hotel neighborhood, especially on weekends when the business travelers disappear), you'll only be twenty minutes from Midtown by subway.

Flexibility in your choice of dates is also a big help. Sometimes, it's the seemingly random events (especially business conventions) that throw the hotel rates out of whack. Sometimes, shifting your vacation by just a couple of days on either end can slash your room rates. And remember, New York City hotels are almost always cheaper on weekends.

How to Use This Chapter

I've arranged this chapter according to the following price ranges for one night in a standard room:

$ $150 and under
$$ $150–$275
$$$ $275–$400
$$$$ More than $400

I've also indicated the neighborhood, using the following abbreviations:

BR: Brooklyn
CH: Chelsea
EV: East Village
GD: Garment District
GV: Greenwich Village
LI: Little Italy
MTE: Midtown East
Q: Queens
SI: Staten Island
TD: Theater District
UES: Upper East Side
UWS: Upper West Side

BX: Bronx
CT: Chinatown
FD: Financial District
GP: Gramercy Park/Flatiron
LES: Lower East Side
MT: Midtown
MTW: Midtown West
SH: SoHo
TBC: TriBeCa
TS: Times Square
US: Union Square
WV: West Village

A ★ indicates a particularly noteworthy hotel within its price range, in that it is more kid-friendly or provides better value than its similarly priced competitors.

I've organized this chapter by price range rather than by neighborhood because price is probably going to be your first and foremost consideration when you select a hotel. Within the price ranges, however, you'll find each hotel designated by its neighborhood.

Although every neighborhood has rooms in every price category, you'll find that you have the most flexibility if you operate in the range of $175 to $300. Anything less will be a squeeze; if you can afford more, you'll have an even wider selection with fewer restrictions, but you'll receive diminishing returns in terms of value.

Where I've indicated "under 12 free" or a similar designation, this pertains to the age of children entitled to free accommodation in a hotel room with their parents. *Don't forget: This age limit is often negotiable, especially at the high-end hotels.* Many hotel managers have confessed to me that this is a guideline and often can be changed at the discretion of the person at the desk. So smile, be nice, and maybe you'll get a few dollars knocked off your bill.

Where the price for a rollaway bed is indicated, that is the charge per night unless otherwise noted.

The price ranges I've indicated begin with a lower number indicating the price of rooms during off-peak dates and range up to a higher number representing room rates for peak-season accommodation (though extraordinary dates, like New Year's Eve, will fall outside the range). I've only considered rooms that can accommodate families. If, for example, a hotel's basic room simply can't accommodate more than two people, the lowest price I've listed is for a suite that will accommodate at least one child.

In general, winter is peak season for most New York City hotels, and summer is low season. But it really varies from hotel to hotel, and I can't lay down any hard-and-fast rules in this regard. Many guidebooks attempt this, but most such information is questionable at best. It's very difficult to generalize about the flow of guests at New York's hotels because so many factors affect it, and they vary by neighborhood and type of hotel. Even veteran hotel managers have told me that they've been blindsided by demand on many occasions.

Finally, please understand that the ranges of room rates I've provided here are only guidelines. Hotels are notoriously cagey when it comes to releasing their room rates, because most engage in "yield management," a practice where rates adapt to supply and demand—just like the airlines. If a hotel anticipates being full on a given night, it will set a very high rate, perhaps higher than what I've indicated here. Likewise, if it's looking as though there will be empty rooms, you'll see the rates plummet (I've witnessed some last-minute bookings at New York's top hotels for a third of the listed price). Thus, even though it's always wise to make your reservations as far in advance as possible, it's also wise to call the hotel repeatedly (and anonymously) as the date of your vacation approaches to see if rates have come down at all.

Money-Saving Tip

Unless a hotel is quite full, the first room rate that the reservationist quotes is really just the opening salvo in a negotiation. Ask repeatedly, "Is that the best you can do?" Also try to negotiate for free local phone calls, included breakfast, waivers of kid-related fees (cribs, etc.), airport transportation (depending on the airport, this alone can save you a hundred bucks), and anything else you can think of. They may say no, but it never hurts to ask!

"$" Hotels: $150 and Under

All of the hotels I've listed here are safe and clean, but they really are budget accommodations. Don't expect concierge service, doormen, swimming pools, or lots of amenities. Some children will be oblivious to this, but others (not to mention their parents) simply won't be happy in most hotels at this level—only you can judge what will work for your family. Still, even in New York, budget hotels offer some benefits. Many have mini-fridges and microwaves in the rooms, and some even offer free Continental breakfast. I've included that information below, but be sure to ask when you make your reservation because policies change constantly, and it's always better to be safe than sorry.

Carlton Arms	$95–$117
160 East 25th Street	**212-684-8337**
(at Third Ave.), GP	**212-679-0680**
www.carltonarms.com	

This former welfare hotel, now catering primarily to artsy types, is an incredible value by city standards. Doubles with private baths and air-conditioning go for a mere $95, triples are $111, and quads are $117. Prices include free rollaways. They usually don't charge for kids (and don't have a firm policy on age), so you're likely to get away with paying for a double (there seems to be no rhyme or reason to this—what can I say, they're artists!). The rooms are very basic, so don't expect many amenities—there are no phones and no air-conditioning. But the staff is friendly, the value is tremendous, the hotel is very safe, and the neighborhood is extremely pleasant. Be sure to book rooms with private baths (there are twenty such rooms available) at least a month in advance because they're the first to go. And let the staff know that you're coming with kids so that you get a room with cheerful art (all walls of the hotel are covered in murals, and each room has a theme—the kids might get a kick out of the Holstein room). As one staff member put it: "We get a lot of Europeans in here—it's sort of like camping."

Comfort Inn Midtown	**$89–$249 double**
129 West 46th Street (between	**212-221-2600**
Sixth Ave. and Broadway), MTW	**800-228-5150**
www.applecorehotels.com (central number)	
www.comfortinn.com (to check for online discounts)	

Renovated in 1998, this small hotel (eighty rooms), boasts an incredible location (a stone's throw from Times Square and the Theater District) and surprisingly reasonable rates. *Cribs (free), rollaways (free); kids under 15 free; Continental breakfast (free), in-room coffeemaker*

Cosmopolitan Hotel	**$109–$159**
95 West Broadway	**212-566-19000**
(at Chambers St.), TBC	**888-895-940**
www.cosmohotel.com	

Don't let the prices scare you away from this modest but clean hotel. All rooms have air-conditioning, cable TV, alarm clocks, and small but tidy bathrooms. Cribs are available for free. Don't expect gigantic rooms or concierge service, but for the price it's hard to do better.

★ *Habitat Hotel*	**$79–$115 (shared bath),**
130 East 57th Street	**$105–$145 (private bath),**
(at Lexington Ave.), UES	**$315–395 (suites)**
www.stayinny.com	**212-753-8841**

Renovated in 1998, this European-style hotel is relatively new on the scene. It's part of the City Life Hotel group, which aims to feature "tourist class, budget hotels that are very affordable but still classy." The hotel is in the heart of Midtown, and 70 percent of the rooms have shared baths, but you can get two adjoining rooms that share a bath that is therefore effectively private. The rooms are small (about 12 feet by 12 feet) but comfortable and clean and include either a queen-size bed or trundle bed. The atmosphere is cheery; the lobby was freshly renovated in 2000, and the restaurant was added in that year. The grand plan is for all rooms to have private baths by the end of 2003. *Concierge, restaurant, complimentary Continental breakfast, suites come with mini-fridges*

City Fact

New York City has more than 62,500 hotel rooms. At an average occupancy rate of 83.9 percent, that means that out-of-towners spend 18,547,000 nights in New York City hotels each year.

Herald Square Hotel	**$120–$140 (two double beds)**
19 West 31st Street (between	**212-279-4017**
Fifth Ave. and Broadway), MTW	**800-727-1888**
www.heraldsquarehotel.com	

After a facelift in early 2000, rooms have firm new mattresses, fresh coats of paint, in-room safes, TVs, and telephones with voicemail. You get a cheerful greeting at the desk. *Cribs (free); kids under 12 free*

Hotel Newton	**$105–$170 suite**
2528 Broadway (between	**212-678-6500**
94th and 95th Sts.), UWS	**888-HOTEL58**
www.newyorkhotel.com/newton	

This AAA-approved hotel is a great value for the money. Located on the desirable Upper West Side, it puts you a block from the 1,

The Upper West Side skyline, from Central Park's reservoir

2, and 3 subway lines and just a short distance to the heart of the UWS's best shopping and attractions. The real values here are the suites (costing less than most double rooms in the City), which come with a microwave and mini-fridge, plus the option for two double or queen-size beds (request these when you make your reservation). *Kids under 17 free*

Portland Square Hotel	**$125 double, $150 triple,**
132 West 47th Street (between	**$160 quad**
Sixth and Seventh Aves.), MTW	**212-382-0600**
www.portlandsquarehotel.com	**800-388-898**

Legend has it that James Cagney lived in this building (as did a few Radio City Rockettes). A family sharing a quad reaps the obvious rewards of the value. *Cribs/rollaways (free)*

Washington Square Hotel	**$123–$188 double-quad**
103 Waverly Place	**212-777-9515**
(at MacDougal St.), WV	**800-222-0418**
www.wshotel.com	

Renovated in 1999, and with regular updates since, this small hotel doesn't have lots of amenities, but the staff is kind and the rooms are clean. Located in a hip neighborhood, this is especially good for pre-teens and teens who will be interested in the goings-on in the Village and nearby Washington Square Park. A word to the wise: Not all of the rooms have windows, so request one that does. *Cribs/rollaways (free)*

Helpful Hint

You may be tempted to beat the system and save a few dollars by seeking accommodations outside the City. Forget about it. The economics just don't work out once you factor in the cost of transportation and the extreme time commitment over and above staying in Manhattan.

Wolcott Hotel	$95–$150 double
4 West 31st Street	$105–$170 suites
(at Fifth Ave.), CH	212-268-2900
www.wolcott.com	800-222-0418

The value here is in the suites. Though the Wolcott doesn't have an official kids-stay-free policy, the charge is overlooked for the suites, which can accommodate two adults and two kids. All of the rooms were renovated in 1998 or 1999, and the exterior of

Insider's Tip

"Always have snacks and drinks on hand in your hotel room. Never, ever, under any circumstances should you allow hungry, cranky kids to force you to resort against your will to room service or the mini-bar, where you'll pay at least a 300-percent markup on all items. Whereas, if you have your own drinks, even if there's no fridge, you can always get ice for free!" —*Dave, father of two*

Top Ten Family-Friendly Hotels

1. Le Parker Meridien (p. 150)
2. The Peninsula (p. 152)
3. Best Western Seaport Inn (p. 126)
4. Ritz-Carlton New York, Battery Park (p. 154)
5. Lyden Gardens (p. 143)
6. Surrey Hotel (p. 157)
7. Habitat Hotel (p. 121)
8. The Regency (p. 153)
9. The Pierre (p. 152)
10. Four Seasons (p. 148)

the building was given a face-lift in the spring of 2000. All suites have mini-fridges, as do some of the queen rooms—request a fridge in advance if you need one, and they'll do their best to accommodate. *Cribs/rollaways (free)*

"$$" Hotels: $150–$275

This is the price range, albeit high, in which you'll maximize the value of New York hotels. This is also where you'll have the most competition for rooms during busy times, so reserve early.

Belvedere Hotel	$140–$220 (up to four people)
319 West 48th Street (between	212-245-7000
Eighth and Ninth Aves.), MTW	888-HOTEL58
www.newyorkhotel.com/belvedere	

Renovated in 1998, it's hard to believe that this modern boutique hotel charges so modestly for its rooms. It's located smack-dab in the Theater District and only two blocks from great cheap eats on Ninth Avenue. The kitchenettes—in every room—are a great bonus. Cribs *($20), rollaways ($20); kitchenette (mini-fridge, microwave), concierge, Continental and full breakfast available, Nintendo video games, kids under 12 free*

★ *Best Western Seaport Inn*	$169–$229
33 Peck Slip (between	**212-766-6600**
Front and Water Sts.), FD	**800-468-3569**
www.bestwestern.com/seaportinn	

This Seaport charmer is in an out-of-the-way corner, down a cobblestone street, which may explain why it has remained one of the City's better-kept hotel secrets. Great values for families at any time of year, every room is equipped with a VCR, adjoining rooms are available, and plenty of rooms have two queen-size beds. For an extra $30, you can get a room with a terrace (ask for one overlooking the Brooklyn Bridge) and/or a whirlpool. For $30, where else can you do that! And the location is not to be overlooked—you'll be right at the South Street Seaport and Pier 17; Chinatown is fewer than ten blocks away; and the Financial District and ferry to the Statue of Liberty are within an easy walk. *Cribs (free), rollaways ($25); kids under 18 free; complimentary breakfast*

★ *Broadway Inn Bed & Breakfast*	$135–$180,
264 West 46th Street (between	**$205–$275 (suites)**
Broadway and Eighth Aves.), MT	**212-997-9200**
www.broadwayinn.com	**800-826-6300**

This hotel was specifically designed with families in mind. The stated aim of this forty-one-room inn is to make you feel as if you're at your "home away from home." And, as at home, there is no elevator (there are only three floors), so be prepared to walk those stairs. In the heart of the Theater District, the intimate charm of the Broadway Inn is a welcome change from some of the chain hotel giants. Built in 1918, this historic building may not look like much from the outside, but the inn itself dates to 1996 and was completely renovated at that time. A fireplace and library welcome you in the lobby (where you can also enjoy the complimentary breakfast), and the rooms are modest, tidy, and comfortable. Each of the eleven suites (which have a pantry with microwave) can easily accommodate a family of four. And though the hotel doesn't have a restaurant (you're better off with the vast selection lining Ninth Avenue), when you check in you'll get discount vouchers for several good area dining spots.

Chelsea Inn	**$79–$109 guest room with shared bath,**
46 West 17th Street (between	**$119–159 studio,**
Sixth and Seventh Aves.), CH	**$169–249 suite**
www.chelseainn.com	**212-645-8989, 800-640-6469**

This country-style inn is housed in a classic turn-of-the-century brownstone. Accommodations range from the guest room with shared bath to the suite, each with a kitchenette (refrigerator, hotplate or stove, coffeemaker), TV, and voicemail. Unless you're traveling with toddlers, the best bets for families are the "guest rooms." Every pair has its own vestibule entry off the hall and shares a bathroom. There are twenty-six rooms, and you'll feel more as if you're in an Old World--style inn or European pension than in a Manhattan hotel. Extended stay rates are available.

Chelsea Savoy Hotel	**$125–$185**
204 West 23rd Street	**212-929-9353**
(at Seventh Ave.), CH	**www.chelseasavoynyc.com**

Built in 1997, the Chelsea Savoy, unlike many hotels in this price range, was actually built to be a hotel. So you'll find that the rooms are practical, well laid out, and fairly roomy. The rates are per room, so if you get a room with two doubles, you can sleep four at no additional charge. The furnishings are a bit chain hotel-like, but everything is clean, new, and well looked after, plus the neighborhood is especially hip and trendy right now. *Cribs (free), rollaways ($50); restaurant, mini-fridge*

Clarion Hotel Fifth Avenue	**$169–$379 double**
3 East 40th Street (between	**212-447-1500**
Fifth and Madison Aves.), MTE	**800-252-7466**
www.clarionfifthave.com	

Tucked away in Midtown, the Clarion is across the street from the City's grandest library, a few blocks from Grand Central Station, steps off Fifth Avenue, and only six blocks from the Empire State Building. Renovated in the fall of 1999, upgrades on technological equipment (like two-line phones and data-ports) don't mean that corners were cut elsewhere—check out the bathrooms and towels, which are downright luxurious for a hotel in this price category. Rooms are configured with either a queen-size bed and a sleeper sofa or two doubles. Refrigerators are available

Top Ten Family-Friendly Hotel Deals

1. **Best Western Seaport Inn (p. 126)**
2. **The Milburn Hotel (p. 135)**
3. **Gracie Inn (p. 140)**
4. **Holiday Inn Downtown (p. 132)**
5. **Habitat Hotel (p. 121)**
6. **Helmsley Middletowne Hotel (p. 131)**
7. **Clarion Hotel Fifth Avenue (p. 128)**
8. **Excelsior (p. 130)**
9. **Novotel New York (p. 136)**
10. **Hotel Newton (p. 122)**

upon request at no additional charge, and in-room coffeemakers will enable you to have a cup before setting out for the day. And as if that weren't enough, local calls (which can really add up) are free. *Cribs/rollaways (free); kids under 18 free; AAA, AARP, senior discounts; concierge, restaurant*

Comfort Inn Manhattan	$144–$249
42 West 35th Street (between	**212-947-0200**
Fifth and Sixth Aves.), GD	**800-228-5150**
www.comfortinnmanhattan.com	
www.comfortinn.com (check for online discounts)	

If tourist sights are a high priority, this location is hard to beat—you'll be around the corner from the Empire State Building and Macy's, a short walk to Fifth Avenue's best shopping, and close to the subway. To get an even better value, you can request a room with a microwave and/or mini-fridge (there are twenty such rooms) or book into a king room with double sleeper sofa (these cost extra, but it's still far cheaper than getting two rooms). And don't forget to ask about special rates and promos, as they are common here. *Kids under 18 free; complimentary Continental breakfast*

Days Hotel Midtown	$99.95–$499.95
790 Eighth Avenue	**(two double beds)**
(at 48th St.), MTW	**212-581-7000**
www.daysinn.com	**800-572-6232**

In the heart of the Theater District and one block from Times Square, don't expect quiet when you step out of the lobby and onto the street because the City doesn't get much busier than this. The guestrooms, which are quite large by Manhattan standards, underwent a full makeover in 2000–2001. This property is no stranger to tour groups, so don't be surprised if you see busloads pulling up in front. *Cribs (free), rollaways ($20); concierge, restaurant, mini-fridge ($20/day)*

Empire Hotel	$199–$700
Broadway (at 63rd St.), UWS	212-265-7400
www.empirehotel.com	888-822-3555

Directly across the street from Lincoln Center, the Empire is ideally located for jaunts into Central Park, the Upper West Side, and Times Square. The lobby of this hotel is grand by any standards, but rooms are a bit small. A deluxe room is big enough to accommodate a rollaway, and the junior suites (with a double bed and a pullout couch) and one-bedrooms are better for more space, if everyone needs to be in close proximity. Don't overlook connecting rooms as a (surprisingly) more economical option to the suites. VCRs and CD players as well as complimentary lending libraries for both are good extras, and renovations were in progress as of 2002. *Cribs (free), rollaways ($25); kids free (ages vary); concierge, restaurant, mini-fridge ($25 per stay)*

★ Excelsior	$149–$369
45 West 81st Street (between Central	212-362-9200
Park West and Columbus Ave.), UWS	800-368-4575
www.excelsiorhotelnewyork.com	

Many of us City residents would kill (and pay a lot) for this location—in the heart of the Upper West Side, less than a block from Central Park, and directly across the street from the new Rose Center (planetarium) at the Museum of Natural History. Surprisingly, the rates at this four-star hotel (converted from apartments) are not as high as one might think. A standard room with two queen-size beds is large enough to house a family comfortably. All one- and two-bedroom suites have pullout couches and computers, while junior suites have only the former. "Park" view rooms (overlooking the museum) cost just $10–$20 more than those without. *Cribs (free), rollaways ($25); kids under 14 free; mini-fridge ($10 per day)*

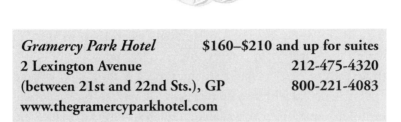

Gramercy Park Hotel	$160–$210 and up for suites
2 Lexington Avenue	212-475-4320
(between 21st and 22nd Sts.), GP	800-221-4083
www.thegramercyparkhotel.com	

"It's very European," the staff informed me, which I'll translate to mean smoky and somewhat campy in nature. Full of artists and rock stars, this hotel is in a great location and a good value if you can handle the smoky lobby and slightly tattered edges. Probably the best feature is that guests have access to the lovely, peaceful, beautifully kept, and private Gramercy Park, which is accessible only to those who reside on the park's boundaries (I've always wanted to go in there!). Some rooms have park views, for which there is no extra charge (just ask), and some also have kitchenettes. I would only advise this hotel for families comfortable with smoking, though. *Cribs (free), rollaways ($10); kids under 12 free; restaurant*

Helmsley Middletowne Hotel	$170–$260 (two beds)
148 East 48th Street (between	$280–$385 (suites)
Lexington and Third Aves.), MTW	212-755-3000
www.helmsleyhotels.com	800-221-4982

This converted apartment hotel offers many of the trappings of a high-end property (multiple phone lines, dataports, plush linens, and fine furniture) but really delivers on value, especially if you're looking to keep your kids close at hand

Taking a break near Central Park

(i.e., in the same room). Two children under 13 years old can share a room with their parents, and even the most modest rooms (read: the cheapest) are quite spacious by New York standards and can be requested with two double beds. Otherwise, one- and two-bedroom suites are also available, though in terms of value, you might be best off with two doubles as an alternative. *Cribs (free), rollaways ($20); kids under 13 free; concierge, mini-fridge*

★ *Holiday Inn Downtown*	**$139–$250**
138 Lafayette Street (at Canal St.), CT	**212-966-8898**
www.holidayinn-nyc.com	**800-465-4329**

If you want to be in the hustle and bustle of it all but Times Square isn't your cup of tea, the Holiday Inn Downtown is a great option. Room rates vary with the seasons, but doubles can accommodate a family, as can the suites with pullout couches. If you want a real New York experience, this neighborhood ensures it—and you'll be close to Little Italy, Chinatown, and the South Street Seaport. *Hint:* Though the Continental breakfast isn't technically included, if you join the Holiday Inn's club (for which there is no charge), you get the breakfast for free as well as free local calls and a daily newspaper. *Cribs (free), rollaways ($15); kids under 18 free; concierge, restaurant*

Holiday Inn Midtown	**$159–$239**
440 West 57th Street (between	**212-581-8100**
Ninth and Tenth Aves.), MTW	**800-HOLIDAY**
www.hi57.com	

If you take comfort in the familiarity of chain hotels, the Holiday Inn Midtown fits the bill just fine. Renovated in 1998, the rooms remain clean and tidy and are of a decent size. It's a bit of a hike to public transportation and attractions, but room rates are very attractive, and you'll surely appreciate the rooftop pool in summer. *Cribs (free), rollaways ($15); kids under 18 free; concierge, restaurant, mini-fridge ($10), rooftop pool (outdoor/seasonal)*

Hotel Beacon	$145–$325
2130 Broadway (between	212-787-1100
74th and 75th Sts.), UWS	800-572-4969
www.beaconhotel.com	

Long one of the UWS's best bargains (though not as much of a secret as it used to be), the Beacon has many charms. A standard room comes with two double beds or a king, one-bedroom suites have a double pullout in the lounge area, and two-bedroom suites can comfortably sleep six. All of the rooms were renovated in 1999; each has a kitchenette with a range, mini-fridge, and coffeemaker; the bigger the room, the more extensive the kitchenette (bigger refrigerator and more accoutrements). The Beacon offers all sorts of discounts (it seems like everyone checking in has some sort of a special deal), so be sure to ask when you call—AAA, seasonal specials, corporate, whatever. *Cribs (free), rollaways ($15); kids under 12 free*

Hotel Metro	$165–$255 double, $225–$400 suite
45 West 35th Street (between	212-947-2500
Fifth and Sixth Aves.), GD	800-356-3870
www.hotelmetronyc.com	

The Metro is, for the price, an absolutely fab hotel. The décor is playful and the rooms are sizeable, but the bathrooms, though spotless, are a bit on the tight side. Perhaps one of the best things about this hotel is the view from the rooftop deck—it's got one of the best views of the Empire State Building I've ever seen. *Cribs (free); restaurant, complimentary Continental breakfast*

Insider's Tip

"Most hotel concierges maintain a list of trusted babysitters who will come to your room and watch the kids for a few hours. It's not cheap, but it may be worth it for that one big night out on the town." —*Albert, hotel concierge*

The Mayflower Hotel	$159–$350
15 Central Park West (between	212-265-0060
61st and 62nd Sts.), UWS	800-223-4164
www.mayflowerhotel.com	

Located directly across the street from Central Park, the Mayflower is a bit worn around the edges, but in what some would consider a comforting way. Formerly an apartment building, the hotel has cavernous rooms that are the primary benefit to guests (my first apartment in New York City wasn't as big as some of the doubles I saw), along with easy proximity to attractions. Double rooms (with two double beds) can comfortably accommodate a family, and suites (with a king or two queens and a pullout) are big enough for gymnastics and tumbling. All rooms come with mini-fridges, and continuous improvements and renovation keep the charming old building up to snuff. *Cribs (free), rollaways ($20); kids under 16 free*

Metropolitan Hotel New York	$159–$389 rooms,
569 Lexington Avenue	$249–$400 suites
(at 51st St.), MTE	212-752-7000
www.metropolitanhotelnyc.com	800-836-6471

This Loews hotel has a very central location, virtually across from the Waldorf and just a few blocks from Madison and Fifth

Avenues (and Sony World of Wonder). Renovated in the fall of 2000, the entire property has undergone a face-lift, smoothing the previously tattered edges. Rooms with two double beds can comfortably accommodate a family, as can the junior suites, which have either one king or two doubles and a pullout couch in the sleeping area. Perched atop the #6 subway and with a good gourmet coffee shop (that is unrelated to the hotel), you can start your day with a cup of java (the kids will have plenty of breakfast choices with bagels and baked goods) and easy transportation via foot or train to the best the City has to offer. *Cribs/rollaways (free); kids under 15 free; mini-fridge upon request (free), concierge, restaurant, children's amenities (pull-out couches, babysitting arrangements available, concierge has lists of nearby children's activities)*

★ *The Milburn Hotel*	$169–$205
242 West 76th Street (between	212-362-1006
Broadway and West End Aves.), UWS	800-833-9622
www.milburnhotel.com	Fax: 212-721-5476

Nestled in the heart of the Upper West Side, The Milburn is perfect for families looking for a good value. The prices are shockingly reasonable considering what you get—a continuously renovated hotel (and regularly undergoing improvements and upgrades), kitchenettes in every room (microwave, range, coffeemaker, mini-fridge), VCR, free video lending library, and Playstation video games upon request (free). A junior suite, with a king-size bed and a rollaway, is the smallest option for a family of three. For larger families or more space (though the rooms are generous by New York standards), one-bedrooms (with two twins, one king, or a queen with a pullout couch) are the better bet. *Cribs (free), rollaways ($10); kids under 13 free; kitchenettes, Playstation video games (free)*

★ *Novotel New York*　　　　　　　　　$169–$359
226 West 52nd Street　　　　　　　　212-315-0100
(at Broadway), MT　　　　　　　　　800-NOVOTEL
www.novotel.com

While all other hotels seem to have vacancies, the Novotel is finding itself booked solid, even during anticipated seasonal lows—and it's obvious why. Fully renovated in 1999, all of the rooms are in top shape and noticeably large by City standards (12 feet by 12 feet, or 10 feet by 14 feet). Rooms have either two doubles or a king and a pullout sleeper, as well as hardwood floors in the bathrooms (the only hotel in New York City that can make this claim), and the added bonus of free full buffet breakfast for the kids (summer rates often include breakfast for parents, too). Check out the outdoor "sky-lobby" that overlooks Broadway, outfitted with chairs for lingering and relaxing. There's free nightly entertainment in the lounge in the lobby, and the hotel welcomes small pets (the reservationist warns, "no horses"). *Cribs (free), rollaways (free); kids under 16 free; concierge, restaurant; mini-fridge (free)*

San Carlos　　　　　　　$195–$265 junior suite,
150 East 50th Street　　$225–$310 one-bedroom suite
(between Lexington and　　　　　　212-755-1800
Third Aves.), MTE　　　　　　　　800-722-2012
www.sancarloshotel.com

The location speaks for itself at this welcoming, modest Midtown hotel. Busy even during the low season, the fair pricing and the convenience of in-room amenities like kitchenettes make the San Carlos a good bet for families. Junior suites can sleep three, and the one-bedroom suites sleep up to five. Also worthwhile: The San Carlos has a sister hotel, the Hotel Bedford, at 118 East 40th Street (800-221-6881; www.bedfordhotel.com).

Travel Inn	$105–$250
515 West 42nd Street (between	212-695-7171
Tenth and Eleventh Aves.), MTW	800-869-4630

The big attractions here are the free parking (wow!) and the large outdoor pool (which is seasonal). A family of up to four can easily stay in one room, with two double beds. For more space or privacy, go for adjoining rooms. The Travel Inn is close to the Circle Line, the Intrepid, and the Javits Center, but not much else (it's even a hike to the subway from this far-west location). So if you have young children or aren't big walkers, you might be better off else-where. *Cribs (free), rollaways ($15); kids under 18 free; free parking*

"$$$" Hotels: $275–$400

Hotels in this range are expensive, to be sure, but they often offer great comfort and convenience. Look especially for good deals on suites and adjoining rooms and for low-season specials (which can drop these hotels to the low end of the price range).

Money-Saving Tip
Remember your frequent flier miles. Many frequent flier pro-grams have tie-ins with the big national hotel chains, and in some cases the exact same number of miles that will buy you a room in Cleveland will also buy you one in New York City!

★ *Beekman Tower*	$274–$360 one bedroom,
3 Mitchell Place	$478–$680 two bedroom
(First Ave. at 49th St.), MTE	212-355-7300
www.mesuite.com	800-637-8483

The Manhattan East Suite Hotels, of which this property is a part, are a real boon to traveling families. The rooms are all, as the name indicates, suites. Accommodations are unusually large for New York, and all have full kitchens. Located virtually on top of the UN, the Beekman Tower was last renovated in 1997 and is still holding up well despite its popularity. The one-bedroom suites range in size from 450 to 650 square feet and can accommodate up to four. The two-bedroom suites run from 700 to 900 square feet and can comfortably sleep six. Take a trip up to the rooftop lounge early one evening for great, unobstructed views of the City. Manhattan East Suite Hotels has several other properties as well; check the Web site for further information. *Cribs (free), rollaways ($20); kids under 12 free; concierge, restaurant*

★ *Crowne Plaza Times Square*	**$199–$469**
1605 Broadway (between	**212-977-4000**
48th and 49th Sts.), TS	**800-2CROWNE**
www.crowneplaza.com	

If it's bright lights, glitz, and glitter that you're after, this forty-six-story glass edifice in the heart of Times Square is the answer to your prayers. The hotel is centrally located near all of the City's attractions (you're pretty much in the middle) and within easy walking distance of Broadway favorites like *The Lion King*. The masterful "ticket and attractions" staff (i.e., the concierge) can help you get tickets even to sold-out shows (though you'll pay for the privilege). Renovated in 1999, the rooms are virtually new and the amenities are excellent—there's even a swimming pool (lap pool with restricted kids hours). Rooms sleep a maximum of four, and children under 18 stay free. If this location is booked, or you're looking for a bit more peace and quiet, you can also try the Crowne Plaza at the United Nations (304 East 42nd St., at Second Ave., 212-986-8800, 800-243-NYNY). *Cribs (free), rollaways ($30); kids under 18 free; concierge, restaurant, mini-fridge ($30), small pets welcome (under 30 pounds), coffeemakers, pool*

★ *Doubletree Guest Suites*	$239–$359
1568 Broadway (at 47th St.	212-719-1600
and Seventh Ave.), TS	800-222-TREE
www.doubletreehotels.com	

If you want to be in Times Square, this is an extremely good option for families. All of the rooms are, you guessed it, suites—so you get more space for your money, and you can keep everyone together without worrying about what's going on in your kids' room next door. The rooms are fully equipped, too, including not one but two TVs, a microwave, coffeemaker, pullout couch, and even hair dryers. This also happens to be an extremely kid-friendly hotel—there's a playroom with all sorts of activities sure to interest and engage children ages three to twelve. *Cribs (free); kids under 18 free; concierge, restaurants*

The Franklin	$295 superior room
164 East 87th Street (between	212-369-1000
Lexington and Third Aves.), UES	877-847-4444
www.boutiquehg.com	

The Franklin, like the other five New York hotels in the Boutique Hotel Group (The Shoreham, The Roger Williams, the Hotel Wales, Hotel 41, and The Mansfield), has been transformed from a questionable property to a beautiful neighborhood hotel. Admittedly, the rooms are small—only the superior rooms can accommodate a crib or a rollaway—but everything is top-notch, from the in-room VCR and CD player to the complimentary "European" breakfast. The sitting room is perfect for breakfast, a snack, an afternoon story break, or a cappuccino (on the house, of course) pick-me-up for rundown parents. *Kids under 18 free*

★ *Gorham Hotel*   **$179–$460**
136 West 55th Street (between   **800-735-0710**
Fifth and Sixth Aves.), MTW   **www.gorhamhotel.com**

The rooms at this classic New York boutique hotel are ideal for families. From the "pillow fight menu" (different-sized pillows with themed pillow cases for evening pillow fights) to the "baby parlors" in the suites (which come complete with stroller, crib, toys, videos, books, and welcome baby amenity), everyone in the family will be happy. Every room has Nintendo and VCRs, and a selection of videos can be delivered to guest rooms. *Cribs (free), cots ($20), mini-fridge, microwave, restaurant, kids under 18 stay free*

★ *Gracie Inn*   **$179–$299**
502 East 81st Street (between   **212-628-1700**
York and East End Aves.), UES

This hotel is more like a mom-and-pop bed and breakfast than an urban hotel. With only twelve rooms (all with efficiency

New York's Top Ten Hotel Swimming Pools

1. Le Parker Meridien (p. 150)
2. The Peninsula (p. 152)
3. Sheraton Manhattan Hotel (p. 147)
4. Travel Inn (seasonal) (p. 137)
5. Millennium UN Plaza (p. 151)
6. Days Hotel Midtown (p. 129)
7. Crowne Plaza Times Square (p. 138)
8. New York Marriott Financial Center (p. 146)
9. Holiday Inn Midtown (seasonal) (p. 132)
10. Trump International Hotel and Towers (p. 158)

kitchens), you'll quickly feel at home in the cozy, somewhat small accommodations. The four one-bedrooms and two duplex penthouses are the best bet for families. The duplexes sleep six, have a VCR and terraces, and one even has a glassed-in Jacuzzi. Continental breakfast is included, and it's delivered to your room. Long-stay discounts are offered (and encouraged) at a shocking rate of 10 percent off per week up to a whopping 40 percent for a four-week stay. *Cribs (free), rollaways ($25)*

Hotel Lucerne	$140–$170 rooms, $220–$370 suites
201 West 79th Street	212-875-1000
(at Amsterdam Ave.), UWS	www.newyorkhotel.com

A relative newcomer to the Upper West Side, the Lucerne opened in 1995 with a complete head-to-toe renovation. A beautiful brownstone landmark (built in 1903), but don't let the age fool you. In your room you'll find the comforts of home with Internet access (via the TV), pay-per-view Nintendo ($5.95 for twenty-four hours), and kitchenettes in the queen and king suites. The location is great for visits to the Children's Museum (four blocks away), the Museum of Natural History (two blocks), and loads of great kid-friendly restaurants like EJ's and the Columbus Bakery. Part of the Empire Hotel Group; see Web site for details on other properties. *Cribs (free); kids under 17 free; concierge, restaurant*

Hotel Wales	$239–$440 and up suites
1295 Madison Avenue	212-876-6000
(between 92nd and 93rd Sts.), UES	877-847-4444
www.waleshotel.com	

You'll find this neighborhood, Carnegie Hill, to be among the quietest in the entire City. Only a block away from Central Park and Museum Mile, this century-old charmer includes in-room VCRs and CD players, and a library of videos for guests to borrow for free. The rooms are small, so only the suites (which have pullout couches) can accommodate families. In addition to the beautiful décor, the rooftop garden, and the historic preservation (the hotel was completely renovated in 1999–2000), the art that adorns the walls is magnificent, including the children's book pictures from *Puss and Boots*. *Cribs (free); rollaways ($20); mini-fridge (upon request); hearty Continental breakfast ($9 adults; free for children 12 and under)*

Helpful Hint

Be sure to tell the reservationist at the time of booking that you're traveling with kids. Many hotels offer free toys, trinkets, and kids' amenities, but they can only provide them if they know the kids are coming.

★ *The Kimberly* **145 East 50th Street** **(between Lexington and** **Third Aves.), MTE** **www.kimberlyhotel.com**	**$219–$449 one bedroom;** **$399–$689 two bedroom** 212-755-0400 800-683-0400

A New York gem, The Kimberly has suites that are perfect for families and also happen to be well priced. The one bedrooms are 600 square feet, sleep four, and have a full kitchen (with dishwasher!) with all of the cookware and utensils you could need. Home improvements and sprucing-up (like new mattresses and carpets) were eagerly undertaken throughout 2000. And the rooms, already well outfitted with high-tech accoutrements, have two-line phones, a fax machine, and data-port as well as two televisions and VCRs upon request. There is no pool; as a hotel guest, you're entitled to the great bonus of free passes to the NY Health & Racquet clubs (located around the City), which do have children's hours (so plan ahead to avoid disappointment). *Cribs/rollaways (free); kids under 17 free; concierge, restaurant, VCR upon request (free)*

★ *Lyden Gardens* $254–$559
215 East 64th Street (between   212-355-1230
Second and Third Aves.), UES   800-ME-SUITE
www.mesuite.com

The size of these rooms alone makes the Lyden Gardens an incredible value, but add to that the full kitchenettes, complete with stove, microwave, coffeemaker, and all of the necessities for cooking and eating, and you've got yourself a perfect setup. On top of that, extended stays (seven to twenty-nine days and thirty days or more) are substantially discounted (more than ⅓ off for seven days or more). You'll need a junior suite (starting at $254) if you want your kids in the same room (two queens and a pullout). Some nice extras include an in-house movie and grocery service (ask at the desk for details). The high level of repeat business (70 percent) and the near-full occupancy level (98 percent) are telltale signs of satisfied customers. Call as far in advance for reservations as possible. *Cribs (free), rollaways ($20); kids under 18 free*

Marriott Marquis $259–$520 and up double,
535 Broadway (between $309 and up, concierge floor
145th and 46th Sts.), TS   212-398-1900
                                                     800-843-4898

Centrally located in the middle of Times Square and considered by many tourists to be one of the City's most luxurious hotels (on the level of a five-star), and certainly one of the favorites, this behemoth (1,946 rooms and 50 floors) won't disappoint those eager to be in the bustle of Times Square. Still, it's hard to forget that you're in a Marriott. Families can comfortably fit into the standard rooms, but depending upon the price variation at the time, you might consider an upgrade to the concierge level, where you get free Continental breakfast, evening appetizers, and a quiet lounge outside of the rooms to sit or play games. *Cribs/rollaways (free); under 18 free; concierge, restaurant*

Melrose Hotel New York	**$139–$340 rooms;**
140 East 63rd Street	**$965–$1,700 penthouse suites**
(at Lexington Ave.), MTE	**212-838-5700**
www.melrosehotel.com	**800-MELROSE**

More like a European boutique hotel than a Manhattan standard, the Melrose once housed the likes of Joan Crawford, Grace Kelly, and Liza Minnelli when it was an all-women's residence. It went through a $40-million renovation in 1998, so you'll see no signs of the previously tattered edges or disrepair, but the hotel still maintains its original class and character. The standard rooms (superior/deluxe and up) are too small for rollaways, but rooms of all sizes can adjoin. *Cribs (free), rollaways ($20); concierge, mini-fridge (upon request)*

The Michelangelo	**$295–$345 executive**
152 West 51st Street	**212-765-1900**
(at Seventh Ave.), MTW	**800-237-0990**
www.michelangelohotel.com	

Just off Seventh Avenue, this hotel is steps away from the activity of Times Square. But in spite of that, tranquility and quiet pervade the moment you step into the lobby. An "Italian" hotel, the décor is luxurious with grand oil paintings, gilded accessories, and large chandeliers. The rooms here are large, and it's the "executive" rooms (600 square feet) that have two beds that can accommodate families. The complimentary Continental breakfast (at the Michelangelo, it's called by its Italian name: *buondi*) is a nice way to start the day—coffee, tea, cappuccino (it's divine; I'd stay here for that alone), and a limited selection of pastries—but it's not a full meal. *Cribs (free), rollaways ($30); complimentary Continental breakfast*

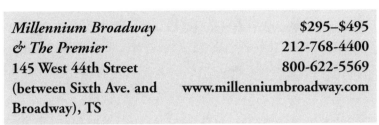

Millennium Broadway	$295–$495
& The Premier	212-768-4400
145 West 44th Street	800-622-5569
(between Sixth Ave. and	www.millenniumbroadway.com
Broadway), TS	

This gigantic Times Square hotel is similar to the others. Though it doesn't actually overlook Times Square, it's just in from the corner of Broadway, so you're not at all removed from the action (which is what you want, otherwise you wouldn't be staying here). The rooms are fairly standard in a familiar and comforting way, and there's always a lot of activity here. *Cribs (free), rollaway ($35); kids under 12 free; concierge, restaurant, pet friendly (very small dogs/cats)*

Insider's Tip

"Use the staff. You're paying not only for your room but also for the salaries of all those people working at the front desk, and often a concierge as well. Especially on longer stays, learn these people's names and utilize their expertise. Many of them are parents, too, and they'll steer you to their favorite local spots." —*Annie, hotel desk staffer*

Next door is the new Premier, which would really only be appropriate with older, well-behaved children (it's really a businessperson's hotel). This lush addition to the Millennium has its own entrance, which is in muted tones, and rather than standing at a desk while reception checks you in, you're invited to sit down for the proceedings. Everything about the Premier is premier, from the beds to the exquisite bathrooms with Aveda bath products. The extensive complimentary breakfast and evening drinks and appetizers in the lounge are very nice extras.

New York Marriott Financial Center $129–$399
85 West Street (between   212-385-4900
Albany and Carlisle Sts.), FD   800-228-9290
www.marriott.com

Seemingly somewhat on the fringe (because it's just off the West Side Highway), this Marriott is actually close to many downtown attractions. A good value, especially during summer months and weekends, the Marriott Financial Center has a modest swimming pool that welcomes kids and nice added touches like cold lemonade on a hot summer day and apples for guests in the lobby. The rooms, if somewhat cookie-cutter in style, are neat and clean— and you can request adjoining doubles for the kids. *Cribs/rollaways (free); kids stay free (ages vary); mini-fridge (free)*

Omni Berkshire Place $239–$419 superior
21 East 52nd Street (between $479–$1150 suites
Fifth and Madison Aves.), MTE   212-753-5800
www.omni-hotels.com   800-843-6664

This very classy four-star– and four-diamond–rated hotel is a bit stuffy, but they're clearly trying to improve upon this because they've recently added an "Omni Kids Rule" program that offers special programs and amenities for children. Favorites include a special children's menu with surprisingly inexpensive children's-sized portions of food, an amenities kids' pack given to children at check-in (coloring books, small toys, a listing of appropriate activities around the City), milk and cookies at turndown, and special backpacks with toys for use during the stay. The superior guestrooms, at 380 square feet, are probably the best option (the one category below superior would be a bit cramped) if you're sharing. *Cribs (free), rollaways ($30); concierge, restaurant, full-service fitness center*

★ *Plaza Fifty*
55 East 50th Street
(at Third Ave.), MTE
www.mesuite.com

$259–$425 one bedroom,
$537–$687 two bedroom
212-751-5710
800-637-8483

The central location of this Manhattan East Suite Hotel (see Beekman Tower) in conjunction with the convenience and affordability of having a fully equipped kitchenette in your suite makes Plaza Fifty a great value for families. Check out the Web site for pictures and especially for the extremely helpful floor plans of the different rooms at the hotel.

Though I've listed only my two favorites of the properties, there is detailed information on all of the ten very respectable Manhattan East Suite Hotels on the Web site. *Cribs (free), rollaway ($20); kids under 12 free; concierge*

Sheraton Manhattan Hotel
790 Seventh Avenue (between
51st and 52nd Sts.), MTW
www.sheraton.com

$290 to $750 and up
212-581-3300
888-625-5144

One of the big midtown generic hotels, the Sheraton Manhattan Hotel has some especially good things to recommend it, such as the swimming pool for starters. Located in the heart of the action, this hotel puts you just a stone's throw from Times Square, the theater district, shopping, and Central Park. You'll also be close to countless subway lines and busses for when you want to jump around the city. Adjoining rooms are available, as are rooms with pull-out sleepers. Specify all special needs (cribs, rollaways, pull-out sleepers, adjoining rooms, mini-fridge, etc.) when you make your reservation. Cribs (free, but when demand is high there is a $10–$20 fee if the hotel has to go off premises to get one for you), rollaway ($15, but ask because sometimes this fee is waived), restaurant, in-room mini-fridge upon request, in-room video games (supplemental charge); concierge; restaurant; fitness center; swimming pool

The Wyndham	$355–$390 two-bedroom suite
42 West 58th Street (between	212-753-3500
Fifth and Sixth Aves.), MTW	800-257-1111

This hotel occupies a prime location in the heart of the hustle and bustle of Midtown, around the corner from Central Park and close to Fifth Avenue's best shopping, the Central Park Zoo, and many museums. With an extremely reasonable price tag, the two-bedroom suites are the best way to accommodate a family; all other rooms can accommodate only two (fire safety regulations) and only the suites connect. The sole problem here is that the staff is often rude, especially the brusque and dismissive management, so if you have a problem you'll likely be on your own. *Cribs (free), rollaways ($15 per night for kids 15 and under)*

"$$$$" Hotels: More Than $400

At these, the most luxurious of the City's hotels, you'll be waited on hand and foot—and you'll pay for it. But if such accommodations are within your budget, these are some of the finest hotels on the planet.

Four Seasons	$455 and up
57 East 57th Street (between	212-758-5700
Park and Madison Aves.), MTE	800-332-3442
www.fourseasons.com	

As historical as the landmark Pierre is, the Four Seasons is modern. Punctuated with high ceilings and light-colored woods,

*One of the City's many
monuments; a favorite for
family snapshots*

nothing is overlooked at this contemporary sister property. In the
heart of Midtown, the bulk of
weekday guests at this classy favorite are business travelers. But if
you're a fan of the Four Seasons'
legendary service, this branch won't
disappoint. Rooms are large by City
standards (averaging about 600 square
feet), and soundproofing goes a long way toward ensuring a good
night's sleep. *Cribs (free), extra bed ($50); kids' amenities*

Learning Tip

Many New York hotels have colorful histories. The Hotel
Chelsea (222 West 23rd St., between Seventh and Eighth
Aves., www.hotelchelsea.com) boasts a bustling lobby filled
with museum-quality works by prominent current and former
residents. Thomas Wolfe wrote *You Can't Go Home Again*
at the Chelsea; Arthur Miller penned *After the Fall* in its
welcoming arms; William Burroughs moved in to work on
Naked Lunch; and in a defining moment of punk-rock history,
Sid Vicious reportedly murdered girlfriend Nancy Spungeon
here. Does your hotel have any interesting history? Even if
it's a new hotel, what building was on the site before?

★ *Le Parker Meridien*
118 West 57th Street (between
Sixth and Seventh Aves.), MTW
www.parkermeridien.com

$380–$630 doubles,
$500–$750 junior suites
212-245-5000
800-543-4300

If you can afford it, I think this is hands-down the best choice for families. From the enormous (the length of one entire city block), naturally lit atrium to the all-day breakfast restaurant, the rooftop swimming pool (where children are *always* welcome), and the team of super professional concierges (who can get you VIP passes to Mars 2112, Jekyll & Hyde, and a few others), you and your children will feel welcome at this Midtown winner. On top of that, $60 million has been poured into renovating the rooms (which I thought were pretty nice already), completed in March 2001. Nice touches include a concierge who is specially attuned to children's needs. But better still is the modified basketball court (by reservation to avoid disappointment) and special swimming classes like "mommy and me" that are open to hotel guests. If your children aren't the "joiner" types, there are plenty of pool toys and swim aides to keep them occupied. There is a lifeguard on duty, but children under 14 must be supervised by an adult. *Cribs (free), rollaways ($30, waived for kids under 12); kids under 12 free; concierge, restaurant*

The Lowell
28 East 63rd Street (between
Madison and Park Aves.), UES

$445 and up
212-838-1400
800-221-4444

The front desk attendants could not be friendlier or more helpful at this UES boutique hotel (though management is on the icy side). You'll be welcomed into the small lobby with smiles and salutations and whisked off to your room or suite (many of which have kitchenettes, balconies, even fireplaces or gardens) in no time. Kids will get a kick out of the fact that Madonna was in

residence for a time but, before moving in, insisted upon having a private gym built in her suite. *Cribs/rollaways (free)*

★ **The Mark**	**$475 and up (specials from $299)**
25 East 77th Street (between	**212-744-4300**
Fifth and Madison Aves.), UES	**800-843-6275**
www.mandarinoriental.com	

Just steps off Madison Avenue, the second you enter The Mark, you'll feel the peace of the place settle over you. Part of the Small Luxury Hotels association, luxury is indeed the name of the game here. Rooms are variable in size, so specify if you intend to have a rollaway brought in (deluxe and up). And if you want a kitchenette, request that at booking, too, because many deluxe (and larger) rooms are fully equipped. Family options range from rollaways to suites and connecting rooms. *Cribs (free), rollaways ($30); kids under 16 free; concierge, restaurant/bar (children's menu)*

Millennium UN Plaza	**$235–$300 rooms,**
1 United Nations Plaza	**$279–550 junior suite**
(at 44th St. and First Ave.), MTE	**212-758-1234**
www.millenniumhotels.com	**866-866-8086**

Perhaps one of the best things about the Millennium UN is the "guaranteed view." Starting on the twenty-eighth floor (the lower floors are occupied by the United Nations), there are no buildings around that are as tall; therefore, every room at the Millennium UN is assured a view of either the East River or the city skyline. Surely there is no other hotel in town that can promise that. The sizeable (remember, Manhattan-sized) pool is another great reason to stay here, as are the peace and quiet of the neighborhood. For theatergoers (or those who just want to get across town in ease and comfort), the hotel also offers free drop-offs in the Theater District. Double rooms can only accommodate two, but it is possible to adjoin two rooms, and the junior suites can sleep four with a pullout couch. For larger families, or those looking for more space, there are also two-bedroom suites. *Note:* All rooms in the East tower were renovated in 2001. *Cribs/rollaways (free for under 18); concierge, restaurant*

The Peninsula	**$560 and up ($350 seasonal specials)**
700 Fifth Avenue (at 55th St.), MTE	**212-956-2888**
www.peninsula.com	**800-262-9467**

Forty-five million dollars later, this landmark hotel is back in business (they closed the whole year of 1998 for the renovation) with renewed spirit (and everything else). Ideal for parents who are combining work with pleasure, the rooms at the Peninsula have all the trappings of the modern office (they say that each room is equipped with $17,000 of technology)—silent fax machine, double-line phones, modem, phone, and ISDN lines. But there's plenty for the kids, too. Special gifts at check-in (the backpack with Velcro pull-off pouch is *sooo* cute) and amenities, like cookies and milk and stuffed animals at turndown, are always winners. The enclosed rooftop pool (with children's hours) and close proximity to Fifth Avenue favorites are also guaranteed to make the kids smile. *Cribs (free), rollaways ($50); kids under 12 free (flexible); concierge, restaurant*

The Pierre	**$465 and up**
Fifth Avenue (at 61st St.), UES	**212-838-8000**
www.fourseasons.com	**800-743-7734**

Ah, the Pierre! A Four Seasons landmark hotel, you'll be hard-pressed to find anything amiss at this exquisite historical favorite. Murals and tapestries adorn the walls, and equally impressive crystal chandeliers hang from the ceilings. Across the street from Central Park, and a stone's throw from FAO Schwarz and the best of Fifth and Madison Avenue shopping, the location

couldn't be better, nor could the friendly and accommodating staff. As a special treat, especially for little (and grownup) girls, try afternoon tea in the Rotunda—I guarantee you, they won't forget it (and neither will you). *Cribs (free), extra beds ($50 for over 18); kids under 18 free; kids' amenities (cookies and milk, coloring books, VCRs, video games, babysitting), pet-friendly, minifridge and microwave (upon request)*

Plaza Athénée	**$480 and up**
37 East 64th Street (between	**212-734-9100**
Park and Madison Aves.), UES	**800-447-8800**
www.plaza-athenee.com	

This peaceful Upper East Side hotel fits right in with the ritzy neighborhood. The staff is helpful, if a bit formal, and rooms are on the somewhat small side—but what each room provides is strictly top-notch. *Cribs (free), rollaway ($40); VCR upon request*

★ *The Regency*	**$375–$650 and up**
540 Park Avenue (at 61st St.), UES	**212-759-4100**
www.loewsregencyhotel.com	**800-235-6397**

This high-end hotel is part of the Loews chain. An extremely kid-friendly property, the Regency also welcomes pets—including dogs of any size (you might still want to leave the Great Dane at home, though). The rooms are well appointed and sizeable, and every effort is made to make your kids feel at home. Small toys are handed out at check-in (tell them you're bringing kids when you make your reservations), and some rooms, like the luxury kings (which come with either a king bed or two doubles), have the convenience of a kitchenette. Some of the larger rooms, like the $650 suite, have a king bed, a pullout couch, sitting and work area, two bathrooms, and plenty of extra space to tumble around in. *Cribs/rollaways (free); concierge, restaurant, toys, pet-friendly (even big dogs)*

WHERE TO STAY

Rihga Royal	$269–$459, $299–$429, $399–$499
151 West 54th Street (between	212-307-5000
Sixth and Seventh Aves.), MTW	800-937-5454
www.righaroyalny.com	

The great thing here is that all of the rooms are suites, and they're all pretty much the same size, regardless of what category level you spring for. There are three levels of suites, all of which are about 500 square feet and have a living room and bedroom separated by French doors and a bathroom with separate tub and shower. The pricing is pretty straightforward—the higher the floor, the more expensive the room. There are also some two-bedroom suites, which range from $600–$1,100. On weekends, every room receives vouchers for $25 or $50 (depending on your category) to spend on food and beverages anywhere in the hotel—including room service—and some of the room categories also include free car service to and from the airport, so be sure to ask when you book. *Cribs (free), rollaways/queen-size pull-outs ($29); concierge, restaurant, kids under 18 free*

The Ritz-Carlton New York, Battery Park	$220–$490,
2 West Street, FD	Suites from $565–$4500
www.ritzcarlton.com	212-344-0800
	800-241-3333

This new (January 2002) thirty-nine-story glass and brick tower Ritz-Carlton Hotel is a great addition to the altered downtown landscape, and it's everything an opulent hotel should be (and the Central Park RC is no exception, either). Your home away from home (and dare I say, perhaps even better)—the RC Battery Park offers 298 luxurious rooms (Art Deco–inspired design with such modern amenities as high-speed Internet access) with fabulous views of New York Harbor, the Statue of Liberty, and Ellis Island; attentive and helpful staff; full-service everything—health club

and spa services (though no one will do your workout for you); complimentary shuttle service in Lower Manhattan; and the list goes on. Children are equally pampered with the Ritz-Kids program—special kid-appropriate amenities are presented to children upon checking into the hotel, a kids' "toy menu" includes games like Monopoly, Battleship, and Candy Land, and favorite kids' movies (with G ratings) are on the ready for viewing. But wait, there's more—the "bath butler" can be called to draw your child's bath (yours, too), turndown tuck-ins with an FAO Schwarz teddy bear (children 8 and under), and twenty-four-hour kids' menu room service is just a phone call away. The hotel also features an expansive art collection with special attention paid to some of New York's most talented artists. The RC Battery Park also houses the new Skyscraper Museum on the ground floor. Ritz-Carlton Club Rooms offer an extra level of privacy and opulence—including a club concierge and butlers and five complimentary food presentations each day, beginning with an extensive Continental breakfast. *Cribs and rollaway beds upon request (free); children under 12 free ($40 for children over 12 in room with parents); concierge; multiple restaurants*

The Ritz-Carlton New York, Central Park	**$395 and up,**
50 Central Park South	**suites $1,395 and up**
(at Sixth Ave.), MTW	**212-308-9100,**
www.ritzcarlton.com	**800-241-3333**

This new (April 2002) Ritz-Carlton (not to be confused with the new Ritz-Carlton in Battery Park downtown) is a most centrally located property (on the site of the former St. Moritz Hotel) perched at the top of midtown, the entrance to Central Park, a stone's throw from the theater district, and close to great shopping (just a few blocks from FAO Schwarz, Fifth and Madison Avenues, and Broadway), Times Square, Lincoln Center, and lots of great restaurants and attractions. As with the RC Battery Park, you will be met with an attentive and helpful staff, luxurious rooms, full service everything—spa, fitness center, restaurants, complimentary Bentley and Mercedes limousine service in Midtown, complimentary use of Burberry trench coats for everyone in the family—including the dog . . . and the list goes on. For small children, there's the P.O.L.O. program—protect our little ones. This includes safety features like outlet covers, corner protectors for sharp corners on beds and tables, first-aid items, and so forth. Children's amenities include coloring books, a small stuffed lion, and games—just pick up the phone and ask. Suites (and nineteen rooms) have the option of adjoining rooms, and all suites, except for Liberty Suites, have pullout couches. Ritz-Carlton Club Rooms offer an extra level of privacy and opulence—including a club concierge and butlers and six complimentary food presentations each day, beginning with an extensive Continental breakfast. *Cribs and rollaway beds available upon request (free); kids under 12 free, 12 and older $75; mini-fridge (free)e; concierge; multiple restaurants (no kids' menu but children can have anything they'd like off the regular menu—$6 at breakfast, $8 lunch and dinner); ask for summer rates*

★ *The Stanhope Park Hyatt*	$499 and up, ($279 summer
995 Fifth Avenue	**and weekend specials)**
(at 81st St.), UES	**212-774-1234**
www.hyatt.com	**800-233-1234**

The Stanhope is a classic, Old World, New York favorite. Located directly across from the Met and Central Park, and only steps from other favorite museums and Madison Avenue boutiques, the Stanhope is a great property for families who enjoy the lap of luxury in a quiet neighborhood. Part of the Hyatt family, the Stanhope renovated rooms in 1999 and continued to update and improve amenities in 2001. A great money-saving feature is the family plan: When parents book one room at the standard rate, they get a second connecting room with two beds at half price. Other options include suites with pullout sleepers. Though there is no children's menu, the chef aims to please, so requests for things like pb&j or macaroni and cheese are met with pleasure. *Cribs/rollaways (free); kids under 18 free; concierge, restaurant/bar, mini-fridge (free upon request), VCR (upon request)*

★ *St. Regis* $690–$815 rooms; $1,200–$11,500 suites
2 East 55th Street (at Fifth Ave.), MTE   212-753-4500
www.stregis.com   800-759-7550

Widely considered one of the very best hotels in the world—Elton John, Michael Jordan, and the Prince of Saudi Arabia all stay here when they're in town. So why not you? An exquisite hotel with extremely attentive service, walking into the St. Regis is like walking into a movie—it's just that nice. Marble bathrooms, double sinks, and separate tub and shower are only the beginning of what you get in these luxurious surroundings. The way it works here is that your wish is their command—all for a price, of course. Fabulous afternoon tea service, with a live harpist and divine pastries that would make any child run in circles—and parents, too. *Cribs (free), rollaways ($95); children's amenities, babysitting*

★ *Surrey Hotel* $298–$830
20 East 76th Street   212-320-8027
(at Madison Ave.), UES   800-ME-SUITE
www.mesuite.com

This all-suite hotel is sister to the Lyden Gardens and a bit more upscale. An equally great value, all rooms have a kitchenette and all of the accoutrements for cooking and eating. The larger suites have a full kitchen (some even have dishwashers, a feature many city residents live without). One- and two-bedroom suites are ideal for families, though connecting studios are also an option. The neighborhood is peaceful and quiet, only one block to Central Park and Museum Mile and close to all of the boutiques on Madison Avenue. Substantial discounts are offered for extended stays (it's no wonder so many guests are quasi-residents), and pets are welcome. *Cribs (free), rollaway ($20); kids under 12 free*

Trump International Hotel and Towers	$325–$1,650
1 Central Park West (between	212-299-1000
59th and 60th Sts.), UWS	888-448-7867
www.trumpintl.com	

Perfectly centered between Midtown and the Upper West Side, the Trump Hotel is everything you'd expect from Donald Trump. No corners cut here. Virtually all of the rooms have fully equipped kitchens, and in case your kids need a video break, the VCR can entertain them while you enjoy the stereo (or telescopes). The fitness center includes a two-lane (it is New York, after all) 55-foot pool, which welcomes children, and the close proximity (directly across the street) to Central Park is another great plus. *Cribs/rollaways (free most of the time; $50 during Thanksgiving and Christmas); concierge, restaurant, kitchenettes*

Waldorf-Astoria (Hilton)	$229–$659 doubles,
301 Park Avenue (between	$329 and up suites
49th and 50th Sts.), MTE	212-355-3000
www.hilton.com	800-925-3673

The president stays at the Waldorf when he's in town, in part because there's a private concrete security bunker underneath and in part because the suites are among the best in the City. This old New York classic is as much of a tourist destination as a classy place to stay. Renovated in 1999, it's a real charmer, though for the money, unless you're feeling nostalgic or need to be in that specific location, you might want, like me, to look elsewhere. *Cribs (free), rollaways ($25); kids under 18 free; concierge, restaurant*

Westin New York at Times Square	**$399–$499 regular**
Corner of West 42nd and 43rd Sts.	**rooms; $479 and up**
(at Eighth Ave.), TS	**executive-level rooms**
212-921-9575	**800-WESTIN-1**
www.westinny.com	

Opened ahead of schedule in October 2002, the Westin New York at Times Square is adjacent to the new E-Walk retail, entertainment, and restaurant complex. The forty-five-story hotel is intended to be not just a finely designed building but also a work of art—the building is a prism split by a curving beam of light. Each of the rooms features wireless Internet access, Westin's signature Heavenly Bed, Heavenly Crib, and it's new Heavenly Bath, along with a full range of amenities, views of Times Square lights and billboards, the Manhattan skyline, the Hudson River—and a very central location for those who want to be smack-dab in Times Square. Children's amenities include gifts for boys and girls, as well as for babies. Pack-n'-plays as well as cots are available. *Kids under 17 free; mini-fridge (free upon request); restaurant*

Money-Saving Tip

Make all your phone calls from the pay phones in the lobby of your hotel. Many New York hotels charge as much as $2 for a local call, which can really add up, especially compared to twenty-five cents for the same service at the lobby payphones. And if you have a cell phone with an included-minutes plan, don't hesitate to use it, even when in your room.

Apartment Stays

In addition to hotels, there's also the option of staying in a furnished apartment. There are obviously some advantages to this choice, not least of which is that you'll feel like a local as you come and go from your place. But ironically, with that freedom also come some drawbacks: There is no concierge to advise you on attractions or make reservations, no maintenance to call when the toilet backs up, no maid service to come and clean up after you, nor any of the other conveniences that come with staying at a hotel (which you can have at the Lyden Gardens, the Surrey, and the Gracie, all of which offer substantial discounts for extended stays). Furthermore, traveling with kids, you might not save as much money as you anticipate because, with three or more people, the smallest rental you can secure is a one bedroom (usually a big jump up in price from a studio).

You might be getting the message that I don't necessarily recommend this form of accommodation. But then again many people really like the idea of staying in a real apartment in New York City, and that's a perfectly respectable view. Certainly, it's well worth researching this option if you think it's right for your family.

Listed here you'll find some of the City's best rental agencies, more of which are springing up every day. I've included only the most reliable, reputable, and long-standing of the bunch. And don't forget, these apartments book up early, so be sure to call as far in advance as you possibly can.

Abode Ltd.	$135–$400
(four-night minimum)	212-472-2000
www.abodenyc.com	800-835-8880

Abode has apartments ranging in size from studios to three bedrooms, all of which require a minimum four-night stay. Apartments include a full kitchen, TV, telephone, answering machine, hair dryer, iron, and clock radio, and some have extras like a microwave, stereo, VCR, fax machine, balcony, whirlpool bath, fireplace, and health club. Apartments are located throughout the City.

Bed, Breakfast, and Books	$125–$250
(two- to three-night minimum)	212-865-8740

Studios and one-bedrooms and a few two-bedroom apartments are available for stays of two to three nights (depending upon the time of year) or longer. Sprinkled throughout the City, all of the apartments are near public transportation and are centrally located to areas of interest. Discounts are available for extended stays. With only thirty units, the stock here goes pretty fast.

Gamut Realty Group Inc.	$170–$700
(three-night minimum)	212-594-5650
www.gamutnyc.com	

Gamut Realty has apartments throughout the City, ranging in size from studios to three bedrooms. Perhaps the largest of all the apartment rental groups, Gamut has more than 900 units in its repertoire, all of which require a minimum three-night stay. The units average between $150 and $250 per night for a one bedroom, and $250 to $350 for two bedrooms. It all depends on the size, location, and swank-factor. Price adjustments are available on extended stays.

New York Habitat	$135–$500
(four-night minimum)	212-255-8018
www.nyhabitat.com	

A pioneer in the field, New York Habitat is one of the most highly regarded agencies—and its rates are very compelling. Prices vary according to location and many other factors, and some apartments are available on a bed-and-breakfast basis.

<table>
<tr><td>Oxbridge
(four-night minimum)
www.oxbridgeny.com</td><td>$140–$225
212-348-8100</td></tr>
</table>

Oxbridge (four-night minimum) www.oxbridgeny.com	$140–$225 212-348-8100

With apartments concentrated on 46th Street (between Fifth and Sixth Aves.) and the Upper East Side, Oxbridge has zeroed in on great locations. Some of the apartments are in blocks, so you could even rent adjoining apartments if they're available. If these neighborhoods aren't to your liking, ask about other locations because Oxbridge has other apartments here and there throughout the City. Like the others, these are self-catering apartments (no maid service) and require a minimum four-night stay.

INDEX TO HOTELS BY NEIGHBORHOOD AND PRICE

CHAPTER

5

Attractions
& Activities

Attractions

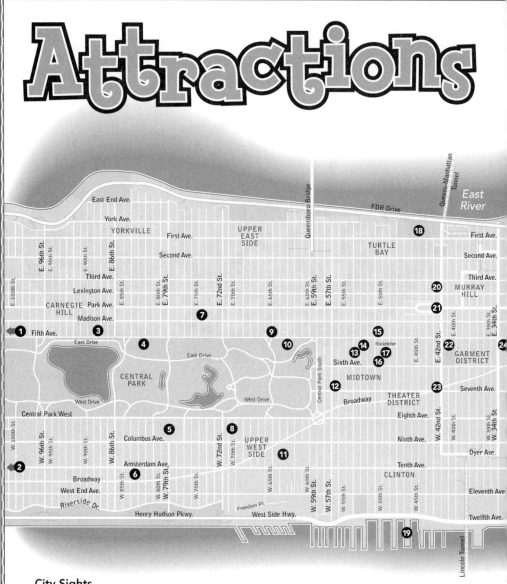

City Sights

Map shows highlights only. See chapter text for more listings.

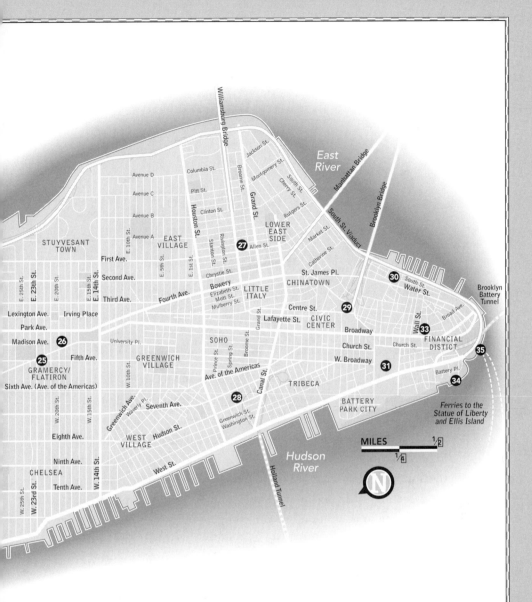

Museums and Zoos

ow that you've decided to visit New York City, it's time to figure out what you're going to do with your time here. There are so many thousands of things to see and do in this ever-changing town that I can't stress enough the importance of advance planning. I've listed more activities and attractions here than a family could possibly do in a year (it's taken me a lifetime of living in and near New York to accumulate all this information), so it's up to you to figure out what your family will enjoy most. For 99 percent of families, a visit to one of the City's several zoos will be sufficient. If you come from a great zoo town like San Diego, though, you may be better off spending your time elsewhere. Or maybe your kids are zoo fanatics and want to visit all of New York's zoos, gardens, *and* the aquarium—so be it, you'll find the information you need here. Here are the two most valuable pieces of advice I have to offer:

1. **Always call ahead.** It is essential that you confirm the location and hours of any attraction you seek to visit. Even the most reliable operations are occasionally forced to close or change their hours on a moment's notice. The last thing in

the world you want to do is waste all that time and energy getting to a destination, only to find it closed or otherwise not up to your expectations. The old adage, an ounce of prevention is worth a pound of cure, certainly applies here.

2. **Always have a backup plan.** Sometimes, no matter how much planning you've put in, and even if you've called ahead, things fall through—or the lines turn out to be so long that you have to back out. Luckily, there's so much variety among New York's attractions that you should be able to fend off heartbreak and disappointment with some creative planning. If things aren't working out at the Guggenheim Museum, try the Whitney. Or just be aware of the shops and restaurants near all your destinations, so you have efficient ways to use your extra time. Act confidently, and your kids may never know you switched to Plan B.

In this chapter, I've listed the major venues for activities in New York City. I designed this book so it could be the only resource you'll need when it comes to planning a trip to New York and choosing your activities. But when it comes to what will be happening at specific places on the specific days you'll be in New York, you won't know until much closer to the actual date of your trip. Thus, when you start planning, you'll want to begin by making a list of desired activities. For some of those activities, like the most popular Broadway shows, you can purchase tickets months in advance. Other spots won't announce their activity schedules until weeks or days before the actual event. But whatever you do, please don't just show up in New York without at least the outline of a game plan—it's really too much of a city for you to wing it.

Here are some resources for planning your New York City activities schedule:

@ For current listings, the most user-friendly sources are *New York Magazine* and *Time Out New York*. They're often available at large chain bookstores like Barnes & Noble, even outside the New York region. Listings run about two weeks in advance of the magazines' dates of newsstand release. Though the physical magazines are much easier to work with, both also maintain Web sites (www.timeoutny.com and www.ny metro.com). For most needs, you probably won't need to go any farther in your research than *New York* and *Time Out*.

🍋 Also very useful are the listings in the free *Village Voice* newspaper (www.villagevoice.com) and the Friday *New York Times* "Weekend" section (www.nytimes.com and www.ny today.com).

🍋 On the Web, CitySearch (www.newyork.citysearch.com) has the best listings, though I still favor the print sources.

🍋 An excellent local monthly is *New York Family*, a magazine specifically targeted at families with kids (www.parenthood web.com). There's also the *Big Apple Parent* paper (www .parentsknow.com) and *ParentGuide* (www.parentguide news.com). These publications are intended mostly for New Yorkers, but tourists can glean some useful information from them as well.

🍋 *Where Magazine* (www.wheremagazine.com) also has good listings, and you'll probably get a free copy in your hotel room.

🍋 In addition, once you land in New York City, you'll be buried under free brochures that list all manner of family-appropriate events. Your hotel lobby and the lobbies of the main tourist attractions should have plentiful collections. Particularly useful are any publications from the NYCVB (Convention & Visitors Bureau).

🍋 If your kids have very specific interests, such as modern art, you'll want to look into specialty publications. I've listed the most important of these in the applicable sections that follow.

℮ But really, despite the wealth of resources available, there's no need to go into research overkill. This book plus a copy of the relevant issues of *New York* or *Time Out* should suffice for planning all but the most unusual trips.

Money-Saving Tip

Use combined attractions passes for big savings. The City-Pass gets you into the Empire State Building Observatory, Circle Line Harbor Cruise, Whitney Museum of American Art, Guggenheim Museum, American Museum of Natural History, Museum of Modern Art, and Intrepid Sea-Air-Space Museum at half the cost of purchasing separate tickets for each. Passes are $38 for adults and $31 for kids ages 12 through 17 (not available to younger kids). You can buy CityPass at the main entrance of any of the attractions or online at www.citypass.net. Less of a savings, but still respectable, is the 34th Street Adventure, available at the Empire State Building or online through www.skyride.com. It includes admission to the Empire State Building Observatory, New York Skyride, and Madison Square Garden's "All Access Tour." It's $33 for adults and $23 for kids ages five through twelve. Don't buy a combined attractions pass, however, unless you really plan and want to visit enough of the included attractions.

City Sights

This section includes a mixed bag of attractions, all of which have that "Only in New York!" quality. Ranging from the Brooklyn Bridge to the United Nations, here is where I've included New York's most unique buildings, monuments, and centers of activity. The really nice thing is that, with many of the listings in this section, there's little or no cost involved—it doesn't, in general, cost anything to look!

I've indicated the neighborhood, using the following abbreviations:

BR: Brooklyn

CH: Chelsea

EV: East Village

GD: Garment District

GV: Greenwich Vilage

LI: Little Italy

MTE: Midtown East

Q: Queens

SI: Staten Island

TD: Theater District

UES: Upper East Side

UWS: Upper West Side

BX: Bronx

CT: Chinatown

FD: Financial District

GP: Gramercy Park/Flatiron

LES: Lower East Side

MT: Midtown

MTW: Midtown West

SH: SoHo

TBC: TriBeCa

TS: Times Square

US: Union Square

WV: West Village

A ★ indicates an attraction that stands out, particularly in relation to the others in its category.

★ Brooklyn Bridge
Connecting the Manhattan and Brooklyn Civic Centers
Manhattan entrance near Park Row and Center Street
(close to the 4, 5, and 6 subways)
Brooklyn entrance near the High Street A and C train station

Something about the Brooklyn Bridge inspires awe in all who lay eyes upon it—Walt Whitman, Hart Crane, me, and everybody else in New York. It's not the world's largest suspension bridge (though it was for a while), and it's not the oldest of its kind (the Roebling Bridge in Cincinnati predates it by several years), but it nonetheless has a certain appeal that combines aesthetics, engineering, and tradition to create what many believe is history's most perfect bridge. Walking across the Brooklyn Bridge is an experience all but the smallest children should have—you can walk one way (allow about half an hour at an average walking pace) and take the subway back, or you can combine the walk with a visit to other Brooklyn attractions. Construction of the bridge began in 1867, and it was completed in 1883. Designed by John Roebling, the project was haunted by misfortune. Roebling was mortally wounded in 1869 when a ferry rammed a waterfront piling on which he was standing. Washington Roebling, his son who took over the project, was taken ill with the bends in 1872. When the Brooklyn Bridge opened, a dozen pedestrians were killed in a stampede started by someone who shouted that the bridge was collapsing. A year later, P. T. Barnum crossed the bridge with a herd of elephants to demonstrate its safety. The situation has improved steadily ever since.

★ *Cathedral of Saint John*	212-316-7540 general info
the Divine	212-932-7347 tour info
1047 Amsterdam Avenue	212-662-2133 event info/tickets
(at 112th St.), UWS	www.stjohndivine.org

Saint John the Divine has been under construction since 1892, and it's still not finished! Even uncompleted, though, it's the world's largest Gothic cathedral, the size of two football fields, with seating for 5,000 worshipers. There are tours offered six days a week (no Mondays) at 11 A.M. (Sundays at 1 P.M.). Admission is $2 for adults, $1 for children. The free New Year's Eve concert is a New York favorite, as is the Blessing of the Animals each October.

Chrysler Building
405 Lexington Avenue (at 42nd St.), MTE

You can't actually ascend the Chrysler Building unless you work there, but chances are you'll pass by it at some point during your visit to New York. It's worth a look (from the outside, as well as inside from the Art Deco lobby that features African marble), because this— is probably New Yorkers' favorite building. Note the radiator-cap ornaments and gargoyles.

★ *Ellis Island*	212-363-3200
New York Harbor	**www.ellisisland.org**

Between 1892 and 1954, seventeen million immigrants passed through Ellis Island. More than 40 percent of Americans living today are the descendants of those immigrants. Renovated and reopened in 1990, Ellis Island is now an absolutely fascinating museum of immigration. The emphasis is on the personal experience of immigration. The "Through America's Gate" exhibit focuses on photographs and oral histories. The "Treasures from Home" exhibit displays family heirlooms, religious articles, rare clothing, and jewelry, all donated by descendants of immigrants. At the American Family Immigration History Center, you can research your family's history. For transportation information, see the Statue of Liberty—the same ferry services Ellis Island and the Statue of Liberty, and you'll likely want to visit both.

★ *Empire State Building*	212-736-3100
350 Fifth Avenue (at 34th St.), MTE	**www.esbnyc.com**

What a colorful history the Empire State Building has. At 102 stories and 1,454 feet, it stood for years as the world's tallest building—and now with the destruction of the World Trade Towers, it is again the tallest in New York. King Kong fictionally scaled it in 1933. A military aircraft really crashed into it in 1945. That funny structure at the top? It was intended as a mooring mast for blimps, but was only used once. Observation decks are on the 86th and 102nd floors, and, even though it's lower, you should give the eighty-sixth-floor deck your attention—many experienced New Yorkers say it's the better

choice. You can see 80 miles from the observation decks on a clear day, and the best times to go are first thing in the morning or late at night (the largest crowds come in the late afternoon and early evening). Also within the building: New York Skyride (888-SKYRIDE or 212-279-9777, www.skyride.com), a flight-seeing simulation that takes you on a virtual aerial tour of New York's major landmarks, but it's not nearly as fun as the real experience of the observation decks.

Take a look at the Empire State Building at night, and you'll see the top of the Empire State Building illuminated by thousands of colored floodlights. The colors change often, to commemorate important holidays and events. Some are easy to figure out: red, white, and blue for Independence Day; green for Saint Patrick's Day. But the building also glows red, black, and green for Martin Luther King Jr.'s birthday; purple, teal, and white for part of National Osteoporosis Month; red, yellow, and green for Portugal Day; blue and white for Hanukkah; green, white, and orange for India Independence Day; and lavender and white for Gay Pride Day. The building is unlit for AIDS Awareness Day. The Empire State Building's Web site (www.esb nyc.com) contains a lighting schedule along with a wealth of other building facts.

Empire State Building hours: Daily 9:30 A.M. to midnight (last chance to purchase tickets is 11:15 P.M.). *It's critical that you call ahead, as the observation decks can be closed in foul weather.*

Helpful Hint

To build anticipation, study the Empire State Building's exterior and lobby first. The best places to view (and photograph) the outside are from the top floor (food court) of the Manhattan Mall (34th St.) and from the base of the Flatiron Building (23rd St.). When you enter the building, be sure to spend some time examining the beautiful details and the mural in the soaring lobby.

Observatory admission: $9 adults, $7 seniors, $4 children under 12, children under 5 free

Skyride hours: Daily from 10 A.M. to 10 P.M.

Skyride admission: $13.50 for adults, $10.50 for kids and seniors

Combined admission: $17 adult, $12 child

Flatiron Building
175 Fifth Avenue (at 23rd St.), GP

One of New York's favorite landmarks, this triangular building (so named because it's shaped like an iron—as in laundry) dates back to 1902 and is only 6 feet across at its narrow end. It contains no specific attractions or events, but it's a great building to observe from the street—then you can turn around and get a phenomenal view of the Empire State Building up the avenue.

Grand Central Terminal   212-935-3960 tour info
42nd Street (at Park Ave.), MTE
www.grandcentralterminal.com

Travelers returning from Europe invariably comment on the beauty of European train stations, but the truth is those stations have got nothing on Grand Central. Though the station, designed by Warren & Wetmore with Reed & Stem, fell into disrepair for many years, it has recently been the beneficiary of a $175-million renovation, and construction continues to this day. The terminal is now again one of the world's greatest public spaces, and many say it's better than it ever was. Observe Jules-Alexis Coutan's neoclassical sculpture, *Transportation,* at the south entrance (the central character is Mercury, the Roman god of travel, among other things). The sky ceiling shows the constellations, lit by fiber-optic cables. Particularly noteworthy and useful for families is the wealth of new restaurants and food stalls, particularly on the new downstairs dining concourse, which features absolutely no chain junk food—just authentic, local, New York fare, including Junior's cheesecake and the Grand Central Oyster bar with its famous, vaulted tile ceilings. There's a tour of Grand Central Station every Wednesday at 12:30 P.M.—meet in front of the main-concourse information booth (you can't miss it). The tour is free, but donations to the Municipal Art Society are accepted.

New York Public Library	212-869-8089
Fifth Avenue and 42nd Street, MTE	212-930-0830
www.nypl.org	

This Beaux Arts edifice was designed by Carrère & Hastings in 1911 and is made of white Vermont marble with Corinthian columns and, in front, the famous lion sculptures: *Patience* (left) and *Fortitude* (right). Mayor Fiorello La Guardia joked, "Read between the lions." The New York Public Library is one of the world's great libraries, with 6 million books, 12 million manuscripts, and 2.8 million photographs. The library also hosts numerous exhibitions and lectures throughout the year—call for details.

Main Reading Room and exhibition hall hours: Monday, Thursday, Friday, and Saturday 10:00 A.M.–6:00 P.M., Tuesday through Wednesday 11:00 A.M.–7:30 P.M. A free one-hour tour is available Monday through Saturday at 11:00 A.M. and 2:00 P.M. (departs from Astor Hall)

New York Stock Exchange	212-656-5165
20 Broad Street (ticket booth), FD	

Note: As of press time, this attraction was closed to the public for security reasons, but it should reopen eventually. Here you can watch all the trading-floor action from a glassed-in observation deck. There are also interactive exhibits explaining how the market works (in a very general sense) and a short film about the

Favorite Public Spaces to Take a Break

One of the great new trends in construction in New York City is the abundance of public spaces carved out of mostly commercial office plazas. Some are indoors, others are outdoors, but all are open to the public for a rest, a snack, or even a low-key picnic.

@ Paley Park—53rd St., just east of Fifth Ave. (outdoors)

@ Sony Plaza—55th St., at Madison Ave. (indoors)

@ Rockefeller Center—47th to 50th Sts., between Fifth and Sixth Aves. (outdoors)

@ Chase Manhattan Plaza—near Liberty and William Sts., Financial District (outdoors)

@ IBM Garden—Madison Ave., between 56th and 57th Sts. (indoors)

@ South Street Seaport and Pier 17—East River, near Fulton St. (indoors and outdoors)

@ Bryant Park—42nd St., between Fifth and Sixth Aves. (outdoors)

@ World Wide Plaza—49th and 50th Sts., between Eighth and Ninth Aves. (outdoors).

NYSE past and present. Very early arrival may earn you a ticket that allows you inside in time for the opening bell at 9:30 A.M., when the whole place goes berserk.

Exchange hours: Monday through Friday 9:15 A.M.– 4:00 P.M.; closed national holidays.

Admission: Tickets are free, but rationed (3,000 per day) and usable only for specified time slots, so arrive early (the ticket booth opens at 8:45 A.M.).

Rockefeller Center   **212-632-3975**
47th–50th Streets (between Fifth and Sixth Aves.), MT

Most of Rockefeller Center was built in the 1930s, at the height of the Art Deco era. It is the world's largest such complex, with eighteen buildings on twenty-one acres of extremely valuable New York City land. If you stand on Fifth Avenue between 49th and 50th Streets, you're looking at the Promenade, which leads to the Lower Plaza, encircled by the flags of every United Nations member country, where you'll find the famous Rockefeller Center ice-skating rink (in winter) and Paul Manship's bronze statue of Prometheus. Also along the Promenade and Lower Plaza are numerous shops and restaurants. This is also where, in the Christmas season, you'll find the famous New York City Christmas tree.

Inside Rockefeller Center:

- The **ice-skating rink** is open October through March. Call 212-332-7654 for details.

- The focal point of the complex is the seventy-story **General Electric Building,** at 30 Rockefeller Plaza, where you can grab a walking-tour brochure at the main information desk.

- **Radio City Music Hall,** at 1260 Sixth Avenue (at 50th St.), www.radiocity.com, is the crown jewel of Rockefeller Center. See Arts for details.

- Many NBC television shows are broadcast from the network's Rockefeller Center studios: *Saturday Night Live, The Caroline Rhea Show,* and *Late Night with Conan O'Brien.* **NBC Studio Tours** run every 15 minutes daily from 8:30 A.M. to 5:30 P.M. (except 9:30 A.M. to 4:30 P.M. Sundays), Easter through Labor Day and Thanksgiving through New Year's, and every thirty minutes Monday through Saturday during the rest of the year. Tickets: $17.50 adults, $15.00

children and seniors (no children under 6 admitted). Reservations recommended. Call 212-664-7174 for details.

@ *The Today Show* broadcasts live from a glassed-in studio on the southwest corner of 49th Street and Rockefeller Plaza on weekdays from 7 A.M. to 9 A.M.

@ And don't miss the **International Building,** on Fifth Avenue between 50th and 51st Streets, with its world-famous statue of Atlas holding up the globe.

Saint Patrick's Cathedral   212-753-2261
Fifth Avenue (at 50th St.), MTE

Saint Patrick's is the largest Catholic cathedral in the United States and the headquarters of the Archdiocese of New York. Designed by James Renwick, it took from 1858 until 1906 to complete. It's named for the patron saint of the Irish, one of New York's principal ethnic groups. A major landmark, its front steps are a great place to meet and people-watch in Midtown. There is, incidentally, a wonderful view of Saint Patrick's from the SFA Café on the top floor of the Saks Fifth Avenue department store across the street.

Hours: Open daily 8:00 A.M.–8:45 P.M.

Shearith Israel Spanish and   212-873-0300
Portuguese Synagogue
8 West 70th Street (at Columbus Ave.
and Central Park West), UWS   www.shearith-israel.org

The oldest Jewish congregation in the United States, Shearith Israel was founded in 1654 by refugees from the Spanish Inquisition. The current building dates back to 1897 and is noteworthy for, among other things, its Tiffany windows.

South Street Seaport   **212-SEAPORT**
At Water and South Streets, FD   **www.southstseaport.org**

The South Street Seaport overlooks the East River and the Brooklyn Bridge and consists of eleven square blocks of historic buildings and piers, plus shops, restaurants, and a museum. It's a great refuge for families because unlike most of Manhattan, the Seaport is relatively manageable.

Within the Seaport:

@ The Seaport hosts **free events** all summer, including concerts, fireworks, and dancing. Call 212-SEAPORT for schedules.

@ The **Pier 17 shopping complex** contains numerous shops and a food court, with a panoramic view that includes the Statue of Liberty and Brooklyn Bridge.

@ The **Fulton Fish Market,** on Fulton Street at the East River, is the nation's largest wholesale fish market. It operates only in the middle of the night, roughly from 12 A.M. to 6 A.M. You can barely tell it's there during the day (except for the smell)!

@ The *Titanic* **Memorial Lighthouse,** at Fulton and Water Streets, commemorates the passengers who lost their lives on April 15, 1912. The *Titanic* was bound for New York on that fateful voyage.

@ The circa-1885 cargo schooner *Pioneer* offers two-hour cruises daily from May through September. Tickets: $20 for adults, $15 seniors, $12 for children. Call 212-748-8786 to confirm times and make reservations.

@ The Seaport is also home to a small but interesting museum, which focuses on maritime history. Museum hours: April to September, Friday through Wednesday 10 A.M.–6 P.M.,

Thursday 10 A.M.–8 P.M.; October to March, Wednesday through Monday 10 A.M.–5 P.M. Tickets: $6 adults, $5 seniors, $4 students, $3 children. Call 212-748-8600.

★ *Statue of Liberty* **On Liberty Island in** **New York Harbor**	**212-363-3200 general info** **212-269-5755 ticket/ferry info** **www.nps.gov/stli**

A gift from France to the United States, the Statue of Liberty was designed by sculptor Frédéric-Auguste Bartholdi, and the engineering was the brainchild of Alexandre-Gustave Eiffel (of Eiffel Tower fame). It is the definitive icon of New York and America. The statue weighs 225 tons and is 152 feet from foot to torch. The nose is 4½ feet long; the index finger, 8 feet.

Ranger guided tours: Thirty to forty-five minute tours explaining the conception, construction, and restoration of one of the world's greatest monuments. Island history and harbor environs and answers to any question you may have are covered by the Stetson-wearing staff. Schedule of offerings posted at Information Center. (Free; available first-come, first-served.)

Note: At the time of publication, only the grounds on Liberty Island are open to the public. The statue, museum exhibit, pedestal, and crown remain closed indefinitely. Check the fol-

Helpful Hint

The Statue of Liberty is one of New York's most popular attractions, so you need to be clever to beat the crowds. Go first thing in the morning. There is a ferry to the Statue of Liberty from New Jersey, which leaves from the front of the Liberty Science Center (see Museums). This ferry is much less crowded than the Manhattan one. Combine your Statue of Liberty visit with a Liberty Science Center expedition for a great day—and save a lot of time. The least busy time of year to visit the statue is in January and February.

lowing Web site for updated visitor and security guidelines for the Statue of Liberty and Ellis Island: www.nips.gov/stli/reopening/index.html.

Allow extra time for security screening—especially if you're carrying bags and backpacks (which are discouraged).

Hours: Ferries run seven days a week year-round (except for Christmas) on a regular schedule, generally between 9:30 A.M.–5:00 P.M., with extended summertime hours. Call 212-269-5755 or go to www.circlelineferry.com for a current ferry schedule.

Admission: The ferry ticket plus admission to the Statue of Liberty and Ellis Island is $10 adults, $8 seniors, $4 children under 17.

Transportation: *Subway:* 4, 5 subway to Bowling Green, or the 1, 9 to South Ferry. Walk downtown (south) through Battery Park to Castle Clinton, where you line up for ferry tickets; you'll then have to wait on a separate line for the ferry (there is a nearby playground where kids can kill some of the time).

Temple Emanu-El	**212-744-1400**
1 East 65th Street (at Fifth Ave.), UES	
www.emanuelnyc.org	

This is the largest Reform synagogue in the world, and the most important. The architecture is a mix of Moorish and Romanesque, which is meant to evoke the commingling of Eastern and Western cultures. Within is a small museum, the Bernard Museum, which has a world-class Judaica collection, including Hanukkah lamps from the fourteenth to twentieth centuries.

Hours: Open daily 10 A.M.–5 P.M.

★ *Theodore Roosevelt Birthplace*	**212-260-1616**
28 East 20th Street (between	
Broadway and Park Ave.), GP	**www.nps.gov/thrb**

I consider this to be one of New York's most delightful attractions. It's small, intimate, and manageable, and the kids can

really learn something without feeling oppressed or overwhelmed. President Theodore Roosevelt was born on this site in
1858. The house contains period furniture, beautiful rooms, and
a collection of Roosevelt memorabilia.

Hours: Monday through Friday 9 A.M.–5 P.M.; closed national holidays. Tours on the hour, beginning at 10 A.M.; last
tour at 4 P.M.

Admission: $3 adults, kids under 18 free

Transportation: *Subway:* Lexington Avenue 6 train to 23rd
Street (which, here, stops on Park Avenue)

Times Square
42nd Street (at Broadway)

It's actually a triangle formed by 42nd Street, Seventh Avenue,
and Broadway (which runs at a diagonal), but it's nonetheless
one of New York's central landmarks. There isn't exactly anything
to do here, but you have to see it—preferably at night.

United Nations   212-963-8687
First Avenue (at 46th St.), MTE
www.un.org

When you're in the United Nations, you're not technically in the
United States. You're in an international zone over which only
the United Nations is sovereign. The complex covers eighteen
acres along the East River. John D. Rockefeller Jr. donated the
land in 1946. There is a beautiful riverside promenade, a rose
garden with 1,400 rosebushes, and sculptures donated by member nations (whose 180 flags fly in alphabetical order in the
plaza). You can have lunch weekdays at the Delegates' Dining
Room, where you'll have a beautiful view of the river, though
you may or may not see actual delegates. Call 212-963-7625 for
reservations. The gift shop sells flags and other international

memorabilia. The UN post office is a must-visit for budding numismatists.

Hours: Guided tours (one-hour long) cover the General Assembly Hall, the Security Council Chamber, the Chagall stained-glass windows, and more. Daily tours every thirty minutes, 9:30 A.M.–4:30 P.M. (closed weekends in January and February).

Admission: $8.50 adults, $7.50 seniors, $6.00 students, $5.00 children (children under 5 not permitted)

Museums

Many people come from around the world for the sole purpose of visiting New York's museums. And, whether you're visiting with toddlers or teens, there's something for everyone. Because you're confronted with a dizzying number of museums, I've tried to help by narrowing down the selection and indicating my top picks by arranging the museums into three categories of appropriateness:

- The two must-visit museums, Best for Children and Families, are my top picks and are listed first. These are the Metropolitan Museum of Art and the American Museum of Natural History (which contains the Rose Center for Earth and Space). I have found that these museums are the odds-on favorites of the greatest number of children and families. I've devoted the longest and most detailed descriptions to these museums, because I want you to be able to use this book as a mini-guide and educational tool. Unless you have a very specific agenda, the truth is that—on a typical New York City vacation—it's possible you won't have the time or inclination to visit any museums other than these.

- The Best of the Rest includes museums that are excellent and highly worthwhile, but, as much as I love every one of these museums, I can't honestly tell you to drag the kids to all of them. You'll have to make choices based on interest, attention span, and availability of time. I provide the highlights of each museum, but the descriptions aren't as in-depth as for my top picks.

@ Specialty Museums are also extremely worthy attractions. I don't mean to judge the value of these museums by placing them in this category, and were I writing a guide for adults, my choices might be different. But I wouldn't necessarily recommend these places for a first-time visitor on a short vacation unless you or your child has a special interest in the particular subject area. These museums tend to be very specialized, off the beaten path, or grownup-oriented. Therefore, these listings are shortest.

Of course, if you're looking for information about a specific museum, you needn't hunt through the categories—all listings are cross-referenced and indexed as well.

Best for Children and Families

★ *American Museum of Natural History*   212-769-5100
and Rose Center for Earth and Space
Central Park West (between 77th and 81st Sts.), UWS
www.amnh.org

Any way you slice it, this museum is a winner for everyone. My favorite museum since I was a young child, the American Museum of Natural History (AMNH) offers something for children of all ages and all interests. With forty-two exhibition halls, the world's largest dinosaur collection, the 563-carat Star of India sapphire, the Hall of Biodiversity, and the replica of the 94-foot blue whale (everyone's favorite), whether you spend thirty minutes or all day there, this museum is a must. Still, although you could easily spend a couple of years exploring this museum, if you have young children, plan to spend, at most, one hour. No matter how enticing the dioramas and the giant elephants are, small legs (the museum is gigantic) get tired, and attention spans wane (you'll be exhausted just reading about everything that's in this place!). If it's a real hit, you can always return later.

For children under 10, the favorites are the whale in the Ocean Life room (first floor), the dioramas (everywhere), the dinosaurs (fourth floor), the African Mammals (third and fourth floors), and the Asian Mammals (second floor). Even toddlers can appreciate the dioramas and will get a kick out of the animals in their "natural" environments.

Here's a quick look at what AMNH has to offer:

- Starting with the first floor main entrance, you'll see the ancient dioramas of the **Pilgrims and Native Americans** in old New York.

- Next, the **Hall of Biodiversity** is dark and soothing. On the right is a giant clamshell. The giant squid and octopus have been the sources of many great novels and bad movies. Children who are in school, and especially those learning about biology, will get a kick (and good grasp) from the classification system on the wall. Younger children will enjoy the specimens (turtles, mammals, birds) that are mounted on the wall. *Note the sea creatures hanging from the ceiling.*

- The **Dzanga-Sangha African Rainfores**t project is an example of what is being done to help preserve the vanishing rainforest. Walk through and even sit down in the rainforest. Even the very young can appreciate the foliage and dim lighting—it simply feels different. Older children can read about and look at pictures of grasslands and savannas and islands. High school students can ponder questions like, *What is an integrated conservation development project?*

- Move along into the **Hall of North American Forests.** This is primarily a pass-through, except for the diorama with the giant earthworm and millipede and the incredible cross-section of the sequoia. This tree, which was cut in 1891, has 1,342 annual rings. It is enormous. After digesting the size and age of the specimen, look at the pointers. Each of those pointers specifies what was happening in history at the time that the tree was that many years old. When put in that perspective, it is mind-boggling.

@ Refuel at **Café 77** if you need a break, drinks, or light fare.

@ By the entrance to the Northwest Coast Indians is the **Haida Indian Canoe.** It was made from a single red cedar log. It is 63 feet long and just over 8 feet wide at its widest point. In the canoe are models of Haida Indians, active in their frozen state, paddling the canoe. Young children will delight in this specimen.

@ Also good for a walk-through (and more if your child has special interests in this area) is the dark, cool **Northwest Coast Indian Hall.** Huge totems line the galleries, each of which has been set up in a separate alcove differentiating specimens and tribes. The collection is vast and varied.

@ The **Hall of Human Biology and Evolution** starts with simple dioramas of prehistoric people and goes on to the more advanced model of the double helix and 3-D holograms of the human body. This hall can be a great area for learning. If attention spans are waning, it's still worth a walk-through, if only for the dioramas and holograms and what it leads you to . . .

@ The **Halls of Meteorites, Minerals, and Gems** are fascinating to children of all ages. The specimens are shiny, and you can touch some of them. Kids in grade school through high school who have spent any time at all studying rocks and minerals will be amazed by the vast collection. The hundreds of labeled specimens are astonishing even to the most avid collector. In this section, my favorite specimens are the petrified trees. Laid out on the floor, without protective glass, are what used to be tree trunks and are now ostensibly rocks.

☙ On the fourth floor, the first stop should be the **Saurischian Dinosaurs,** but en route, walk through the **Vertebrate Origins Hall.** You don't even have to stop, but kids might want to check out the skeletons and shells of the giant sea turtles and crocodiles. As you walk from one hall to the next, and as your children likely race ahead, the walls of the passageway are lined with black-and-white photographs of various dinosaur excavations. Projects all over the world are featured, including some in Mongolia, Wyoming, and Egypt.

☙ As you walk into the dinosaur hall (the room gets lots of natural light, so it's an extremely pleasant place to spend some time), you'll likely hear exclamations of "cool!" or "excellent!" As well as squeals of delight. These guys are gigantic. To put things in perspective a little, take a few moments to have a discussion. Ask younger kids: *If you stood next to the Apatosaurus skeleton, how high could you reach? Compare your leg with his. How many times bigger are his bones than yours? Who do you think is smarter, you or the dinosaur?*

☙ Around the corner is the **Dinostore,** which seems as good a place as any to buy a museum souvenir if you're planning to do so. The selection includes books, T-shirts, stuffed animals, jewelry, mugs, postcards, pens, and so forth.

☙ The third floor has two highlights: The first is the **Reptiles and Amphibians exhibit.** You can view this room in five minutes. The big attractions are the 23-foot skeleton of the reticulated python; the Komodo dragon; the 14-foot, 7-inch American crocodile; the Galapagos tortoise; and the 12-inch American alligator. Ask your children: *How many* *vertebrae do you think this python has? How about in its tail? How many does a human have?* (The python has 321 vertebrae in the body and ninety-one in the tail; humans have twenty-four total.)

@ Second, and perhaps most beloved in the museum by the young, is the **Hall of African Mammals.** From the third floor you get a good view of the eight East African elephants standing in the middle of the enormous room, a hint of what's coming downstairs. Take a quick spin around to view the dioramas upstairs—warthogs, ostriches, and cheetahs—but spend most of your time below on the second floor with the close-up view of the elephants and the other animals. At the far end of the room is a pair of tusks, found in Kenya in 1939 and weighing in at 169 pounds. *For younger children, an excellent school report or presentation topic is the difference between African and Asian elephants.*

If you're overwhelmed or don't have a lot of time, you can take one of the museum's free highlights tours. They're offered daily at quarter after the hour from 10:15 A.M. to 3:15 P.M. Of the host of other tours and programs, many are free, so be sure to stop by an information desk when you arrive at the museum. Even if you aren't interested in a tour (and with toddlers and younger children, I'd advise that you're best off on your own), at least you'll know in case you want to join one. For those interested in a self-guided highlights tour, pick up a copy of the World Culture Hour Tour. You can always skip ahead or skip some exhibits altogether if the troops are getting restless.

At all times the museum has special exhibits, such as the recent fighting dinosaurs and the comeback of the Butterfly Conservatory: Tropical Butterflies Alive in Winter (tropical butterflies free-flying in a walk-in vivarium), as well as two feature IMAX films. There is an additional charge for special exhibits and IMAX films.

If that isn't enough, the AMNH also offers educational programs, workshops, and field trips on such topics as bird watching, wildlife in art, and dinosaur shadow theater. These programs are usually on weekends and have fees starting at $15 for one adult with one child. Check the Web site or call ahead to have a schedule mailed.

The Rose Center for Earth and Space has received a tremendous amount of attention since the opening of its new multimillion-dollar facility. Truly a sight to behold at any hour, it is especially striking when illuminated at night. Entry into the Rose Center is included with admission to the AMNH. But the biggest attraction—the Space Show in the Space Theater—costs extra. Narrated by Tom Hanks, this twenty-minute show brings audiences "the clearest possible images of the night sky, along with a three-dimensional visual exploration." But be warned: This show is very advanced—most kids won't be able to keep up, no matter how soothing Tom Hanks' voice is—and it's very expensive ($19.00 for adults, $14.00 for seniors and students, and $11.50 for children, including admission to the museum). So, unless your children are extremely interested in astronomy or are at least 10 years old, I'd say save it for the next trip, when they can appreciate it more. Better just to have a walk around the Rose Center (which offers many free exhibits) and see the Big Bang show (which is also free) and pick up a copy of *Our Place in Space, A Kid's Guide to the Universe*. But there's already so much to see and do in the AMNH that unless your kids are in the double digits agewise, I'd be inclined to spend most of my time elsewhere.

Hours: Daily 10:00 A.M.–5:45 P.M., On Fridays, the Rose Center is open until 8:45 P.M.

Suggested admission: $10.00 adults, $7.50 seniors/students, $6.00 children 2–12

Transportation: *Subway:* B, C to 81st Street; 1, 9 to 79th Street. *Bus:* M79 to CPW

★ *Metropolitan Museum of Art*   **212-535-7710**
Fifth Avenue (at 82nd St.), UES   www.metmuseum.org

Some would argue that the Met, with three million works of art, is the most magnificent art museum in the world. Though it is not quite as large as the Louvre or the British Art Museum, certainly it has the most encyclopedic collection on the planet. So, what do you do? How do you tackle this monster? How do you get the most out of your visit to the Met with your children?

The best strategy is to select a couple of galleries or a handful of works on which you'd like to concentrate, view those, and call it a day. The thing about the Met is that you can't see the whole thing—not in a day, a week, or a month. It's just that big, which is why children and adults alike should relax and concentrate on what they enjoy most or what they'd like to learn about. Once you've figured out what interests you most, you can set about focusing on those few things.

Still, with *three million* works of art (and rotating special exhibits), how do you narrow down the selection? It's actually not as difficult as you might think. There are four ways to handle it:

1. If you don't want to do any advanced planning (though to get the most out of your visit, you might want to reconsider), pick up a floor plan and select one of the tried-and-true exhibits, like the Arms and Armor gallery on the first floor. This will be a guaranteed hit with most children ages 4 and up. Other favorites include the Temple of Dendur and the costume collection.

2. Go to the Met's Web site (www.metmuseum.org), select a few pieces of art, and learn about them. You don't need to learn enough to write a dissertation, just enough to help your children appreciate and enjoy the art and encourage them to think about the pieces they're seeing. Ask them some questions: *How does this piece make you feel? What do*

you think it's made of? How old do you think this work of art is? Have you seen anything else that reminds you of this mask/ costume/painting? Beyond toddlers, children of any age can answer most of these questions, and, as they do, they'll be thinking about the art and looking at it more carefully than if they just stood before it with no guidance at all. This way, you are helping your child absorb and enjoy the art, not just dragging him or her around the museum by the hand.

3. Join one of the programs for kids. These programs, usually run on weekends, are free with admission to the museum. "Look Again!" is a family program that takes place on Saturday and Sunday. There is usually a tour and discussion of three or four works of art (while standing or sitting in front of each piece), followed by a storyteller or a drawing project, followed by a related movie for those who are still interested. Children are first engaged by the two team leaders with a description on the piece, then further lured in with pointed questions to get them involved, thinking, and interested. The program is for children ages 5 through 12, though a few younger ones sometimes participate, as well as older siblings (it was plenty interesting for the adults who were in tow, too). Weekend family films are thirty minutes, and special events include multihour celebrations and festivals ("Greek Family Festival" and "Mexico: A Spanish Family Program" are two of many examples) where your children can stay for as long as they're interested. Other programs include "Hello, Met!" "Discoveries," and *"Programas en Español para las Familias"* (programs in Spanish for families). And new programs are being added all the time. Call in advance (212-570-3932) for a listing of family programs, check the Web site, or ask to be added to the mailing list. The programs are real winners for children, and adults will find that they learn plenty, too.

4. Enter the museum at the Uris Center for Education (at 80th Street—this is also where all of the children's and family programs begin) and read through or pick up some of the special educational guides. There's *Kids Pick, 10 Works of Art,* a particularly useful brochure that highlights children's top ten picks in the museum, including a photo and description of each piece. *Museum Kids* is available, as is *Rooms with a View, A Museum Search* (in both English and Spanish), which is sort of like a treasure hunt through the museum (without the running, touching, and racing). *Family Guides* are also extremely worthwhile. One recent family guide, set up in the form of a hunt, focused on tea sets. There are four objects. The "clue" for the fourth says: "Walk down the corridor, past the canopied bed, until you are in a gallery with two lion sculptures. In the corner just at your right, look for a teapot with a dragon spout. This one is made of real gold and a sparkling material called rock crystal." The guide also specifies all the pertinent details, such as where the pot originated, when it was made, and how the museum acquired it. Also near the Uris Center entrance is a library with plenty of resources and a good collection of children's books, perfect for a break after the museum or before. Another great trick about entering through the Uris Center is that it's far less crowded; there is a coat and stroller check (again, fewer people); bathrooms right by the entrance (not so by the main door); and the library, ideal for a story or a break. This alone is worth the slight detour.

I've found that younger kids respond better to three-dimensional objects than they do to paintings. Thus, with small children, it may make sense to focus your visit on sculptures and artifacts, rather than on paintings, drawings, and other two-dimensional renditions.

The museum is enormous, and it's easy to get lost, so don't be afraid to ask for directions before your kids start to lose it. Don't push the envelope. Budget a realistic amount of time to spend in the museum (about an hour is reasonable) and stick to it—if you have to leave early, do it. If you've got young kids in tow (even teens), and you've been in the museum for an hour and they're still doing well, it's still time to get out and onto the next thing. It's difficult for children (and adults) to spend much more than an hour looking at works of art, and better they should leave wanting more than leave never wanting to return.

Remind children that:

ℯ The museum and the art are there for them to enjoy, but a museum is a *quiet place,* like a library. Other people, many of whom are serious students and lovers of art, don't appreciate loud, shrieking children running around the galleries.

ℯ The art, no matter how big, small, or nice it is, is for viewing with the eyes and is not to be touched. There are alarms on many pieces, not for theft, but as warning to guards and viewers that they've had "a touch." Explain that the reason is not for the guards at the museum to be mean, but rather because the oils from our hands, no matter how clean we are and how much we wash, damage art. Over time, the more people touch the art, the more damage is done, and the art deteriorates and disintegrates. Obviously, we don't want that to happen, so please: no touching.

ℯ Running in the museum is not appropriate behavior. If your children are too young to understand this, you might want to let them enjoy the comforts of their strollers (which are allowed every day except for Sunday) for the hour while you enjoy the art. If they are in the running phase, you may want to skip the visit altogether because obviously, if they can't stand still, they can't focus on the art. Don't forget, a museum can be a difficult place for a young child, and only you know whether it's appropriate for yours.

I encourage your children to read *From the Mixed-Up Files of Mrs. Basil E. Franweiler*, by E. L. Konigsburg, if they haven't already (or they can watch the film version, *The Hideaways*). It's perfect for children ages 9 to 12, but younger readers will get it too, and older children will read it in a breeze. I guarantee they'll all appreciate the museum more after reading the book. And, for those who are too young to read, or aren't motivated to do so, start the book a few weeks before departure and read a chapter to the kids each night. It's well worth the effort, and you'll enjoy the exercise (and the story), too.

Hours: Tuesday through Thursday and Sunday 9:30 A.M.–5:30 P.M., Friday and Saturday 9:30 A.M.–9:00 P.M. No strollers allowed Sunday (back carriers available at 81st St. entrance coat-check area)

Admission (includes same-day entrance to The Cloisters): $10 adults, $5 seniors and students, free for children under 12 when accompanied by an adult

Transportation: *Subway:* 4, 5, 6 to 86th Street.

The Best of the Rest

American Museum of the Moving Image	718-784-0077
35 Avenue (at 36th St.)	718-784-4777
Astoria, Q	www.ammi.org

Recently home to *Sesame Street, The Cosby Show,* and earlier to the Marx Brothers, the Museum of the Moving Image makes its home in what is part of the Kaufman Astoria Studios. "Behind the Screen" is the central exhibit in the museum, which details, from start to finish, how a movie is made, marketed, and showcased. For those who are more inclined to *do* rather than to *look,* there are interactive elements. Learning about and trying out sound-effects editing is always a hit with older kids—especially when put in the context of film production. The collection has more than 1,000 items on display, from costumes to high-tech gadgets and nostalgia kitsch. Screenings are free with the cost of admission. Free exhibition tours are offered Tuesday through Sunday at 2 P.M.

Hours: Tuesday through Friday 12 P.M.–5 P.M., Saturday and Sunday 11 A.M.–6 P.M.

Admission: $8.50 adults, $5.50 seniors and college students, $4.50 children 5–18

Transportation: *Subway:* R to Steinway Street

Brooklyn Children's Museum (BCM)   **718-735-4400**
145 Brooklyn Avenue   **(museum hotline)**
(between Saint Marks and Prospect Pl.), BR
www.bchildmus.org

The first children's museum in the world, the Brooklyn Children's Museum has been the benchmark of children's interactive and innovative exhibits for more than one hundred years. If you can get beyond the one major drawback—it's between two subway lines (and close to neither) and difficult to get to without a car—it's a great destination for kids.

From the moment your children climb the steps, they'll be drawn to the museum like bees to honey. The entrance is a nineteenth century subway kiosk, and directly inside the door kids are enticed into the heart of the museum by the "people tube," a huge drainage pipe, that runs to the depths of the 35,000 square foot, four-floor underground facility, complete with neon accents and a stream.

The wonderful thing about the BCM (and the now-more-than 200 others around the country and the world that have used the BCM as a model for their own children's museums) is that it's about hands-on, interactive exploration and learning. This is not the "hush, don't talk, don't touch, don't run" kind of a place, nor is it the "clobber your kid over the head with educational programming" kind of a place. What the BCM is, is a place where children, from toddlers to teens, can learn about life and the world around them, their neighbors, the environment, culture, arts, and science through exhibits, touching, special educational and/or family programs, and exploration.

Though a best-kept secret (perhaps because of its less-than-ideal location), BCM continues to strive to keep pace—changing and evolving with the world and the needs of children as we embark upon the twenty-first century. Some favorite activities and exhibits include Can You Tell Me How to Get to Sesame Street?, Make a Pizza, Sing a Rap Song, Around the Block, Jump Rope, All Bark, MusicMix, Plants and People, the Mystery of Things, Produce a Movie, and Together in the City.

During the summer, the museum holds many special events. The Early Learner Performance Series with Puppet Theatre Inside Out and Fun on *Sesame Street* are big hits. But these exhibits and programs change, so if one of the above programs is gone by the time you arrive, don't despair; something equally exciting and entertaining will have replaced it.

Hours: BCM is always closed on Monday and Tuesday. Summer hours: Saturday and Sunday 10:00 A.M.–5:00 P.M., Wednesday and Thursday 12:00 P.M.–5:00 P.M., Friday 12:00 P.M.–7:30

Brooklyn Children's Museum

P.M.; September to June, Wednesday through Friday 2:00 P.M.–5:00 P.M., Saturday through Sunday 10:00 A.M.–5:00 P.M.

Admission: $4

Transportation: *Trolley:* Free shuttle service from Grand Army Plaza to BCM at fifteen minutes past the hour from 10:15 A.M. to 4:15 P.M., Saturday and Sunday. *Subway:* Take the 1, C, or A train. *Bus:* Take the B43 or B44 to Saint Mark's Avenue, or take the B45, or B65to Brooklyn Avenue.

Brooklyn Museum of Art　　　　　　718-638-5000
200 Eastern Parkway (at Washington Ave.), BR
www.brooklynart.org

If you're only going to visit one art museum on your visit to New York City (and you're staying in Manhattan), I'd have to suggest the Met because, well, it's the Met. The Brooklyn Museum of Art (BMoA), however, is a tremendous museum in its own right, with a magnificent edifice housing its equally grand art collection. What you'll find in the collection is far more extensive than what you'd see in most other cities in the country. It's only because it sits in the shadow of the Met that the Brooklyn Museum of Art does not get the recognition that it deserves (of course, on the plus side, that makes for smaller crowds, too).

The permanent collection includes about two dozen American period rooms (1675–1928), which is still popular with kids, although always frustrating because you can't actually go in, walk around, touch, and sit on the pieces. It helps to put history and time in perspective. The Egyptian collection, especially the mummies, is always a big hit, and the Impressionists—Monet, Degas, Cézanne—are not to be overlooked.

Most recently, the BMoA received a tremendous splash of attention for a controversial exhibit involving dung and images of religious figures. For less controversial exhibits, the BMoA has also received a great deal of press and recognition for its temporary exhibits: Monet and the Mediterranean, Maxfield Parrish 1870–1966, Impressionists in Winter, Masterpieces of Fashion (a great costume exhibit), The Jewels of the Romanovs, and modern works like From Hip to Hip Hop: Black Fashion and the Culture of Influence.

"First Saturday," a program that runs (you guessed it) on the first Saturday of each month, is something your older teens might get a kick out of. It's from 5 P.M. to 11 P.M. Admission is free, and the program includes some form of entertainment. It could be film, poetry, jazz, dance, and so forth. I'd certainly call first to see what's on the calendar because it can be pretty weird stuff—experimental, sort of out there, you know, the stuff that New York City is known for. There are also special programs for kids, so call ahead or check the Web site for information.

Hours: Wednesday through Friday 10 A.M.–5 P.M., first Saturday of the month 11 A.M.–11 P.M., each Saturday thereafter 11 A.M.–6 P.M., Sunday 11 A.M.–6 P.M.

Suggested admission: $6 adults, $3 seniors and students, children under 12 free

Transportation: *Subway:* 1, 2 to Eastern Pkwy/Brooklyn Museum

★ *Children's Museum of Manhattan*	212-721-1234
212 West 83rd Street (between	www.cmom.org
Broadway and Amsterdam Ave.), UWS	

The Children's Museum of Manhattan is a great destination for kids to touch, learn, and play. Designed specifically *for* kids (they say ages 2 to 12, but it's more like 2 to 8 or 10), this museum encourages hands-on participation. Exhibits like Body Odyssey are presented in language and formats that kids can understand—it's scientific discovery rather than textbook discourse. There's plenty of stuff for toddlers (and even babies) in the 4-and-under play area, and the carpeted reading room is a nice place for a break if

Intrepid Sea-Air-Space Museum

energy levels are getting too high, or too low. The Early Childhood Center has a range of activities, too. Time Warner Media Center is a hit with older kids—especially when they get to produce their own television show or videos. The animation program is also popular. Every day there is a calendar of events with special programs: Storytellers, face painting, and holiday projects entertain and delight just as much as the regular collection. Here, as at all museums, exhibits change: Dr. Seuss, John Lennon's Real Love: Drawings for Sean, Maira Kalman's Max (A Dog), and WordPlay are a few of the recent winners. If they're gone when you arrive, something equally wonderful will be in their place. *Note:* The museum is very popular with locals, so to avoid the crowds, don't visit it on weekends and holidays if at all possible.

Hours: Wednesday through Sunday 10 A.M.–5 P.M. (Summer hours, Tuesday through Sunday 10 A.M.–5 P.M.)

Admission: $6 children and adults, $3 seniors

Transportation: *Subway:* 1, 9 to West 86th Street or B, C to West 81st Street

---

★ *Intrepid Sea-Air-Space Museum*   212-245-0072
West 46th Street (at Twelfth Ave.), Pier 86, MTW
www.intrepidmuseum.org

It takes a while for the facts to sink in: This, the USS *Intrepid*, what is now a museum (and National Historic Landmark) sitting in the Hudson River, was once an active aircraft carrier from which fighter planes actually took off and—harder still—upon which they landed. It's not until you go up on the flight deck that the vastness of the vessel begins to register (especially when the kids have to walk from one end to the other—or run, as the case may be) and yet ironically, at the same time, it seems oddly small: How exactly is it that pilots landed fighter jets on this so-called runway? (Very carefully!)

I had never visited the *Intrepid* before I started working on this book. It didn't strike me as interesting. But having been there I can't believe it took me so long—this is simply an amazing spot for kids.

There's plenty of great stuff to see before you venture up to the flight deck, and a lot of it is participatory. This museum, in particular, is a good one at which to arrive early, otherwise your kids will either have to wait in long lines (to do things like sit in the cockpit of the A-6) or worse, skip some of the attractions altogether.

@ After you pay admission and climb the stairs to the **Hangar Deck,** directly inside is the **A-6 cockpit challenge.** It's a simulated flight program used to train A-6 pilots to land planes on aircraft carriers. Anyone can sit in the cockpit, and adults and children alike are eager to give it a go.

@ Nearby are mannequins adorned in uniforms; there's the landing signal officer, marine detachment, steward's mate, and hell-diver pilot. You'll see more uniforms throughout the exhibit, and they're worth a quick look in passing (and longer with kids who are really into this sort of thing).

@ The **cockpit orientation trainer** allows you to climb into a 4D-2N and check out the cockpit. It's amazing how small the space is considering how tall our pilots are. Then there's the Sparrow, which you can also climb into (which is billed as the "free world's most versatile medium range radar guided missile").

@ Take time to pause at the **Iwo Jima Monument,** which was sculpted after the famous photo (Raising the flag atop Mount Suribachi, 23 February 1945). *If your child is old enough to understand the implications of bombs and war, this might be a good time to have a short discussion.*

@ The **Famous Flying Machines** exhibit is pure fun. The basket for the hot air balloon (climb on in) and the Human Powered Flight Challenge encourage you to pedal your way to flight. Read the panel about Bryan Allen, who pedaled the Gossamer Albatross (similar to what your child has or is about to climb into) 22.5 miles across the English Channel. It makes the experience that much more interesting and educational.

@ For older children, there are computer information stations where with the press of a button (entertaining for youngsters too, just for the button pushing), you can access files of photographs, videos, and print information on all of the armed services. For military junkies, there is also a station with narrated videos on aircraft carriers, tanks, helicopters, fighter planes (Blue Angels and Joint Strike fighters are but a few), and attack submarines.

@ The two things that are available at an extra charge are the **dog tags** from $0.95 to $4.95 (for military stainless steel and upward) and the ***Intrepid* flight simulator.** The flight simulator gets the longest lines by far, so if the museum is crowded and your kids are determined to get on board, go there first. The cost of the ride is $5.00, and as much as some kids love it, others (and parents) don't. A sign explains: "The simulator is used to test and train commercial airline pilots. Simulator training helps produce more skilled up-to-date pilots, which result in safer operations." There is also a telling notice posted out front: "Dynamic, high speed motion simulation. You must be able-bodied to ride this simulator. You must hold tightly to the rails and do not stand or smoke during the flight. You should not enter the simulator if any of the following apply: (1) Prone to motion sickness; (2) neck, back, or heart problems; (3) you're pregnant; (4) claustrophobia; (5) under 3 years old. Simulates acceleration, deceleration, slow and sharp turns, and dives. Motion is synchronized to a computer-generated film. It runs five minutes and holds fifteen people." Sounds horrible, but many kids love it.

℮ Before you go upstairs to the flight deck, walk straight back to the outside deck. If it's a nice day, you'll get a great view of the river and downtown to the Statue of Liberty. If you're having lunch, you can grab something from the **Stars & Stripes Café** or eat what you've packed along and have a seat. There are tables and soda machines for a nice outside lunch.

℮ Upstairs are the main attractions, especially for the little ones. Outside voices are acceptable here, and there's plenty of room for burning off some extra energy. Look for the **A-12 Blackbird,** "the world's fastest airplane." If everyone isn't completely exhausted, there's also the submarine USS *Growler* and the destroyer USS *Edson*.

Hours: April to September, Monday through Friday 10 A.M.–5 P.M., Saturday and Sunday 10 A.M.–7 P.M.; October to March, Tuesday through Sunday 10 A.M.–5 P.M.

Admission: $13 adults; $9 veterans, seniors, and students; $6 children 6–11; $2 children 2–5

Transportation: *Subway:* A, C, F to 42nd Street. *Bus:* M42 crosstown

> ★ *Liberty Science Center (LSC)*   201-200-1000
> 251 Phillip Street   www.lsc.org
> Liberty State Park, Jersey City, NJ

It's well worth the trip to the LSC (and it's a fun ride on the ferry, too), and it can easily be combined with a trip to the Statue of Liberty and Ellis Island to boot (see Statue of Liberty, in City Sights, for details). LSC is a great opportunity for hands-on learning and play, all within the framework of science and technology. The building itself looks really "cool" and futuristic, and your kids will get the futuristic feel simply by walking inside. IMAX films are a big draw, as are the exhibits, temporary and permanent. There's no shortage of things to see and do. Specials like Animal Eyes: What Do Animals Really See?, Scream Machines: The Science of Roller Coasters, and Electric Space really get kids (and parents) excited about learning (probably because they think they're just having fun). Call in advance for special programs and activities or check the Web site.

    Hours: Daily 9:30 A.M.–5:30 P.M.

    Admission: $10 adults, $8 seniors and children

    Transportation: *Ferry:* from World Financial Center to Colgate Center. Connect to Lafayette-Greenville bus to LSC.

> ★ *Lower East Side Tenement Museum*   212-431-0233
> 90 Orchard Street (at Broome St.), LES   www.tenement.org

This museum is an excellent depiction of what life was like for the multitudes of poor immigrants arriving in America, many of them not speaking as much as a word of English. They expected to find streets paved with gold, but instead encountered hard work and squalor. Here, in this five-story tenement house, there lived, from 1863 to 1935, 10,000 people from twenty-five countries. A visit here will help your children imagine the hardships of the immigrant's life and also illustrate the City's earlier history.

If you've had a visit to Ellis Island, don't forget to point out that this, the Lower East Side, is where many of the immigrants made their first homes before moving on to a better life.

You can see the museum only with a guided tour, and because group size and tours are limited, it helps to reserve ahead of time. Each of the tours (there are four) lasts an hour and highlights different aspects of life. The Visitors' Center also has a few small exhibits, including photos, videos, and a model tenement, so it's worthwhile to arrive a bit early and check those out.

Hours: Tenement tours depart Tuesday through Friday at 1 P.M. and approximately every forty minutes to 4 P.M., Thursday hourly 6 P.M.–9 P.M.; Saturday and Sunday approximately every half-hour 11:00 A.M.–4:30 P.M.

Admission for one tenement tour: $9 adults, $7 seniors and students

Transportation: *Subway:* F to Delancey Street; J, M, Z to Essex Street

Museum of the City of New York	212-534-1672
1220 Fifth Avenue (at 103rd St.), UES	**www.mcny.org**

This is the place to be if you're interested in exploring New York's long history, starting with its modest beginnings as a Dutch trading post in the seventeenth century to its current incarnation as the most visited city in the world. Through photographs, maps, costumes, memorabilia, toys, furniture, and other artifacts, the museum cleverly links the past to the present (and the future). Kids will be especially drawn to New York Toy Stories, a collection of toys and dolls that were owned (and well loved) by generations of New York children.

Hours: Wednesday through Saturday 10 A.M.–5 P.M., Sunday 12 P.M.–5 P.M.

Suggested admission: $7 adults, $4 seniors, students, and children, $12 families

Transportation: *Subway:* 6 to 103rd Street

Museum of Jewish Heritage 212-968-1800
A Living Memorial to the Holocaust
18 First Place, Battery Park City, FD www.mjhnyc.org

More than fifty years after the MoJH was proposed, it was finally born. Everything about it is striking: its location (on the water at the south end of Battery Park), its six-sided building, and its contents. Jewish Life a Century Ago, The War Against the Jews, and Jewish Renewal are all within the permanent exhibits. Moving in their simplicity, stories are told through life's simple objects, photographs, and documents. The videotaped testimonies of Holocaust victims, survivors, and their families (all of which were chronicled by Steven Spielberg's Survivors of the Shoah Visual History Foundation) are especially powerful. Special exhibits are also scheduled, recently including Roman Vishniac's gripping Children of a Vanished World.

Hours: Sunday through Wednesday 10:00 A.M.–5:45 P.M., Thursday 10:00 A.M.–8:00 P.M., Friday and evenings of Jewish holidays 10:00 A.M.–5:00 P.M.

Admission: $7 adults, $5 seniors and students, children under 5 free.

Transportation: *Subway:* 1, 2 to Wall Street; N, R to Whitehall Street, J, M, Z to Broad Street.

★ *The Museum of Modern Art* 212-708-9480
45-20 33rd Street (at Queens Blvd.) www.moma.org

An extensive expansion has temporarily closed MoMA. The expansion will provide the museum with 50 percent more gallery space, and construction is expected to be complete in 2005. On the bright side, however, MoMA has opened a branch of the museum, MoMA QNS in—you guessed it—Queens. A full exhibition schedule will continue in the Queens location and, lest you feel like you'll be settling, rest assured, there will still be a whopping 65,000 square feet of gallery space for you to peruse with your children. There is also a café.

Hours: Monday, Thursday, Saturday, Sunday 10:00 A.M.–5:00 P.M., Friday 10:00 A.M.–7:45 P.M.

Admission: $12.00 adults, $8.50 students (with current identification) and seniors (65 and over), under 16 free when accompanied by an adult. Pay what you wish Friday 4:00 P.M.–7:45 P.M.

Transportation: *Subway:* 7 local to 33rd Street, Queens (look for MoMA logo atop a low blue building; also don't hesitate to ask someone if you're confused). *Bus:* On weekends there is also a shuttle bus service called Artlink. This shuttle service operates Saturday and Sunday. Catch the bus on West 53 Street (between Fifth and Sixth Aves.) in Manhattan to MoMA QNS. Another bus travels from MoMA QNS to P.S.1 and other Queens destinations. For further information, call 212-708-9750 or visit www.queensartlink.org.

Museum of Television & Radio 25 West 52nd Street (between Fifth and Sixth Aves.), MTW www.mtr.org	212-621-6800 212-621-6600, operator assistance

Ideal for malcontent teens, kids who need a TV break (while satisfying parents who want culture), and those who especially enjoy television and radio as art, the Museum of Television & Radio will be a sure hit. Here there are no pictures on the walls, plaques to read, or people telling you not to touch and to hush. You can take one of the daily tours if you so desire or, better yet, pick up a copy of the day's schedule and either pop into one of the screening rooms or select programs (from among the more than 100,000) that you've always wanted to see again or wished you had seen in the first place. Those who are overwhelmed with the selection and unsure of what to choose can try the highlights option (only 500 selections of TV and radio programs), from which you can break your selection down further by category, title, search, and so forth. Ideal for children who can sit still quietly (you sit in a room with a bunch of TV monitors, each person or group of people watching their own programs with headsets), selections range from *Sesame Street* to *Star Trek* to *Gilligan's Island.* If all of this seems like a little too much fluff (it really is culture though, like it or not), during your two-hour time slot at the monitor, you can also select great moments in history. Search for the Beatles' first appearance on the *Ed Sullivan Show,* old television commercials like Dinah Shore singing about Chevrolet (a total hoot), Roosevelt's address to Congress in 1941 (after the bombing at Pearl Harbor) about entering WWII, footage of the first astronauts walking on the moon, and TV classics that capture an era: *MASH, Leave it to Beaver, I Love Lucy* (chocolate factory), and *Mr. Rogers.* Everyone except perhaps toddlers will find something that appeals, and it's a nice chance to bring the family together—or to allow children to sit at their own consoles with their own selections—doing something the kids most likely won't associate with museums and culture. But I warn you, when you return home and ask the kids to turn off the TV, be prepared to hear, "But television is culture; I'm educating myself here!"

Hours: Tuesday, Wednesday, and Friday through Sunday 12 P.M.–6 P.M., Thursday 12 P.M.–8 P.M. On Friday, theaters stay open until 9 P.M.

Admission: $6 adults, $4 seniors and students, $3 children under 13

Transportation: *Subway:* B, D, F 47th–50th Streets/Rockefeller Center; N, R to 49th Street

★ *New York City Fire Museum*   212-691-1303
278 Spring Street (between Varick and Hudson Sts.), SH
www.nycfiremuseum.org

Always a huge hit with the little kids (and the big ones too, when no one's looking), the Fire Museum features vintage trucks and equipment (fire houses, fire boats, fire gear), as well as fire-related folk art, paintings, photographs, and memorabilia. Poles and bells from firehouses—it's the stuff that children's fantasies are made of! Don't miss the fire-safety education tours (call ahead). Nothing makes quite the impact as a lesson on fire safety in this place.

Hours: Tuesday through Saturday 10 A.M.–5 P.M., Sunday 10 A.M.–4 P.M.

Suggested admission (donation): $4 adults, $2 seniors/ students, $1 children under 12

Transportation: *Subway:* C, E to Spring; 1, 9 to Houston Street

---

The New York City Police Museum   212-480-3100
100 Old Slip at South Street (between Water St. and South St.), FD   **www.nycpolicemuseum.org**

Opened in February 2002, the museum depicts the history of the NYPD and also presents a look at the world of law enforcement through the eyes of its officers. It presents members of the NYPD performing their service to the community. Exhibits include fingerprinting and forensic art stations, an arrest record display of famous criminals, an array of weapons, a drug awareness display, and a tactics simulator.

Hours: Tuesday through Saturday 10 A.M.–5 P.M.

Admission: Suggested donation: $5 adults, $3 seniors, $2 children (6–18)

Transportation: *Subway:* 4, 5 to Bowling Green; 1, 2 to Wall Street; N, R to Whitehall, South Ferry. *Bus:* M15 to Wall Street

---

The New York Transit Museum   718-694-5100
www.mta.nyc.ny.us/museum

Located in a decommissioned subway station in downtown Brooklyn, the NY Transit Museum is currently undergoing a major renovation (to be completed in 2003). The renovated building will feature a new art gallery, a classroom for children's workshops, a computer lab, a reference library, and a few other bells and whistles. A new permanent exhibition on the history of surface transportation is scheduled for the Brooklyn museum— buses and trolleys will be installed using elements of a New York City intersection—and the display will also include more than 200 trolley models. In the interim, the Gallery Annex at Grand Central Terminal will continue to offer exhibits free of charge. Call or check the Web site for updates on the opening date, hours, directions, and prices for the new museum.

★ *Solomon R. Guggenheim Museum*   212-423-3500
1071 Fifth Avenue (between 88th and 89th Sts.), UES
www.guggenheim.org

At this museum, perhaps the most photographed edifice in the neighborhood (Carnegie Hill), it's irresistible not to consider the possibility of roller skating, sledding, skateboarding, or banister-riding down the six-story spiral interior that is the Guggenheim Museum.

The building was designed by Frank Lloyd Wright, and the permanent Guggenheim collection and special exhibits feature modern art. Even if you're all arted out, step inside the lobby for a look up. The building really is magnificent, and it only enhances the manageable collection of art.

Special exhibits tend to occupy the walls of the central spiral, whereas permanent collection pieces (Chagall, Kandinsky, Picasso, Degas, Van Gogh) are in rooms off the swirl. Special offerings include a free highlights tour daily and free family films (check the Web site or call ahead for the current offerings). Jazz in the rotunda is always a big hit. The exhibits do vary though, so check the calendar before you shell out the big bucks to go in.

You can also visit the Guggenheim Museum SoHo (575 Broadway at Prince St., 212-423-3500), which is trendier but not nearly as impressive.

Hours: Sunday through Wednesday 9 A.M.–6 P.M., Friday and Saturday 9 A.M.–8 P.M.

Admission: $12 adults, $8 seniors/students, under 12 free; pay what you wish Friday 6 P.M.–8 P.M.

Transportation: *Subway:* 4, 5, 6 to 86th Street

Whitney Museum of American Art   212-570-3676
945 Madison Avenue (at 75th St.), UES   877-WHITNEY
www.whitney.org

The brainchild of artist Gertrude Vanderbilt Whitney, the Whitney Museum of American Art actually came into being in a somewhat haphazard manner. A collector herself, Whitney offered her collection to the Met, and the Met turned it down (I guess the curators weren't interested in twentieth-century American art at the time— wonder how they feel about it now?), so she started her own museum. Unveiled in 1966 in its current incarnation, the Whitney is a striking edifice (if only because it looks to me somewhat like a futuristic prison), especially for Madison Avenue. Dedicated to preserving, collecting, interpreting, and exhibiting twentieth- and twenty-first century art, the Whitney is one of the greatest advocates of the art of our times. The museum focuses special attention specifically on the work of living artists (after all, why should the dead ones get all the attention?). If you really want to expose your children to what's au courant, the Whitney is a good bet—and it's very manageable, too. The permanent collection includes Georgia O'Keeffe, Edward Hopper, Jasper Johns, George Bellows, Roy Lichtenstein, and many other notable twentieth-century artists. Free gallery tours are offered daily, and the restaurant at the Whitney, Sarabeth's, is a winner, as is the counter service, also catered by Sarabeth's. You can enjoy a great cappuccino outside in the moat, while your children burn off some steam.

Hours: Tuesday, Wednesday, Thursday, Saturday, Sunday 11 A.M.–6 P.M., Friday 1 P.M.–9 P.M.

Admission: $12.00 adults, $9.50 seniors/students, under 12 free; pay what you wish Friday 6 P.M.–9 P.M.

Transportation: *Subway:* 6 to 77th Street. *Bus:* M1, M2, M3, M4, M30 to 75th Street; M79 crosstown

---

| *Whitney Museum of American Art*
at Philip Morris **(Midtown branch)**
120 Park Avenue (at 42nd St.), MT | **212-663-2453** |

Features a small gallery (with changing exhibits), a sculpture court, and free gallery tours.

Hours: Monday through Friday 11:00 A.M.–6:00 P.M., Thursday 11:00 A.M.–7:30 P.M.

Admission: Free

Transportation: *Subway:* 4, 5, 6 to 42nd Street

Specialty Museums

| *American Craft Museum*
40 West 53rd Street (between
Fifth and Sixth Aves.), MTW | **212-956-3535 weekdays**
212-956-3690 weekends
www.americancraftmuseum.org |

Depending upon the exhibit, this small museum is a good one to pop into, if only for fifteen minutes (children under 12 are free). Founded in 1956, it's the country's oldest establishment to be singularly dedicated to contemporary crafts. The gift shop is great; I've been known to stop in for a browse and leave with a bundle. Gallery talks are regularly scheduled and families are welcome.

Hours: Tuesday through Wednesday, Friday through Sunday 10 A.M.–6 P.M., Thursday 10 A.M.–8 P.M.

Admission: $8 adults, $5 students and seniors, children under 12 free; pay what you wish Thursday 6 P.M.–8 P.M.

Transportation: *Subway:* E, F to Fifth Avenue

Asia Society   **212-517-ASIA**
725 Park Avenue (at 70th St.), UES   www.asiasociety.org

Specializing in contemporary Asian and Asian American art, the Asia Society was established in 1956 to unite us through art and promote better understanding of and communication among Americans and Asians. Through performances, films, lectures, conferences, and, of course, art exhibits, the Asia Society (including people of Asia and the Pacific) aims to present Asia to Americans.

Hours: Tuesday through Saturday 11 A.M.–6 P.M. (to 8 P.M. on Thursday), Sunday 12 P.M.–5 P.M.

Admission: $4 adults, $2 seniors, children under 13 free; Thursday 6 P.M.–8 P.M. free

Transportation: *Subway:* 6 to 68th Street/Hunter College

Children's Museum of the Arts   **212-941-9198**
182 Lafayette Street (between   **212-274-0986**
Broome and Grand Sts.), LI   **www.cmany.org**

This is definitely a place you'll want to call ahead of time if you want to get involved in one of the special programs. Here workshops designed especially to encourage and bring out kids' (18 months to 10 years) creativity are the biggest draw, but there are also plenty of hands-on activities like dress-up for the younger kids and computer graphics for the older ones. Programs include storytelling, sing-alongs, plays, skits, and art projects like puppet-making.

Hours: Wednesday through Sunday 12 P.M.–5 P.M.; Thursday until 6 P.M.

Admission:$5; pay what you wish Thursday 4 P.M.–6 P.M.

Transportation: *Subway:* N, R to Prince Street; 6 to Spring Street

---

The Cloisters   212-923-3700
Fort Tryon Park (north end), Upper Manhattan
www.metmuseum.org

Part of the Met, The Cloisters is a bit of a schlep (it's in northern Manhattan), but you can get there via public transportation, it's included with your entry to the Met (same day), and if your kids (or more likely, you) have always dreamed of seeing the famous unicorn tapestries, this is the only place to do it. The kids will get a kick out of the architecture (there are cloisters from medieval monasteries and a Spanish apse brought *intact* from Europe). Free guided tours are offered Tuesday through Sunday at 3 P.M.

Hours: November to February, Tuesday through Sunday 9:30 A.M.–4:45 P.M.; March to October, Tuesday through Sunday 9:30 A.M.–5:15 P.M.

Suggested admission: $10 adults, $5 seniors and students, free for children under 12 (includes same-day entrance to the Metropolitan Museum of Art and vice versa)

Transportation: *Subway:* A to 190th Street, then a ten-minute walk north along Margaret Corgan Drive, or pick up the M4 bus at the station. *Bus:* M4 to Fort Tryon Park-The Cloisters

---

Cooper-Hewitt National   212-849-8400
Design Museum
2 East 91st Street (at Fifth Ave.), UES   www.ndm.si.edu

Housed in the Carnegie Mansion, this museum is magnificent to look at. I've been known to walk inside just to feel the grandness of the place (a girl can dream, can't she?) and of course pop into the gift shop for a quick browse. The yard alone gives me palpitations. Part of the Smithsonian Institution, the Cooper-Hewitt's exhibits are often funky and offbeat. The exhibit that included brightly colored tents in the yard was unlike any other I had ever seen, as were the toasters. If nothing else (depending upon the exhibit), the art can be engaging and fun and open your eyes and those of your children to a different way of looking at art. And after all, isn't that what it's really all about?

Hours: Tuesday 10 A.M.–9 P.M., Wednesday through Saturday 10 A.M.–5 P.M., Sunday 12 P.M.–5 P.M.

Admission: $8 adults, $5 seniors and students, free for children under 12; Tuesday 5 P.M.–9 P.M., free to all

Transportation: *Subway:* 4, 5, 6 to 86th Street

Forbes Magazine Galleries   212-206-5548
62 Fifth Avenue (at 12th St.), GV

Toy soldiers, model boats, old Monopoly sets, toy cars, and, of course, the bejeweled Fabergé eggs, were all part of Forbes's collection. Even though they can't touch, the kids are sure to be delighted by this collection, and it's free, too (what a guy he was, Mr. Forbes), so everyone can be elated.

Hours: Tuesday, Wednesday, Friday, Saturday 10 A.M.–4 P.M.
Admission: Free
Transportation: Subway: L, N, R, 4, 5, 6 to 14th Street/Union Square

---

The Frick Collection   212-288-0700
1 East 70th Street (at Fifth Ave.), UES   www.frick.org

They don't love kids here. Children under 10 aren't even allowed to set foot inside this place (I wonder if they'll card you). So if you're traveling with a young family, this isn't the place for you. That being said, this collection really is magnificent (with works by Picasso, Titian, Rembrandt, Michelangelo, Turner, and Vermeer) and manageable, and the facility itself is breath-taking (it was indeed Frick's residence). Could you just imagine?

Hours: Tuesday through Saturday 10 A.M.–6 P.M., Friday until 9 P.M., Sunday and minor holidays 1 P.M.–6 P.M.

Admission: $10 adults, $5 seniors and students. *Children under 10 not admitted;* children under 16 must be accompanied by an adult.

Transportation: *Subway:* 6 to 68th Street/Hunter College

International Center of *Photography (ICP)* **1133 Sixth Avenue (at 43rd St.), MTW**	**212-768-4682** **www.icp.org**

ICP is New York City's preeminent collector of photography. Dedicated to all aspects of photography, from exhibits to seminars and classes, this museum is a must for photo buffs and aspiring photographers.

Hours: Tuesday through Thursday 10 A.M.–5 P.M., Friday 10 A.M.–8 P.M., Saturday and Sunday 10 A.M.–6 P.M.

Admission: $6 adults, $4 seniors, $1 children under 13

Transportation to ICP: *Subway:* 6 to 96th Street

Transportation to ICP Midtown: *Subway:* B, D, F trains to 42nd Street

Japan Society **333 East 47th Street (between First and** **Second Aves.), MTE**	**212-832-1155** **www.japansociety.org**

Featuring highly regarded exhibitions of Japanese art, the society also offers programs that include lectures, films, concerts, and classes.

Hours: Tuesday through Sunday 9:00 A.M.–5:30 P.M.

Suggested admission: $5

Transportation: *Subway:* 6 to 51st Street; E, V to Lexington Avenue

The Jewish Museum **1109 Fifth Avenue (at 92nd St.), UES**	**212-423-3200** **www.jewishmuseum.org**

The collection at the Jewish Museum chronicles 4,000 years of Jewish life. From ancient artifacts to modern art, the two-floor permanent exhibit, Culture and Continuity: The Jewish Journey, is the museum's heart and focal point. Touring exhibits are constantly on display, so there's a continuous flow of regulars as well as guests from out of town. The scope of the exhibits is tremendous—enlightening, overpowering, touching. The gift shop is a worthwhile stop for Judaica, books, and posters.

Hours: Sunday, Monday, Wednesday, Thursday 11:00 A.M.–5:45 P.M., Tuesday 11:00 A.M.–8:00 P.M.; Friday 11:00 A.M.–3:00 P.M.

Admission: $8.00 adults, $5.50 seniors and students, free for children under 12; pay what you wish Tuesday 5 P.M.–8 P.M.

Transportation: *Subway:* 4, 5 to 86th Street; 6 to 96th Street

Madame Tussaud's	**800-246-8872**
234 West 42nd Street (between Seventh	
and Eighth Aves.), MTW	**www.madame-tussauds.com**

It's at the extreme edge of the definition of "museum," but Madame Tussaud's wax museum is always a favorite attraction for kids. Located in the heart of Times Square, it's easy to combine a visit to Madame Tussaud's with a trip to the theater, or a walk (or gawk) around the neighborhood. The more than 250 lifelike figures offer a great opportunity to work in a little history and pop-culture lesson while focusing on the personalities from entertainment, music, sports, politics, and world history.

Hours: Open 365 day a year. Doors open everyday at 10 A.M., and the last ticket is sold at 8 P.M. Madame Tussaud's occasionally closes early for private parties, so be sure to call in advance to confirm hours.

Admission: $22 adults, $19 adults over 60, $17 children 4–12; prices include the virtual reality movie, *New York, New York*

Transportation: *Subway:* A, C, E, and S trains (Port Authority/Eighth Ave.), 1, 9, 2, 3, B, D, F, Q, N, R; *Bus:* M57,

M16, M42, M11, M27, M104. All subways and buses stop within a few blocks of the museum.

El Museo del Barrio   212-831-7272
1230 Fifth Avenue (at 104th St.), UES   www.elmuseo.org

The only museum in America whose central focus is Puerto Rican, Latin American, and Caribbean art, El Museo's aim is to preserve the cultural heritage of Puerto Ricans and Latin Americans living in the United States. The permanent collection includes paintings, historical photographs, hand-carved religious figurines (*santos de palo*), sculpture, and other creative displays. New exhibitions highlight contemporary Latin art and artists.

Hours: Wednesday through Sunday 11 A.M.–5 P.M.

Suggested admission: $5 adults, $3 seniors and students, children under 12 free

Transportation: *Subway:* 6 to 103rd Street

Museum for African Art   212-966-1313
593 Broadway (between Houston and Prince Sts.), SH
www.africanart.org

You can't help but be drawn to this museum from the outset. The interior was designed by Maya Lin, the same architect who designed the Vietnam Memorial, and, with exhibits like Hair in African Art and Culture and Liberated Voices: Contemporary Art from South Africa, it's not difficult to see why MfAA is so engaging. A leader in organizing exhibits dedicated to historic and contemporary African art and culture, the MfAA brings to New York its own identity of art and culture.

Hours: Tuesday through Friday 10:30 A.M.–5:30 P.M., Saturday–Sunday 12:00 P.M.–6:00 P.M.

Admission: $5.00 adults, $2.50 seniors, children, and students

Transportation: *Subway:* N, R to Prince Street, 6 to Spring Street, B, D, F to Broadway-Lafayette

Museum of American Folk Art	212-265-1040
45 West 53rd Street, MTW	**www.folkartmuseum.org**

A great representation of the American folk-art tradition. The quilts, part of the museum's most popular exhibit (textiles), will make any sentimentalist's fingers start to twitch. These quilts put the sewing class you took in Home Ec into perspective. The gift shop here is full of great originals, and there are usually some nice "dollies," far more authentic and cuddly than those at Toys "R" Us.

Hours: Tuesday through Sunday 10 A.M.–6 P.M., Friday until 8 P.M.

Admission: $9 adults; $5 seniors and students

Transportation: *Subway:* E, V to 50th Street

National Museum of the	212-514-3700
American Indian	212-514-3888
George Gustav Heye Center	
1 Bowling Green (at Broadway), FD	**www.si.edu/nmai**

Housed in the magnificent U.S. Customs House, the collection at the Museum of the American Indian is the oldest and one of the best in the country. Sadly, it's only a temporary fixture in its current home. As part of the Smithsonian Institution, the collection will find its new and permanent home on Independence Mall in Washington, D.C. (in 2004). Until then, there is plenty to see, most of which was collected independently (and eventually donated) by George Gustav Heye. In addition to the comprehensive original collection, there are also special exhibits and programs including storytelling, music, and dance presentations. Not to be missed are the Especially for Kids events. Call ahead for a calendar of current programs.

Hours: Sunday through Wednesday and Friday through Saturday 10 A.M.–5 P.M., Thursday 10 A.M.–8 P.M.

Admission: Free
Transportation: *Subway:* 4, 5 to Bowling Green

New York Hall of Science   718-699-0005
47-01 111th Street
Flushing Meadows/Corona Park, Q   www.nyhallsci.org

The NYHoS touts itself as New York's only Science Playground and backs the claim with the largest collection of hands-on science and technology exhibits in the City. It's a big hit with kids because it's all hands-on. There are 200 interactive exhibits to examine, touch, and explore, and every child will definitely find something of interest. A few all-time favorites include being "swallowed" by a giant bubble, the antigravity mirror (can you guess what will happen?), and composing music by dancing in front of light beams. During the summer, the Outdoor Science Playground is open. Geared toward children 6 and up, the playground outside has plenty of room and opportunity to slide, seesaw, spin, jump, and climb—all lessons in physics but, more important, tons of fun. And for the under-5 set, don't overlook the Discover Place play area, designed especially with them in mind. *Note:* If you're traveling with older kids, those who have seen the movie *Men in Black,* keep a look out for the Unisphere: it really does exist, and no, it wasn't actually destroyed in the movie.

Hours: Tuesday through Wednesday 9:30 A.M.–2:00 P.M., Thursday through Sunday 9:30 A.M.–5:00 P.M. July to August, Monday 9:30 A.M.–2:00 P.M., Tuesday through Friday 9:30 A.M.–5:00 P.M., Saturday and Sunday 10:30 A.M.–6:00 P.M.

Admission: $7.50 adults, $5.00 children and seniors; $2.50 kids ages 2–4. Thursday through Friday 2 P.M.–5 P.M. free

Transportation: *Subway:* 7 to 111th Street, Queens

The New-York Historical Society   212-873-3400
2 West 77th Street (at Central Park West), UWS
www.nyhistory.org

Since 1804, the New-York Historical Society has been the definitive repository of New York. The collection includes manuscripts, sculpture, paintings, books, decorative arts, photographs,
prints, architectural documents, and other objects that catalog
the city's history. The focus, though primarily on New York, also
includes general American history, culture, and art. Ongoing exhibits include Kid City and Glimmers of the Past. If you get a
chance to see Times Square in Pictures, you'll view the fascinating evolution of Times Square from what it was a century ago to
its current incarnation.

> **Hours:** Tuesday through Sunday 11 A.M.–6 P.M.
> **Admission:** $6 adults, $4 seniors/students, under 12 free
> **Transportation:** *Subway:* B, C to 81st Street; *Bus:* M10 to
77th Street, or M79 to 81st Street Central Park West

Pierpont Morgan Library   212-685-0008
29 East 36th Street (at Madison Ave.), MTE
www.morganlibrary.org

This is one of my personal favorite museum spaces in the City.
Interestingly enough, the Morgan Library remains something of
an undiscovered New York treasure. It not only houses one of the
world's most important collections of rare books and bindings,
master drawings, original manuscripts, and personal writings (including a working draft of the U.S. Constitution with handwritten notes; handwritten scores by Beethoven, Mozart, and
Puccini; and Voltaire's personal household account books), but it
also features special exhibitions. Recent exhibits include From
Bruegel to Rubens, Treasures from the Royal Tombs of Ur, and
Collecting for the Centuries. The building alone is worth a look

inside (a grand old mansion), and it's also a great place for a light lunch or afternoon tea.

Hours: Tuesday through Thursday 10:30 A.M.–5:00 P.M., Friday 10:30 A.M.–8:00 P.M., Saturday 10:30 A.M.–6:00 P.M., Sunday 12:00 P.M.–6:00 P.M.

Suggested admission: $8 adults, $6 seniors/students, children under 12 free.

Transportation: *Subway:* 6 to 33rd Street or any subway to 42nd Street-Grand Central. Bus: M2, M3, M4, Q32 to 36th Street

P.S. 1 Contemporary Art Center	**718-784-2084**
22-25 Jackson Avenue (at 46th Ave.)	
Long Island City, Q	**www.queensmuse.org**

Originally a public school (hence the name), P.S. 1 is the world's largest contemporary art museum. What's featured here is art from the United States and abroad that's so contemporary, it's not yet collected in most other museums. If you have a budding artist in the family, this museum could be an interesting stop—and most definitely unlike any other your child has probably ever seen. A high-profile merger with the Museum of Modern Art was announced recently, so P.S. 1 should start getting more attention soon.

Helpful Hint

Insider's Hour, a program coordinated by the New York Convention and Visitors' Bureau, runs July 1– September 30. Many of the City's top cultural institutions participate: The American Museum of Natural History, Guggenheim, Intrepid, New York Botanical Garden, and more. The one-hour tours give a quick exposure to the best that each institution has to offer. Pick up a Summer *Insider's Hour* brochure at the NYC Visitor Information Center (Seventh Ave. at 53rd St.) or contact www.nycvisit.com to get a brochure by mail.

Hours: Thursday through Monday 12 P.M.–6 P.M. (Hours vary in summer, so call ahead.)

Suggested admission: $5 adults, $2 seniors/students/artists

Transportation: *Subway:* E, V to 23rd Street/Ely Avenue; 7 to Court House Square/45th Road

Galleries:
The Museum Alternative

As opposed to art museums, which are in the business of preserving art, galleries are in the business of selling art—by showcasing the most important artists, especially new ones. Thus, for those children—teens in particular—who have an exceptionally high level of interest in art, New York's dizzying array of art galleries (we have more galleries even than museums—in other words, a whole lot) are a resource you shouldn't pass up. Most galleries have no problem with children, as long as they're well behaved. An added bonus: Galleries charge no admission!

A Few Key Galleries in the Major Gallery Districts

A ★ indicates a gallery that has been particularly excellent over the years, though individual shows may vary in quality.

57th Street Galleries

ACA Galleries
41 East 57th Street (at Madison Ave.)
212-644-8300

Andre Emmerich
41 East 57th Street (between Madison and Fifth Aves.)
212-752-0124

Blum-Helman
20 West 57th Street (between Fifth and Sixth Aves.)
212-245-2888

Tips for Getting the Most Out of New York's Art Galleries

@ Before coming to town, consult the Friday *New York Times* "Weekend" section for a listing of shows that will be on during your visit. If you want to do more in-depth research, take a look at the *Art Now Gallery Guide*, published monthly or online at www.galleryguideonline .com. Plan your gallery itinerary around what you learn from your research.

@ Plan to wander around a single gallery neighborhood, stopping in for a few minutes at each of several nearby galleries. The major clusters of galleries are in SoHo, along 57th Street, and along upper Madison Avenue (there are also many galleries in Chelsea and the East Village). In certain gallery-rich buildings, like 41 East 57th Street, you can get into the elevator and just go from floor to floor, sampling what's of interest and passing over what isn't.

@ Don't be discouraged from visiting galleries by their reputation for being snooty or unfriendly. The truth is that if you visit at a time when they aren't busy (midweek; first thing in the morning), any given gallery's staff will give you a nice greeting—and maybe even show you around a little.

@ Children under 12 should be extra-carefully supervised because galleries have no barriers between observers and the art.

Marchian Goodman Gallery
24 West 57th Street (between Fifth and Sixth Aves.)
212-977-7160

Learning Tip

A visit to a gallery makes a great topic for a school report. Ask the gallery for a brochure, which will contain detailed information about the works on display, and focus the report on the work of one artist.

Marchlborough
40 West 57th Street (between Fifth and Sixth Aves.)
212-541-4900

★ PaceWildenstein
32 East 57th Street (between Park and Madison Aves.)
212-421-3292

Robert Miller
41 East 57th Street (at Madison Ave.)
212-980-5454

★ Sidney Janis Gallery
110 West 57th Street (between Sixth and Seventh Aves.)
212-586-0110

Tatistcheff and Company
50 West 57th Street (between Fifth and Sixth Aves.),
    8th floor
212-664-0907

Madison Avenue Galleries

Gagosian
980 Madison Avenue (at 76th St.)
212-744-2313

Hirschl & Adler Galleries
21 East 70th Street (at Madison Ave.)
212-535-8810

★ M Knoedler & Company
19 East 70th Street (between Madison and Fifth Aves.)
212-794-0550

Terry Dintenfass
20 East 79th Street (at Fifth Ave.)
212-581-2268

SoHo Galleries

Barbara Gladstone
99 Greene Street (between Prince and Spring Sts.)
212-431-3334

Charles Cowles
420 West Broadway (between Prince and Spring Sts.)
212-925-3500

Curt Marcus Gallery
578 Broadway (between Houston and Prince Sts.)
212-226-3200

Gagosian
136 Wooster Street (between Houston and Prince Sts.)
212-228-2828

John Weber
142 Greene Street (between Houston and Prince Sts.),
   3rd floor
212-966-6115

★ Leo Castelli
420 West Broadway (between Spring and Prince Sts.)
212-431-5160

Mary Boone Gallery
417 West Broadway (between Spring and Prince Sts.)
212-431-1818

★ Max Protetch Gallery
560 Broadway (at Prince St.)
212-966-5454

Metro Pictures
150 Greene Street (between Houston and Prince Sts.)
212-925-8335

★Paula Cooper
155 Wooster Street (between Houston and Prince Sts.)
212-674-0766

Postmasters
80 Greene Street (at Spring St.), 2nd floor
212-941-5711

PPOW
532 Broadway (at Spring St.), 3rd floor
212-941-8642

Insider's Tip

"Younger people are typically interested in art that's closer to their own age, style, or aesthetic. Galleries that show the younger, or emerging, artists are particularly suitable. The larger galleries tend to show more contemporary or modern art and are easier for the uninitiated to visit. Smaller galleries, or galleries specializing in, say, Old Master drawings, will be more intimidating and less fun for younger people."
—*Robert Schonfeld, art dealer*

★Sonnabend Gallery
420 West Broadway (between Spring and Prince Sts.)
212-966-6160

Sperone Westwater
142 Greene Street (between Houston and Prince Sts.)
212-431-3685

In addition to galleries, don't forget the auction houses, which are among the best free entertainment in town and often have objects on view that are of interest to kids (carousel animals, toys, baseball cards, rock-and-roll memorabilia, etc.).

Christie's
20 Rockefeller Plaza
212-636-2408
www.christies.com

Sotheby's
1334 York Avenue (at 72nd St.)
212-606-7000
www.sothebys.com

William Doyle Galleries
175 East 87th Street (between Lexington and Third Aves.)
212-427-2730
www.doylenewyork.com

Zoos and Gardens

You wouldn't think such a densely populated urban area would have so much open space, but New York has some amazing—and huge—zoos and gardens. The jewel in the crown is the Bronx Zoo, of which New Yorkers are understandably proud. To this I give the lengthiest coverage. Remember, you can combine your Bronx Zoo visit with a New York Botanical Garden visit and a trip to Arthur Avenue (see chapter 3) for a full, wonderful day in the too-often-overlooked

Coney Island

Bronx. Likewise, you can combine the Aquarium with Coney Island and Little Odessa/Brighton Beach (see chapter 3) for a great Brooklyn adventure.

> ### *Bronx Botanical Garden—*
> ### See New York Botanical Garden

> ### ★ *Bronx Zoo Wildlife Conservation Park*   718-367-1010
> ### Fordham Road (at Bronx River Pkwy.), BX   www.wcs.org

Set on 265 acres of woods, ponds, streams, and parkland, with more than 6,000 animals from 665 species, the Bronx Zoo is every child's fantasyland (and the nation's largest urban zoo). Because of the zoo's enormous size, you really need a strategy for your visit, lest you find that the troops have run out of gas before they've seen the things they'll enjoy most.

Highlights of the zoo include the Congo Gorilla Forest (for which there is an additional charge of $3), the Children's Zoo (additional charge of $2), the World of Reptiles, Africa, Jungle World, and Wild Asia. This is not even the tip of the iceberg. Everyone has a personal greatest-hits list, but these are some of the favorites of the more than two million visitors coming through the zoo each year.

Note: If you're on a tight budget and don't wish to/can't spring for the exhibits with extra fees, don't feel compelled to do so. Your children will still have a great zoo experience—there is *plenty* to see and do without paying the extra fees. If you are going to pay for one extra, for youngsters I'd suggest the Children's Zoo; for older kids I'd go for Congo. On the bright side, during the winter months the fee for Congo drops to $1 to compensate for the reduced number of animals you can view.

If you're coming via public transportation on the bus or subway, you'll enter through gate B, which is a perfect place to begin. You can start with the Monkey House, the Zoo Center (elephants, rhinos, and tapirs), and the Children's Zoo. Here's a good basic itinerary, beginning at the Children's Zoo.

- The **Children's Zoo** has some animals for petting, like goats and chickens, in a farmlike setting (pens and barns), and you can buy feed to really endear yourself to the animals. There are also some great climbing apparatus, like the rope spider web and the tree house with swirling slide. One of the most amusing things (to me, at least) is the prairie dog burrow. Prairie dogs are running around on this hill, and if the children go underneath the hill, they can poke their heads through Lucite domes and at once be like a prairie dog poking its head out of its burrow, and at the same time, watch the real prairie dogs scurrying around their habitat. Another nice feature of the Children's Zoo is the opportunity for learning. Children can compare their jumping distance with that of a bullfrog or sit down in a heron's nest. Want to see what it feels like to be a turtle? Slide into one of the brassy shells. Along the pathways are questions on plaques; as you proceed, the questions are answered. The signs are easy to read and understand.

- The star of the **Elephant House** has to be Samuel R. II, a young female elephant who made her first appearance in 1993. She is watched over by Tus, the matriarch of the herd. Nearby neighbors include the tapirs, Carrie and Snuffles, who are a part of the zoo's participation in the Species Survival Plan.

- If you need a ride, the **Zoo Shuttle** is right outside the Zoo Center (which houses the elephants). Transportation options within the zoo include the Zoo Shuttle train, the Skyfari aerial tram, and the Bengali Express Monorail (all of which cost $2 each way). The different shuttle options each go to different destinations.

- When you need a break: The zoo has plenty of picnic areas, and you're free to bring in any food, snacks, and drinks you like—but be warned, carrying too much heavy stuff will become a burden quickly because the zoo is both huge and hilly.

❧ If you're still on foot, **World of Reptiles** isn't too far away, and it's a nice dark, cool building with lots of slithering, hopping residents. Probably the most famous of the reptiles is Samantha, the 25-foot reticulated python, who weighs in at a handsome 223 pounds. When the zoo acquired Samantha, she was only 23 feet long. I am also a big fan of the fluorescent tree frogs—blue, green, or red with black spots—it's sort of like being in Alice's Wonderland.

❧ Have a look around the **Himalayan Highlands.** This exhibit's star is the endangered and elusive snow leopard. The Bronx Zoo has had snow leopards since 1903, with seven generations of cubs born at the zoo—seventy-eight in all so far! As you look at the snow leopards with your kids, share this: Bronx Zoo snow leopard cubs have been sent to zoos in Australia, Canada, England, Russia, and Japan, as well as many zoos within the country! If your child is missing school and needs to write a report, suggest pertinent snow leopard topics (the history of the species, the conservation efforts, the countries in which it now lives). The zoo is a great place to start doing that research firsthand.

❧ The **Big Bears** are back to back with the snow leopards, and kids always love the grizzlies and polar bears. If it's summertime, don't expect the bears to be too active during the day. Look in the dark shady places to spot them or try to visit the exhibit early or later in the day when temperatures are a bit more agreeable to the creatures with fur coats.

❧ This might be a good time to make your way to the **Wild Asia** exhibit and hop on the Bengali Express Monorail (May through October) for a narrated ride. The trick here is that you've got to keep your eyes peeled for the animals, or you'll miss them as you travel slowly by (the monorail snakes along on a track above the animals). In this exhibit are the hard-to-miss Asian elephants, Indian rhinoceros, red pandas, Gaurs, a selection of deer (don't expect too much excitement here even if there is a great variety—most children have the attitude that "if you've seen one deer, you've seen 'em all").

@ **Jungle World,** which re-creates an Indonesian scrub forest, isn't far and with as many as 780 animals from 99 species, everyone should be able to find something to love. Jungle World has 280 reptiles, amphibians, and fish, including Indian gharials and mudskippers—you'll have to find them to find out what they are. The 55 mammals include white-cheeked gibbons and black leopards. Ah, and the birds. The 100 birds are complete with laughing thrushes, hornbills, and Bali mynahs. If the Reptile House didn't satisfy all desire for scales and slithers, there is also a collection of arthropods—350 animals to be exact, with millipedes topping the list. Anyone feel like counting the millipede's feet?

@ Over in **Africa** you'll find the timeless favorites. Who doesn't love the lions, cheetahs, and giraffes? Zebras, blesboks, nyalas, okapis, and ostriches are on hand, too. The names alone are the stuff that entertainment is made of.

Stretching some limbs at the Bronx Zoo's Children's Zoo

So, what's left? Plenty, but the final must-see exhibit is the **Congo Gorilla Forest.** For starters, the money you pay as you enter the door is actually donated to projects funded by the WCS (Wildlife Conservation Society, founded in 1895 as the New York Zoological Society and the consortium of the Bronx Zoo, New York Aquarium, Central Park Wildlife Center, Queens Wildlife Center, and Prospect Park Wildlife Center) and better still, as you exit the exhibit, you get to choose how your dollars are spent. This is a good platform from which to discuss the notion of conservation with your children if you haven't already done so.

As you walk along the path you'll see a sign telling you to look for hidden signs of life: dung, anthills, skeletons, and so forth. Who can spot the skull just behind the sign? How about the millipede farther along the trail, embedded into the dirt wall? Look for the colobus monkey forest—can you spot the monkeys in the trees? What colors are they? What feature helped you to spot *them?* The Red River hogs are wonderfully ugly to the point of being adorable. Do you see that dirt area right in front of the glass (in which they're probably sleeping)? Every night, when the hogs are most active, they root around and dig up that entire area. Each morning the zookeepers have to put the dirt back in place!

An eight-minute film describes a little bit about what the WCS does, and then the curtain goes up, and you get the dramatic exposure of the gorillas. They're in their habitat, hidden from view first by the movie screen and then by the black curtains. When the curtains part, there's an audible gasp from the audience, and everyone rushes along the path to see the gorillas (we're glassed in, not them). Another hit of the Congo exhibit is the pygmy marmosets. They are the smallest primates in the world. You could easily cup one in the palm of your hand. It's dark and they're small, so they're a bit difficult to spot, but they're extremely active, so a minute or two of dedicated watching should prove fruitful. Nearby, games like Compare Your Weight to a Primate, Create a Gorilla Reserve, and Measuring Up (comparing your handprint with those of the inhabitants) bring the animals closer to home and make the experience more personal.

A day at the zoo is magnificent and exhausting. Some tips to help you avoid the crowds: Avoid free Wednesday, if at all possible. If you want to capitalize on the free entry (who doesn't), winter, spring, and fall are certainly going to be better than summer. If you are visiting in peak season (summer), arrive as early as possible so that you can enjoy at least some of your time at the zoo with fewer human inhabitants. And, try to schedule your visit during the week, when there's less human traffic. During winter months, not only are crowds sparser and rates lower, but grizzlies, snow leopards, and Mexican gray wolves are also more active. Some animals are not on exhibit because of the temperatures, but you'll find that there's still plenty to see and do. And you can always schedule an Insider's Hour tour (January to March and July to September) by calling 718-220-5141.

Hours: November to March, daily 10:00 A.M.–4:30 P.M.; April to October, Monday through Friday 10:00 A.M.–5:00 P.M., weekends and federal holidays 10:00 A.M.–5:30 P.M.

Admission: January third through March $5 adults, $3 seniors and children under 12; April through October $9 adults, $5 seniors and children under 12; November through January third $7 adults, $4 seniors and children under 12; Wednesdays free all year

Transportation: *Bus:* If you're not driving, the Liberty Line's BxM11 express bus is by far the easiest, most comfortable, and safest way to get from Manhattan right to the zoo's entrance gate. Pick-up points are along Madison Avenue, the cost is $3 each way, and you can use your MetroCard to pay (if it isn't an unlimited card). Call 718-652-8400 for a schedule and updated prices.

Brooklyn Botanic Garden   718-623-7200
1000 Washington Avenue (Eastern Pkwy.), BR www.bbg.org

With names like Daffodil Hill, Shakespeare Garden, Lily Pool
Terrace, Bluebell Wood, and Children's Garden to lure you, how
can you stay away? Just down the road a piece from the Brooklyn
Museum of Art, you'll find this beautiful garden oasis in the
middle of Brooklyn. Regardless of what time of year you arrive—
though many claim that the garden is at its most spectacular in
May when the cherry trees are in blossom—you'll find plenty to
see and smell (take the kids to the Fragrance Garden, designed
especially for the blind—perhaps they'd like to try sniffing their
way through the garden with their eyes closed, rather than seeing
their way through). Have an interest in bonsai trees (perhaps on
account of watching the *Karate Kid* too many times)? The Stein-
hardt Conservatory is home to the renowned Bonsai Museum.
Whether you're indoors or out, the 12,000 plant specimens
should keep everyone happily engaged, at least for a while. Free
tours are conducted at 1:00 P.M. on Saturday and Sunday. Call in
advance for tours in languages other than English.

   Hours: April to September, Tuesday through Friday 8:00
A.M.–6:00 P.M., Saturday and Sunday 10:00 A.M.–6:00 P.M.; Oc-
tober to March, Tuesday through Friday 8:00 A.M.–4:30 P.M.,
Saturday and Sunday 10:00 A.M.–4:30 P.M.

   Admission: $3 adults, under 16 free; Tuesday and Saturday
10 A.M.–12 P.M. free

   Transportation: *Subway:* 2, 3 to Eastern Parkway/Brook-
lyn Museum; D to Prospect Park

★ Central Park Wildlife Center/   212-861-6030
Tisch Children's Zoo (Central Park Zoo)
Fifth Avenue (at 64th St., in the Park)   www.wcs.org/zoos

The Central Park Zoo (that's what we locals call it; this
"Wildlife Center" business is new, and we're not too quick to

change) is the perfect zoo destination for young children. Smack dab in the middle of the City and lower Central Park, this zoo is a perennial favorite because it's small, manageable, easily accessible (so it doesn't really matter if kids get cranky after an hour, or even fifteen minutes), and specifically geared toward kids. The setup is extremely engaging: Just inside the gate, kids are met with a view of sea lions gliding around their spacious (and glass—ideal for peering and for short people) tank, and just beyond there are monkeys who are far less interested in us than we are in them. Nearby are the famed polar bears (one of whom made headline news—no small feat in New York—due to his obsessive "pacing" and resulting psychiatric analysis; and no, Woody Allen didn't write the story) and perky penguins. The Tropic Zone is a junglelike environment in which the humans are the trespassers. Birds of every imaginable color fly and chirp overhead. If you're lucky, one might land near enough for one of the kids to snap a picture. Don't miss the daily sea lion and penguin feedings, either.

Among preschoolers, the Tisch Children's Zoo is a great hit. Complete with a playground, animal exhibits, and a petting zoo, no child (big or small) can resist the call of the llamas, potbellied pigs, goats, bunnies, and other gentle creatures.

Hours: April to October, Monday through Friday 10:00 A.M.–5:00 P.M., Saturday and Sunday 10:30 A.M.–5:30 P.M.; November to March, daily 10:00 A.M.–4:30 P.M.

Crabbing at New York Aquarium

Admission: $3.50 adults, $1.25 seniors, $0.50 children 3–12, under 3 free

Transportation: *Bus:* M1, M2, M3, M4 to 65th; M66 to Fifth Avenue

---

★ *New York Aquarium*   718-265-3400
West 8th Street (at Surf Ave.), Coney Island, BR   www.wcs.org

---

Because of the travel time from Manhattan (sixty to ninety minutes, depending upon where in Manhattan you're coming from), it's best to coordinate a visit to the aquarium with a trip to the amusement park (this is no Six Flags—expect more of a roving carnival atmosphere than a Disney World) and beach at Coney Island, the nearby playgrounds, and a wander around Little Odessa (see chapter 3). The whole package is ideal for a full summer's day outing, but the fall and spring are also very nice times to visit. The tradeoff for fewer people in fall and spring, however, is that most of the rides and games aren't open. A nice, mild winter day is not to be overlooked, either. Chances are you'll have the clean beach all to yourself, perfect for building sand castles and playing on the jungle gyms. Most of the aquarium's exhibits are indoors.

The New York Aquarium, though not the best in the country, is actually perfect for young children who have short attention spans and delight in the big sea creatures—as well as in the simple pleasures of seeing colorful tropical fish.

@ Upon entering the aquarium, the **shark tank** will impress even the jaded teens who are tagging along. Circling the large tank are large sharks—big enough so that you wouldn't want to encounter them anywhere else—and rays as big as any I've ever seen. When the kids have sated their viewing needs, wander through the darkened den of tanks. The squeals of delight let loose by toddlers echo through the hall and entertain older children and adults equally.

- Outside, the **California sea otters** steal the show. Oh, how I wish I could swim like that! You can also view the penguins, seals, and walruses from the outside viewing area and then go inside to the underwater viewing to get a good look at all of the same creatures in action. Seeing them swim around like that really puts your child's swim team in perspective. The same underwater viewing area also holds some magnificent visual treats like the seahorses—especially the dragon seahorses from Australia. Just try to spot one of those. Also not to be missed is the octopus tank with two enormous octopuses. It might take everyone's eyes a few minutes to adjust to the darkness of the tank, but it's worth the effort to try to spot them. The inhabitants are surprisingly large and certainly the stuff that stories of the deep are made of.

- From April through October, the **touch tanks** are active with horseshoe crabs and other nonstinging creatures. Children can "pet" and pick up the creatures, as long as they treat them very gently.

- One of the best exhibits for its educational value is **Discovery Cove.** Here there are sea creatures coupled with questions and information to enhance the aquarium experience and to help children think about the creatures and their environment. Exhibits include Different Ways to Breathe, Different Mouths for Different Diets, Protection, Vision, Bottom Walkers, and Hearing (listen to aquatic sounds like the "singing" of dolphins and whales).

- Outside are more big hits: The **beluga whale tank,** with plenty of belugas for everyone to see (did you know that *beluga* means "white" in Russian?), and the dolphins are highlights. During the winter, the dolphins reside in the Oceanic Exhibit.

- From an educational point of view, the exhibit on the **Hudson River** is a great tool, especially for older children. The big map on the wall details the route of the Hudson River and how it flows from way upstate (it starts up in Canada, actually) down into New York City and the Atlantic Ocean. This would make a great report topic for an older child. It also places the aquarium in the context of the New York region and brings the exhibits a little closer to home.

Note: The zoo has plenty of outdoor picnic areas for breaks and lunch (packed or purchased) and also *lots* of clean bathrooms. Be sure that everyone uses one before you head to the boardwalk because there bathrooms are few and far between at best.

Hours: Daily 10 A.M.–5 P.M.

Admission: $8.75 adults, $4.50 seniors and children 2–12, free for children under 2

Transportation: *Subway:* D, F to West 8th Street in Brooklyn

---

★ *New York Botanical Garden*   718-817-8700
200th Street (at Southern Blvd.), BX   www.nybg.org

If I had to choose only one botanical garden to visit on my trip to New York City, it would have to be this one. A National Historic Landmark, the 250-acre New York Botanical Garden is one of America's most beautiful and engaging (public) gardens. The beautifully manicured grounds are ideal for an autumn stroll or a spring fling, and the ponds, waterfalls, streams, wetlands, and grassy knolls are only the beginning. What lies beyond are the twenty-eight specialty gardens and plant collections, the Enid A. Haupt *A World of Plants* Conservatory, and, perhaps best of all, the Everett Children's Adventure Garden with forty hands-on plant discovery activities (spread throughout 12 acres of gardens and wetlands) and the Family Garden, where kids can plant, water, weed, and compost firsthand.

Because the garden is so big and the travelers range in size from small to tall, you should consider the transportation options within the garden before you set out. To be sure, if you don't want to hoof it entirely, it's best to call ahead to be certain the tram is running.

Hours: April to October, Tuesday through Sunday and Monday holidays 10 A.M.–6 P.M.; November to March, Tuesday through Sunday and Monday holidays 10 A.M.–4 P.M.

Admission: $3 adults, $2 seniors and students, $1 children 2–12; Wednesday and Saturday 10 A.M.–12 P.M. free; extra charges for Everett Children's Adventure Garden, Enid A. Haupt Conservatory, and T. H. Everett Rock Garden and Native Plant Garden

Transportation: The easiest way is by Garden Shuttle (running weekends, April through October) between the Museum of Natural History, the Met, and the Botanical Garden—call 718-817-8700 for reservations and information. *Train:* Take Metro North 212-532-4900 from Grand Central Station to the New York Botanical Garden station. *Subway:* take the D or 4 train to Bedford Park Boulevard and walk east eight long blocks.

Parks

A Guide to Central Park

The south and north borders of Central Park are 59th Street to 110th Street. Fifth Avenue and Central Park West mark the park's east and west boundaries.

Whenever people ask me, "How can you stand living in Manhattan, surrounded by all those tall buildings?" I answer: "Central Park!"

Occupying 843 acres, Central Park is more than a park to most city dwellers—it's a lifeline to a quiet refuge, culture, sports, wildlife, and nature. It's also where New Yorkers do most of their plain old hanging out.

Designed by Frederick Law Olmsted and Calvert Vaux as the first such park in the City, Central Park was intended to be a refuge from the hustle and bustle of city life right from the

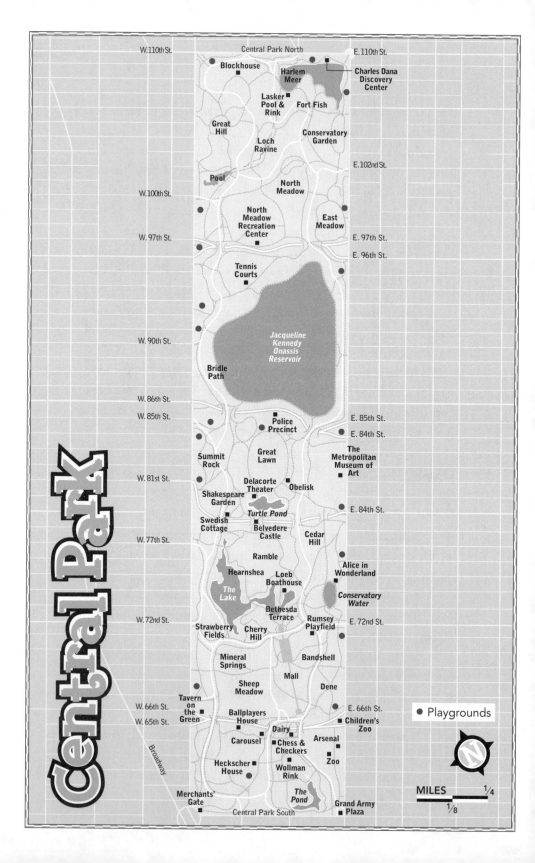

beginning. The prophetic Olmsted, as if he were gazing into a crystal ball, predicted in the late 1850s that the City would become built up and that, with no natural environments left, Central Park would be the oasis that it has become for City dwellers.

Personally, I use the park almost every day for a run or a walk or just some peace and quiet. As soon as the plan was approved, people began using the park. The lower end was developed first with the children's district, and the work progressed north from there. The park was actually completed in 1872. By that time there were already a recorded several million visitors per year utilizing the grand open space. Now reports estimate that twenty million visitors pass through Central Park annually.

In the south the park gets more concentrated traffic (both pedestrian and vehicular), and as you progress north, the numbers tend to dwindle (except when there are concerts and special events in and around the north meadow). Circling the entire park is a paved road called the Park Drive. The Park Drive is a six-mile loop, and it is open to vehicular traffic during morning and afternoon rush-hour periods. The roadway transverse cutting across the park at 72nd Street makes up what is known as the "lower loop." The lower loop has extended hours for vehicular traffic and is also the primary route of horse-drawn carriages (otherwise known as Hansom cabs).

Central Park is a place in which you could easily get lost—in a good way. At the same time, there are always plenty of people about (especially on spring, summer, and fall weekends) within shouting distance, even if not in view, if you should find yourself ready to exit the park and in need of directions. But Central Park works pretty much the same as the rest of the City, with main east-west arteries to get from one side of the park to the other (in this case, paved paths) and north-south pathways, too. The paths may meander a bit, but generally, when you come to a clearing, especially in winter, you should be able to spy the city skyline and orient yourself in the direction you wish to be going. If all else fails, just ask. I get stopped for directions almost every time I enter the park and not only do I not mind helping, but also I actually enjoy pointing people in the right direction and answering their questions (if I can).

Working from the south, favorite attractions (and, really, these are only my favorites!) include:

- **Wollman Rink,** which is open for ice-skating in the winter, is located parallel to 63rd Street.

- The **Dairy,** a great source of information, postcards, and calendars of park events, is also housed in a lovely little cottage (formerly a dairy) and is on the 65th Street cross-town path.

- Just in from Fifth Avenue (coming off of Fifth is the best way to enter, unless you're meandering your way down through the park along the path that parallels Fifth Avenue) at 64th Street is the **Central Park Zoo,** a guaranteed winner (see Zoos).

- Right off the Park Drive (at about 64th St.) from the East Side is the famed **Carousel**. The Carousel is by far one of the greatest rides around. It costs $1 per ride, and don't be surprised if your kids ask to ride again and again. I never pass up an opportunity to ride the Carousel in Central Park—and it goes really fast, too.

- On the West Side at 66th Street is **Tavern on the Green.** It's pretty when it's all lit up (the restaurant keeps lights on its trees all year round), especially in winter when the trees are barren without their leaves.

- Directly across from Tavern is the **Sheep Meadow,** a huge green field where people come to relax with books, for picnics, and to take naps.

- Just in from the Central Park West (CPW) entrance at 72nd Street is the famous **Strawberry Fields.** The commemorative plaque is surrounded by benches where people often come to ruminate about the Beatles and John Lennon's awful demise. No matter what time of year, you'll always find bouquets of flowers (just outside the park is the Dakota, where John and Yoko lived and in front of which John was murdered in 1980).

@ The 72nd Street transverse, which has along side of it a paved sidewalk shaded by giant old trees, is a good route to take to get to the Bethesda Terrace, which overlooks the **Bethesda Fountain.** This is a great place to take a break, to watch the people wander by, to eat an ice cream, to play with the dogs that so love the fountain, and to watch the rowers go by.

@ Just north of the fountain along the pathway is the **Loeb Boathouse,** where you can rent rowboats and bicycles for use in the park.

@ At 74th Street (across the Park Drive toward Fifth) on the East Side is the **Model Boat Pond.** Here children play with remote-controlled boats (many of which are rented at the building on the pond) that are set up on the water during the week. On weekends, the heavy hitters come out, and it's mostly adults (who, in my opinion, take themselves a bit too seriously) who navigate their remote-controlled sailboats around the pond. All of those boats (many of which really are magnificent—remember, they take themselves and their boats very seriously) gliding about are quite a sight.

@ Directly north of the Boat Pond is perhaps the most beloved statue in all of Central Park: **Alice in Wonderland,** with the mushroom and some of her compatriots. Well loved and well rubbed, these brass statues are climbed upon, photographed, and polished by adults and children alike, who insist upon a lengthy visit with the Wonderland characters.

ℯ Just below the Great Lawn (between 81st and 85th Sts.), where people relax and play ball games (also where many of the free concerts in Central Park are held), is **Belvedere Castle.** To the right or left of the southern end of the lawn, follow the pathway that leads up to the castle. After the short climb, you'll be rewarded with not only great views of the park and the City skyline, but also the opportunity to bird-watch and peek into the small museum/information center that is housed inside. Pick up one of the brochures, such as Birds from Belvedere, which not only shows some of the many birds that you can see in the park, but also identifies the buildings that dot the skyline and other points of interest in the park.

ℯ Below the castle is **Turtle Pond** and to the left (looking down from the castle) is the Delacorte Theater, which is home to free Shakespeare in the Park performances during summer.

ℯ Off the West Side's Park Drive (at 79th St.) is the **Swedish Cottage Marionette Theater.** A touring company since 1939, the puppeteers settled into the Swedish Cottage in 1947 but continued to tour until 1971, when the cottage was turned into a theater, and the company kicked off it's first season at home with *Cinderella*. The cottage was renovated in 1997 to be more historically accurate, and, at the same time, state-of-the-art stage and lighting equipment was installed. The company does one production per year, which changes annually in October. Reservations are required (tickets are $5 per child and $6 per adult). Recent productions include *Hansel and Gretel* and *Peter Pan*.

ℯ If you were to exit the park on the 81st Street Path to the West Side (the one that runs south of the Great Lawn, across the Park Drive and west), you would come out at Central Park West and 81st Street, or the northern reaches of the **Museum of Natural History.**

e On the East Side, at about 81st Street, is **Cleopatra's Needle,** commonly referred to simply as "The Obelisk." The Obelisk was a gift from Egypt and is the oldest single nonnatural thing in Central Park. It dates back to 1600 B.C.

e On the other side of Park Drive is the unmistakable and unmissable **Metropolitan Museum of Art.** At 85th Street on the transverse (the roadway that runs from one side of the park to the other) is the Police Precinct.

e Just above the precinct, at about 87th Street, is the southern end of the **Central Park Reservoir,** where each day thousands of people come to run (including presidents when they're in town). The dirt track around the reservoir is 1.6 miles long, with two water fountains at the southern end. A nice view (and a favorite of tourists) is at the 90th Street entrance to the park. Cross the Park Drive and walk up the stairs to see the reservoir and the skyline that peeks out from the West Side.

e North of the reservoir are the **East Meadow, North Meadow Recreation Center (NMRC),** and **North Meadow** (all at approximately 97th Street, from east to west). The NMRC offers all sorts of wonderful free family programs (such as woods and water hikes, family sports and fitness), so be sure to call ahead or pick up a copy of the calendar at the Dairy. The North Meadow is a playing field, and both the North and East Meadows have been the site of many free concerts and speakers (Garth Brooks, Sting, and the Dalai Lama have been here).

e At East 105th Street on Fifth Avenue is the **Conservatory Garden.** This magnificent gated garden is a favorite destination of brides and grooms and wedding photographers— and it's easy to see why. You'll be hard-pressed to get out of the garden without seeing at least one, if not two or three, wedding parties in pose. Obviously, depending upon the season, the number of blooming plants will vary, but the roses are lovely, as are the blossoming trees and even the little lily pond.

℮ Even farther north, though very few tourists ever venture up here, is the **Lasker Pool and Rink** (in the summer it's an outdoor public pool and in the winter it's a skating rink) and the **Charles A. Dana Discovery Center.** The Dana Center offers free family programs, the favorite and most well known of which is probably the Catch-and-Release Fish Identification & Fly Tying Demonstrations, but Songs of Central Park and Beats of the Trees are also hits.

℮ Throughout the park are sprinkled twenty **playgrounds.** Most are on the periphery so that you can reach them easily from the streets and avenues without having to traipse into the center of the park for playtime. There are two north of Tavern on the Green, one just south of 72nd Street off Fifth Avenue, another at about 76th Street, one at the bottom of the Met, and one just above it. Four additional playgrounds are situated along Fifth Avenue just inside Central Park. On the West Side bordering Central Park West, going north from Tavern on the Green, is a playground (located at 81st St.) and two more around 85th Street. There is one at 90th Street near the reservoir (look for the Hippopotamus Playground), another at 91st Street, and a third at about 97th Street. Two more playgrounds north of 97th Street border the Park. For more details, stop by the Dairy, which has maps of Central Park, complete with playground locations. Also stop by the Dairy to pick up a schedule of free walking tours of Central Park, which go year-round, rain or shine (call 212-360-2726 two hours in advance for a status report if the weather is really extreme).

Top Ten Favorite Things to Do in Central Park

1. Ride the carousel

2. Visit the Central Park Zoo

3. Go ice-skating at Wollman Rink

4. Take a horse-drawn carriage ride

5. Look out from the Belvedere Castle

6. Take in a puppet show at the cottage

7. Play at the Hippopotamus Playground

8. Visit Strawberry Fields

9. Rent inline skates or bikes and ride along the park drive

10. Visit (and climb on) the statues of Alice in Wonderland

If you can believe it, these are really only the highlights of Central Park. There's always so much going on in all the different corners that it's easy to stumble upon something any day of the week.

An important word of caution: Central Park, though extremely safe during the daylight hours, should not be entered at night. It's not even that there have been many unfortunate incidents in Central Park in recent years, but it's nevertheless a vast open space that is deserted at night, and there's no reason to tempt fate. So unless you're attending one of the concerts or special events at night (to which hundreds and thousands of people flock and where you'll have plenty of company), it's best to stay out of the park from sunset to sunup.

Contact Information

Central Park Conservancy General Information: 212-360-3444; 800-281-5722 for the hearing impaired

Alice in Wonderland Statue: just north of Boat Pond

Belvedere Castle, The Henry Luce Nature Observatory (midpark at 79th St.): 212-772-0210

The Charles A. Dana Discovery Center (110th St. and 5th Ave.): 212-860-1370

The Dairy (midpark at 65th St.): 212-794-6564

Bicycle Rental (at the Boathouse): 212-517-3623

Boathouse (boat rentals and gondolas): 212-517-3623

Carousel: 212-879-0244

Conservatory Garden: 212-360-2766

Conservatory Water (Model Boat Pond at 74th St.): 212-673-1102

Fishing at Harlem Meer—Catch & Release: 212-860-1370

Harlem Meer Performance Festival: 212-860-1370

Horseback Riding (Claremont Stables): 212-724-5100

Metropolitan Opera in Central Park: 212-362-6000

New York Philharmonic in Central Park: 212-875-5709

North Meadow Recreation Center (midpark at 97th St.): 212-348-4867

Shakespeare in the Park (Delacorte at the Public Theater): 212-539-8655

Skating—Lasker Rink: 212-534-7639

Skating (ice skating & inline skating at Wollman Rink): 212-396-9203

SummerStage Music Festival: 212-360-2777

Swedish Cottage Marionette Theater: 212-988-9093

Tennis Courts: 212-280-0205

Weddings Hotline: 212-360-2766

Wildlife Center & Tisch Children's Zoo: 212-439-6500

The Central Park Conservancy is a not-for-profit organization founded in 1980 that manages Central Park under a contract with the City of New York/Parks & Recreation.

Other Parks

Battery Park
State Street and New York Harbor, FD

As you weave your way through the skyscrapers that make up downtown, it's hard to imagine that there is a park nearby. But there, on the West Side, hidden from view and tucked along the Hudson River, is Battery Park. You might find yourself here almost by accident if you're headed for the ferry to the Statue of Liberty (Castle Clinton National Monument—an early fort—is where you buy tickets). A fine place for a break, picnic, or stroll, Battery Park is well used by people from all walks of life (which is why it's such a great place for people-watching)—Wall Street's most promising and prominent, tourists, and residents of Battery Park City. If your kids are old enough to have seen *Desperately Seeking Susan* (Madonna's first, and most awful, movie), many scenes from the movie were filmed right here.

Transportation: *Subway:* N, R to Whitehall Street; 1, 9 to South Ferry; 4, 5 to Bowling Green

Prospect Park   718-965-8951
Grand Army Plaza (borders: Prospect Park West/
Parkside Ave./Flatbush Ave.), BR   www.prospectpark.org

Many Manhattanites never venture to parks beyond the borders of the small island. And it's a shame, because Prospect Park, approximately two-thirds the size (562 acres) of Central Park, is less crowded and equally as enticing as Central Park. Also designed by the famed team of Olmsted and Vaux after the completion of Central Park, Prospect Park is viewed by many people as being as nice as (if not nicer than) Central Park. Its fans consider it the jewel of Brooklyn.

From Grand Army Plaza, you'll enter through (under, around, in-sight-of) the Soldiers' and Sailors' Memorial Arch (1892) honoring Union veterans. Park highlights include the Litchfield Villa on Prospect Park West, the Lefferts Homestead (718-965-6505), and a Dutch farmhouse dating back to 1777 (it's now a museum specializing in children's education programs). The Friends' Cemetery, a Quaker burial ground, is worth a look if anyone in your group is into that sort of thing (ancient headstones can be pretty fascinating). And not to be missed are the carousel and the Prospect Park Wildlife Conservation Center (450 Flatbush Ave., 718-399-7339, www.wcs.org) where kids can be kids and enjoy the animals (wallabies, baboons, prairie dogs, red pandas, sea lions, and domestic animals) and special programs at the zoo ($3.50 adults, $1.25 seniors, $0.50 children 3–12, under 3 free).

Transportation: *Subway:* 2, 3 to Grand Army Plaza (walk 3 blocks down Plaza Street West to Prospect Park West)

Riverside Park
72nd to 158th Streets

Riverside Park is an oasis along the Hudson River. And guess who designed it? Once again, it's Olmsted and Vaux. Olmsted brilliantly planned this refuge for city dwellers in what is now one of the world's most populated urban environments. Especially nice for a walk along the waterfront (my favorite walk is along the public marina—where people actually live on houseboats!), there are also lots of places to play: basketball, tennis, and volleyball courts; softball fields; and playgrounds.

Snug Harbor Cultural Center   718-448-2500
1000 Richmond Terrace (between Tysen and
Snug Harbor Rd.), SI

Only about two miles from the ferry landing, Snug Harbor Cultural Center houses the Art Lab, a historical museum, Staten Island Botanical Garden, Staten Island Children's Museum, Performing Arts, Education Center, and the Newhouse Center for Contemporary Art. Entry to the grounds is free, and it's worth a wander around to have a look at the twenty-eight historic buildings, a collection of nineteenth-century Greek Revival, Beaux Arts, Second Empire, and Italianate architecture.

What used to be the Sailors' Snug Harbor maritime home and hospital for retired sailors is now a thriving 83-acre parkland and cultural center. It's best to call ahead before you make the trip to find out about special programs, concerts, activities, and exhibits, of which there are plenty, especially for kids.

Transportation: Staten Island Ferry to SI. Pick up the S-40 bus (ask to be let off at Snug Harbor) or a taxi.

Union Square Park
14th–17th Streets (north and south) and
Park Avenue South–Broadway (east and west), US

In reality, there isn't all that much park to Union Square Park, but to see it alive and bustling on greenmarket days (Monday, Wednesday, Friday, and Saturday), you can understand just how important this small park is to us city folk. Aside from the greenmarket, probably my favorite things about this park are the dog runs; there's one for big dogs and one for small. I enjoy staking out a nearby bench, perhaps with a drink, a friend, or both, and watching the dogs at play (after all, they live in a crowded city, too). If that's a little too mundane for your kids (or they're petrified of dogs, as I was as a tot), the park is often full of performers

Union Square Green-market

of various sorts, and it's a welcome place to take a break in the midst of all the hustle and bustle.

Transportation: *Subway:* 4, 5, 6, L, N, R to 14th Street/ Union Square

Washington Square Park
At the bottom of Fifth Avenue, bordered by Washington Square North, Washington Square South, MacDougal Street, Wooster Street, GV

This is another park without all that much green, but it is an open area (with dog runs) and lots of activity. Many famous movies have been filmed here, including *Searching for Bobby Fisher* (this is where all of the chess game scenes in the park take place—look around, it's for real) and the opener in *When Harry Met Sally* (when Meg Ryan, after driving from University of Chicago with Billy Crystal, drops him off in front of the Washington Arch). Older kids might be impressed by the Greenwich Village scene that thrives here: Lots of kids dressed in black with pierced everything, New York University students, skateboarders, musicians, and the occasional unsavory character. Although perfectly safe during the day, this park is best avoided after dark.

Transportation: *Subway:* A, C, E, B, D, F, Q to West 4th Street/Washington Square

Wave Hill   718-549-3200
West 249th or 252nd Street (at Independence Ave.), BX
www.wavehill.org

This 28-acre public garden and cultural center (situated north of Manhattan in the Bronx) overlooks the Hudson River. If you should be so lucky as to visit on a sunny afternoon, a crisp autumn day, or a balmy spring morning, you'll perhaps see why the likes of Mark Twain and Theodore Roosevelt decided to make their homes here. Perhaps because of its location, this remains one of the city's best-kept secrets. A dream for botanical garden lovers, Wave Hill offers all sorts of special programs for children and families (like Family Art Project, where kids explore the gardens with an artist/naturalist and then create paintings and collages with their own inspiration). Other programs touch upon forestry, horticulture, environmental education, performing arts, and landscape history.

Hours: Tuesday through Sunday 9:00 A.M.–4:30 P.M.; extended in summer (check ahead)

Admission: $4 adults, $2 seniors and students; free in winter and Saturday and Tuesday mornings during summer

Transportation: *Subway:* 1, 9 subway to 231st Street; transfer to the bus, Bx7 or Bx10; ask to be let off by Wave Hill. Liberty Lines' Manhattan-Riverdale Express *Bus:* (718-652-8400) BxM1 or BxM2 to 252nd Street and walk west across the parkway bridge, following the signs.

Theater and Shows

Many people feel that a trip to New York City isn't complete without a visit to a Broadway show. But with tickets nowadays starting at $60 for the cheapest seats, and with the most desirable shows requiring booking months in advance (or payment of exorbitant markups to ticket agents), you need to have a plan.

The two most effective strategies for getting tickets are:

1. Plan far, far ahead—this will allow you to get good seats at exactly the show you want, though you'll pay full price.

2. Make a last-minute decision—in which case your reward for flexibility will be great savings.

The best ways to get discounted tickets:

@ The Theater Development Fund (TDF) operates two TKTS half-price booths, one in Duffy Square (five blocks straight up Broadway from Times Square) and the other at the South Street Seaport. (It goes without saying that the location at Two World Trade Center, listed in many out-dated guides, no longer exists.) You can't decide what you're going to see in advance—you just have to go to one of the two TKTS booths, read what's on the board for the day, and wing it. It helps to familiarize yourself with all the major shows in advance (pick up a copy of *New York Magazine* or *Time Out New York*) because you'll have to make an on-the-spot, split-second decision. Tickets for Broadway and off-Broadway performances are half price (plus a service charge of $2.50 per ticket). Cash only. Call 212-221-0885 or visit www.tdf.org for the most up-to-date information. (*Note:* Every Monday afternoon, the TDF Web site posts the shows that were available at the TKTS booths during the previous week. This may help give you some ideas of what might be available.)

@ For the Duffy Square TKTS branch, located at 47th Street and Broadway, hours are Monday through Saturday (for evening tickets) 3 P.M.–8 P.M., Wednesday and Saturday (for matinee tickets) 10 A.M.–2 P.M., Sunday (matinee and evening tickets) 11 A.M. to closing.

ℰ The Lower Manhattan TKTS branch is at the corner of Front Street and John Street at the South Street Seaport (the southeast corner of 199 Water Street in the building that also houses Abercrombie and Fitch). In addition to day-of-performance tickets, a limited number of matinee tickets are sold one day prior to performance date at the Lower Manhattan TKTS only. Hours are Monday through Saturday 11:00 A.M.–6:00 P.M.; Sunday 11:00 A.M.–3:30 P.M. Unlike the Duffy Square branch, the Lower Manhattan TKTS doesn't have special hours for sale of matinee versus evening tickets—all tickets are sold at all times. Lines also tend to be quite a bit shorter (though you should still plan to spend a half-hour or more waiting) at the Lower Manhattan branch.

Remember, though, Broadway isn't the be-all and end-all of New York theater. The City is also rich in off-Broadway and off-off-Broadway theaters, where the spectacles tend to be less elaborate and less expensive, but no less fun. And there are also some theaters that cater specifically to kids and families. Sometimes you'll find the best experiences at these alternate venues. For current listings see *New York Magazine, Time Out New York, the Village Voice,* or the Friday *New York Times* "Weekend" section.

Insider's Tip

"Afternoon matinee performances are usually much better for most kids than evening performances. At night, a show may not end until 10:30 P.M. or later, and kids can get tired, cranky, and fidgety. Most shows have their matinees on Wednesday and on weekends." —*Jane Matthews, educator*

Theaters for Kids and Families

★ *New Victory Theater*   646-223-3020
229 West 42nd Street (between Seventh and Eighth Aves.), TD
www.newvictory.org

Theater targeted exclusively toward kids and families. A range of performances, including plays, music, dance, puppetry, mime, and circus arts. Performers come from around the world to perform at New Victory.

Kay Playhouse at Hunter College   212-772-4448
68th Street (corner of Lexington Ave.), UES

Eccentric performances using paper bags and cardboard boxes as props. January through March only.

★ *Tada! Youth Ensemble Theater*   212-627-1732
15 West 28th Street (between Fifth Ave. and Broadway), GP
www.tadatheater.com

Performances by kids for kids, as opposed to most children's theater, which uses adult actors. The performances are very professional.

Theatreworks USA   212-627-7373
2162 Broadway (at West 76th St.), UWS
www.theatreworksusa.org

Classic children's plays (*Oliver Twist*, *Treasure Island*) every weekend from September through March.

The Arts

New York City is the world capital of the performing arts, and you could easily see a different musical performance every night of the year. As with all aspects of planning your vacation, when selecting arts performances, it helps to do your homework and be selective. *Time Out New York* tends to have the best arts listings, along with *New York Magazine* and the Friday *New York Times* "Weekend" section.

Music

Brooklyn Academy of Music	718-636-4111
30 Lafayette Avenue, BR	**www.bam.org**

BAM, as we call it, is a mecca for dance, film, music, theater, and opera seven days a week. Though you'll have to schlep to Brooklyn to experience the wonders of BAM, it's almost always worth the trip. A real gem for those who are willing to wander off the beaten path, BAM offers several family-appropriate performances each month.

Carnegie Hall	212-247-7800
156 West 57th Street (between Broadway and	
Seventh Ave.), MTW	**www.carnegiehall.org**

One of America's most beloved and beautiful concert halls, the William Barnet Tuthill–designed Carnegie Hall is one of the most acoustically wonderful performance venues in the world. Acts range from classical to jazz. Carnegie Hall presents several Saturday afternoon children's concerts each year—call for schedules. There's also an hour-long tour available Monday, Tuesday, Thursday, and Friday at 11:30 A.M., 2:00 P.M., and 3:00 P.M. (performance schedule permitting).

Learning Tip
Named for Andrew Carnegie, who paid for most of the construction, Carnegie Hall opened in 1891. If you had been alive then, you could have gone to Carnegie Hall to see Tchaikovsky conduct his own works!

Lincoln Center   212-875-5000
Broadway, from 62nd to 65th Sts., and beyond, UWS
www.lincolncenter.org

Lincoln Center took six years (1962–1968) to build and is currently the largest performing arts center in the world. The various venues within have a total of 18,000 seats. Standing on
Broadway (the avenue) and facing the fountain, to your left is
the New York State Theater, where the New York City Ballet and
New York City Opera perform. The central building is the Metropolitan Opera House, home to the Metropolitan Opera and
American Ballet Theatre (the murals you see through the arched
windows are by Marc Chagall). To your right is Avery Fisher
Hall, where you'll find the New York Philharmonic Orchestra.
Also within the complex are several additional performance areas
for theater, film, and music. Lincoln Center has several very ac-
tive youth programs, including the Little Orchestra Society and
Young People's Concerts at Avery Fisher Hall; Growing Up With
Opera at the Metropolitan Opera House; and Jazz for Young
People and Meet the Music at Alice Tully Hall. And of course
there are frequent tours. Call for schedules.

92nd Street Y   212-415-5607
1395 Lexington Avenue, UM   www.92ndsty.org

A major New York cultural institution, this is a great place to expose kids to the riches of New York intellectual life—you won't
find many tourists here. The Y is famous for its lectures and interviews, readings by award-wining authors, dance performances,
and concerts, including classical, cabaret, jazz, and popular
music.

Radio City Music Hall   212-247-4777
1260 Sixth Avenue (at 50th St.), MT   212-632-4041
www.radiocity.com

With 6,000 seats, Radio City is America's largest indoor theater. The chandeliers weigh 2 tons! Best known for the Rockettes and its Christmas and Easter extravaganzas, Radio City also plays host to concerts and events year-round. One-hour tours ($16 adults, $10 children under 12) usually leave from the main lobby every half-hour Monday through Saturday 10 A.M.–5 P.M. and Sunday 11 A.M.–5 P.M. Call for schedules.

Dance

Alvin Ailey American Dance Theater   212-247-0430
Performances at City Center   212-767-0590
130 West 56th Street, MTW   schedules and details
www.alvinailey.org

The amazing Alvin Ailey dancers—unquestionably the foremost African American dance company—perform at City Center as well as at other venues, including Lincoln Center.

American Ballet Theater   212-362-6000
Lincoln Center (see Music) at the Metropolitan Opera House
www.abt.org

Though the company is artistically considered the lesser (by just a little bit) of the two Lincoln Center ballet troupes, many viewers find these performances more pleasant and accessible (there isn't as much experimental dance going on here as at the New York City Ballet). Performance season is May through June.

Joyce Theater   212-242-0800
175 Eighth Avenue (at 19th St.), CH   www.joyce.org

A world-class modern dance theater, with a particularly strong children's outreach program.

New York City Ballet   212-870-5570
Lincoln Center (see Music) at the New York State Theater
www.nycballet.com

The New York City Ballet needs no introduction. This is where the legendary George Balanchine created his masterworks, and where *The Nutcracker* is performed every December. Just be sure you choose your show carefully—many of the performances are very modern and abstract, and may not appeal to kids other than die-hard dance fanatics. Performance seasons are April through June and November through February.

Film

You'll find no shortage of movie theaters in New York City (all local papers have complete listings, as does 777-FILM), but frankly it seems a waste of time to see the same movie in New York City that you could see at your local cineplex. There are, however, three gigantic IMAX theaters in the area, which you might not find as easily at home.

IMAX Dome Theater at the   201-200-1000
Liberty Science Center
Liberty State Park, Jersey City, NJ   www.lsc.org

See the separate entry on Liberty Science Center under Museums.

IMAX Theater at the   212-769-5100
American Museum of Natural History
79th Street (at Central Park West), UWS   **www.amnh.org**

See the separate entry on the Museum of Natural History under Museums.

★ *Sony IMAX Theater*   212-336-5000
68th Street (at Broadway), UWS

The biggest (eight stories high) and best, with many 3-D offerings.

In addition, check with Lincoln Center (see Music) for the latest schedules for the weekend Movies for Kids series, which emphasizes the classics. There are also weekend children's film series at the Metropolitan Museum of Art (see Museums) and the New York Public Library (see City Sights).

Puppetry

In Central Park, don't miss the Crowtations on weekend afternoons at the Bethesda Fountain (at the middle of the 72nd St. transverse) and the shows at the Swedish Cottage (Park Drive West at 81st St.). See Central Park.

Lenny Suib Puppet Playhouse   212-369-8890
Asphalt Green Center
555 East 90th Street (between York and East End Aves.), UM
www.asphaltgreen.org

Saturday puppet shows (at 10:30 A.M., 12:00 P.M., and 1:30 P.M.) from the legendary Lenny Suib, who has been delighting audiences for decades.

Puppetworks—Park Slope   718-965-3391
338 Sixth Avenue (at 4th St.), Park Slope, BR
www.puppetworks.org

Classic fairy and folk tales performed daily. Puppetworks uses all hand-carved wooden marionettes. Shows sell out far in advance, especially on weekdays when school groups often take up all the seats. So plan ahead. Audience members can mingle with the puppets and puppeteers after the show.

Circuses

Three major circus troupes come to New York City annually. Locations and show times vary, so check with each circus for up-to-the-minute schedule information.

The Big Apple Circus   212-268-2500
ww.bigapplecircus.org

The most kid-friendly and intimate of the New York circuses, everybody loves this one.

Cirque du Soleil   www.cirquedusoleil.com

The famous French circus, now a multinational franchise. It's the most adult of the circuses, and younger children may even find parts of it too scary.

Ringling Bros. Barnum &   800-755-4000
Bailey Circus   www.ringling.com

The original three-ring circus extravaganza. It can be a bit overwhelming—it's huge—but it's not called the Greatest Show on Earth for nothing. At Madison Square Garden every spring.

Just for Kids–Or Maybe Not!

Crafts

| *The Craft Studio* | 212-831-6626 |

1657 Third Avenue (between 92nd and 93rd Sts.), UES

Stop in for an arts and crafts project, and the kids take their completed work with them. Each child selects a plain plaster ($11.95 and up), wood, or terra-cotta ($14.95 and up) piece. You pay by the piece, and everything is covered in that price, including supplies and time. Kids can paint, glue, sparkle, and adorn their piece until they are satisfied with the outcome. Afterward the art is sprayed with a shellac coating and voilà! The project is ready for the road.

| ★ *Little Shop of Plaster* | 212-717-6636 |

431 East 73rd Street (between First and York Aves.), UES

If I had to choose one of the three shops for a craft outing, I'd most likely go with this one, especially if the kids are varied in age. It offers a variety of materials to work with—pottery (which starts at $17.95), T-shirts ($14.95 and up), and plaster pieces ($11.95 and up). Your artist can take the piece home when it's complete, except for the pottery, which has to be fired here (and usually takes a week, but shipping arrangements can be made).

Our Name Is Mud

1566 Second Avenue (between   212-570-6868
    81st and 82nd Sts.), UES
506 Amsterdam Avenue (between   212-579-5575
    84th and 85th Sts.), UWS
59 Greenwich Avenue (Seventh   212-647-7899
    Ave. at 11th St.), WV
www.ournameismud.com

Kids love this! Our Name Is Mud is a great activity for any age kids, especially on a rainy day. You buy a piece of ready-made pottery and paint it at the "Paint Bar" any way you want. You pay for the piece and $5 per half-hour for the time. The only catch is that usually the pieces aren't ready for a week (because they have to fire them). If your visit is a short one, call in advance and ask about exceptions—sometimes pieces get fired more quickly, depending upon volume.

Makeup Makeovers

One of the greatest activities of all time for young and teen girls has got to be the opportunity to have a makeover. Girls who wear no makeup at all and those who wear it all the time will appreciate the exercise because it's so much fun. All of the big department stores do makeovers by appointment (and charge a fee), and some do casual makeup application at the counter if you catch a representative in the right mood (no appointment). A few places that are especially good with kids follow. In all instances, be sure to *call well in advance for an appointment* to avoid disappointment.

Barney's	212-826-8900
Madison Avenue (at 61st St.), UES	

If you're planning on buying any makeup, the women who work the makeup counters at Barney's are very generous with their time. When I went to buy makeup for my wedding at the Clinique counter, the woman who helped me was extremely kind and patient (she didn't talk down to me) and helped me not only with lipstick (about which I was totally ignorant), but with some other products as well. Even though I'm an extreme cynic (I know that the more she helps me, the more she sells and the better for her), I appreciated her efforts and attention. She did her job well, and I walked away a satisfied (and made-over) customer—having only bought one lipstick. For the best shot at the most attention (smaller crowds), go during the day and midweek, when only the idle rich (and the other half of New York with odd schedules) are at play.

Bloomingdale's	212-355-5900
1000 Third Avenue (between 59th and 60th Sts.), UES	

Numerous makeup artists work their magic in the Bloomingdale's makeup department. You might want to describe your daughter a bit when you make your reservation (age, if she wears makeup, and how much) so that you get the best person for the job.

Face, Stockholm	
226 Columbus Avenue	**212-769-1420**
(at 70th St.), UWS	
687 Madison Avenue (at 62nd St.), UES	**212-207-8833**
110 Prince Street (at Green St.), SH	**212-966-9110**

The staff could not be nicer at this minimalist makeup gallery. They look a little bit intimidating from the outside, but the moment you enter the store, you're made to feel welcome.

Henri Bendel	212-247-1100
712 Fifth Avenue (at 55th St.), MTE	

Ok, so I admit it. This is where I had my makeover when I turned sixteen. My older cousin, who lived in Brooklyn at the time, decided that it would be the perfect gift for my sweet sixteen—me, the short-haired athlete who could barely spare the time to towel dry my hair (let alone apply makeup). She took me to Bendel's, a store I had never so much as set foot in, and we had a total field day. Because of my coloring (fair skin, fair hair), I didn't end up looking that much different than when I started, but that was a good thing—they checked me out, realized I had never worn any makeup at all, and worked from there. Of course, I got suckered into buying all sorts of expensive and fancy makeup (with my hard-earned babysitting money), but you don't have to, and to this day I still use one of the products that I discovered there.

> ### *Laura Geller Make-Up Studios*   212-570-LIPS
> **1044 Lexington Avenue (between 74th and 75th Sts.), UES**

At Geller, beauty is the name of the game. Laura is the big gun here, so if you want a lesson with her, you'll have to pay big bucks to get it ($250 for an hour). But there are also plenty of other makeup artists in the studio with whom you can book an appointment, and the price tag, though still a bit steep, is $150. They also offer makeup parties for children and teens. While you're at it, if anyone needs a facial, they do those too. Call ahead for appointments.

High-Tech Fun

> ### *Lazer Park*   212-398-3060
> **163 West 46th Street (at Broadway), MTW**

Lazer Park's digital entertainment center includes high-tech hits like Lazer Tag, BattleTech, and loads of outrageous video games.

> ### *Sony Wonder Technology Lab,*   212-833-8100
> ### *Sony Plaza*
> **550 Madison Avenue (at 56th St.), MTE**
> **www.sonywondertechlab.com**

Sony Wonder is a hit with kids of all ages (except perhaps for pre-kindergarten). It's a cutting-edge, hands-on, interactive technology zone, and it's free! After kids have personalized a "swipe card" at "Log-in," they are free to explore communications technology as a "Media Trainee." Create a musical composition, take a cyber journey, examine the inner workings of innovative technology, experiment with robotics, or experience High Definition in the seventy-two-seat theater. And, upon "Log-out," each kid is presented with a graduation certificate for becoming a technology pro. There are also scheduled special events, so call or check the Web calendar for listings.

Hours: Tuesday through Saturday 10 A.M.–6 P.M., Thursday 10 A.M.–8 P.M., Sunday 12 P.M.–6 P.M.

Admission: Free

Transportation: *Bus:* M1, M2, M3, M4, M5, M57. *Subway:* 4, 5, 6 to 59th Street; E, F to Fifth Avenue

Helpful Hint

For kids who can't live without their video game fix, one of the best selections by far is at ESPN Zone in Times Square. For more information, see the Theme Restaurants section.

Participatory Sports

Chelsea Piers   212-336-6666
23rd Street (on the Hudson River, from 17th to 23rd Sts.), CH
www.chelseapiers.com

Chelsea Piers has filled a gap in NYC so big that no one seems to be able to figure out how we managed without this place for so long. I guess it's the old story of you don't know what you're missing until you have it. An enormous 30—acre "sports village," Chelsea Piers has something for everyone in the family. In no other single place in New York City will you find such extensive facilities and equipment dedicated to sports and fitness as here. Choose from among golf, soccer, dance, gymnastics, batting, inline skating, bowling, rock climbing, skate park with ramp, swimming, and lacrosse. Starting to get the idea? Prices vary (and they do run high), so to avoid disappointment and bankruptcy, call in advance for prices and the children's schedule.

Claremont Riding Academy   212-724-5100
175 West 89th Street (between Columbus and Amsterdam Aves.), UWS

Skilled riders, ages 10 and up, can take a horse out for a ride in Central Park. Claremont is one of the City's unexpected finds. There, right in the middle of the Upper West Side, is a stable and riding academy. These same folks that teach city kids to ride can also set you and your family up with horses for an outing in the park. You've got to follow their rules, which they'll run through with you over the phone (when you call at least two days in advance to reserve) and when you get there. Even though the stable's hours are long, park rides are only allowed during daylight hours. Therefore, during the winter, horses have to be in by 4:30 P.M. And safety is a big issue for the staff at Claremont—no riding in the park when the ground is icy and no outings when the mercury is above 90 degrees. Helmets (you can borrow one or bring your own) and hard shoes are required and no shorts or sneakers are allowed (riders will be turned away if they are not appropriately attired). Riders must be experienced in English style; there are no Western saddles available. For avid equestrians, riding in Central Park, with the leaves turning red, yellow, and orange all around, is one of life's great moments.

Hours: Monday through Friday 6 A.M.–10 P.M., Saturday and Sunday 6 A.M.–5 P.M.

Cost: $50 per hour per horse

Transportation: *Subway:* 1, 9, B, C to 86th Street

For inline skate rentals, see Blades Board & Skate (under Sports) in chapter 7.

Rockefeller Plaza Rink   212-332-7654
Fifth Avenue (between 49th and 50th Sts.), MTE

This is undeniably the most glamorous, famous, and romantic ice-skating rink in the city, and maybe even the world. The stuff that Hollywood movies have been made of, lacing up skates and going for a spin is sort of like living in a dream. It's especially wonderful when the Christmas tree is set up and illuminated. The best time to go is early in the morning during the week, before the crowds come. I've often seen people skating before work, and the rink is virtually empty. By far the worst time to skate is during the Christmas/winter vacation, but if you must, call for hours and rise and shine to beat the crowds. Hot Chocolate at Serendipity (if it's open yet) is a perfect finish to the experience.

Admission: The prices seem to be changeable (in the upward direction) but last word was: Monday through Thursday $8.50 adults, $7.00 kids under 12; Friday through Sunday $11.00 adults, $7.50 kids. Rentals are available. Call for updated details on hours (and prices).

Transportation: *Bus:* M1, M2, M3, M4 to 49th Street. *Subway:* B, D, F, Q to 47th–50th/Rockefeller Center.

See also Central Park, under Parks, for ice-skating.

Family-Friendly Nightlife: Comedy Clubs

Nightlife in major cities isn't typically family-friendly, centering as it does around the bar scene. But New York's multitude of comedy clubs can provide the perfect evening of entertainment for families, especially those traveling with teens. Be sure to call ahead and learn about the act and the club's specific policies. Some comedians can get pretty raunchy; others keep it clean. It's also important to call ahead because clubs change their admissions policies from time to time, or allow under-18 customers only on certain days or at certain times.

Caroline's Comedy Club	212-757-4100
1626 Broadway (between 49th and 50th Sts.), MT	

Very slick, modern club. Entertainers have included Joy Behar, Sandra Bernhard, and Gilbert Gottfried.

Helpful Hint

For families traveling with independent teens who have a particular interest in other forms of nightlife, there are some music and dance clubs that allow underage patrons to attend at certain times and on certain nights of the week. These fluctuate wildly, so the best way to find out what's going on when you're in town is to check *Time Out New York* and then call the club in question to inquire about its policy.

Chicago City Limits   212-888-5233
1105 First Avenue (at East 61st St.), UES

Wonderful improvisational comedy with lots of audience participation.

Comedy Cellar   212-254-3480
117 MacDougal Street (between 3rd and Bleecker Sts.), GV

A real old-time comedy club in a basement, in business for twenty years.

Comic Strip Live   212-861-9386
1568 Second Avenue (between 81st and 82nd Sts.), UES

Reliable comedy in a neighborhood bar/lounge atmosphere with several acts nightly.

Dangerfield's   212-593-1650
1118 First Avenue (between 61st and 62nd Sts.), UES

It is indeed owned by Rodney himself.

Freestyle Repertory Theater	212-642-8202
Various locations	

An utterly zany improv company.

Gotham Comedy Club	212-367-9000
34 West 22nd Street (between 5th and 6th Aves.), GP	

This Flatiron District club has hosted comedians ranging from Chris Rock to David Brenner.

Professional Sports

There's nothing like attending a sporting event in New York City, where fans are surely the world's most enthusiastic. It's usually pretty easy to get early-season baseball tickets in the upper decks, but basketball and football can be more of a challenge (in some cases impossible without resorting to scalpers). In any event, for the best seats, it's best to plan far ahead.

Baseball

If you're in New York during baseball season, even if you're not a die-hard baseball fan, I strongly recommend attendance at a Mets or Yankees home game as one of the best New York experiences available. I suggest you bring some snacks and sandwiches to avoid paying outrageous sums for stadium junk food, and that you agree with the kids in advance that you won't be purchasing overpriced souvenirs at the ballpark. You can get all that stuff in Manhattan at the clubhouse shops (or you can buy hats and T-shirts for a fraction of the cost, about $5, on the street; see chapter 7).

The New York Mets	718-507-TIXX
Shea Stadium, Flushing, Q	**www.mets.com**

To get to Shea Stadium, take the #7 train (it stops along 42nd Street in Manhattan) eastbound (toward Queens) to the Willets

Point/Shea Stadium stop. Allow for about forty-five minutes on the train. There's also a quicker Long Island Railroad commuter train that departs from Penn Station, but you get more of the true fan experience when you take the subway. Shea Stadium also has ample parking for those with cars.

The New York Yankees	**718-293-4300**
Yankee Stadium, BX	**www.yankees.com**

To get to Yankee Stadium, take the #4 (Lexington Avenue), C (Eighth Avenue), or D (Sixth/Eighth Avenue) trains to 161st Street/Yankee Stadium. Though the neighborhood isn't great, it's safe enough when you're traveling with 60,000 other fans. Driving to Yankee Stadium is not advised, because the parking situation is very inconvenient. *Note:* For the diehard fan or baseball junkie, there is a fascinating one-hour Yankee Stadium tour at noon every day (except game days) in season. Check the Web site or call for details.

Basketball

The New York Knickerbockers (Knicks)
Madison Square Garden Center
Seventh Avenue (from 31st to 33rd Sts.)
212-465-6741
212-465-MSG1 for Madison Square Garden info
www.nba.com/knicks
www.thegarden.com

The New York Liberty (WNBA)
Madison Square Garden
212-465-6741
212-465-MSG1 for Madison Square Garden info
www.wnba.com/liberty
www.thegarden.com

All tickets for events at Madison Square Garden are sold through Ticketmaster (212-307-7171).

The New Jersey Nets
Continental Airlines Arena
East Rutherford, NJ
800-7NJ-NETS
www.nba.com/nets

Hockey

New York Islanders
Nassau Coliseum (Long Island)
800-882-ISLES
www.newyorkislanders.com

New York Rangers
Madison Square Garden
212-465-6741
212-465-MSG1 for Madison Square Garden info
www.newyorkrangers.com
www.thegarden.com

New Jersey Devils
Continental Airlines Arena
East Rutherford, NJ
201-935-6050
www.newjerseydevils.com

Transportation: For all events at the stadiums and arenas in East Rutherford, NJ (Giants Stadium, Meadowlands, Continental Airlines Arena), buses run from the Port Authority Bus Terminal, located at 42nd Street and Eighth Avenue. New Jersey Transit buses leave two hours before game time, and return up to one hour after the game. $3.25 one-way fare. Twenty minute travel time. For more information, call 212-564-8484.

Football

You'll need good connections or a very large wallet to pry loose even the least desirable football tickets, but for those who simply must attend . . .

The New York Giants
Giants Stadium
East Rutherford, NJ
201-935-8111
www.giants.com

The New York Jets
Meadowlands Arena
East Rutherford, NJ
516-560-8200
www.newyorkjets.com

Soccer

Metrostars
Giants Stadium
East Rutherford, NJ
201-935-8111
www.metrostars.com

Tennis

If your kids are into tennis, this is the most incredible spectator tennis experience available in America. Tickets are wickedly expensive, though.

U.S. Open
USTA National Tennis Center
Flushing Meadows-Corona Park
Flushing, NY
212-239-6250 U.S. Open ticket info
888-OPEN-TIX (888-673-6849) tickets through Telecharge
Follow the directions to Shea Stadium.

Flea Markets

Visiting New York's flea markets is a great way to combine the best of sightseeing, shopping, and people-watching. The following are some of the best.

Annex Antique Fair & Flea Market   212-243-5343
(Chelsea Flea Market)
Sixth Avenue (at 26th St.), CH

Antique furniture, jewelry, used clothing, old books, and bric-a-brac (and lots of it) fill the parking lot. Prices are often sharply reduced at dusk.

Hours: Saturday and Sunday, sunrise to sunset.

NoHo Flea Market
Broadway (between East Fourth and Great Jones Sts.), EV

As a teenager, this was always one of my favorite markets, especially around Christmas time. Jewelry, T-shirts, funky clothes, sky's the limit. Perfect for bringing hip gifts home to give to (and impress) friends.

Hours: Saturday and Sunday

SoHo Antique Fair   212-682-2000
Broadway and Grand Street, SH

A wide range of goods—especially antiques and crafts.

Hours: Saturday and Sunday

Spring Street Flea Market
Spring and Wooster Streets, SH

I've browsed this crowded SoHo lot for more than fifteen years. The stock is changeable, depending upon the season—gloves and hats in winter are standard, as are sunglasses and silver jewelry in summer. Good entertainment and not as pricey as the rest of SoHo.

Hours: Saturday and Sunday

West 76th Street Flea Market (Greenflea)
Columbus and 76th Street, UWS

A combination of furniture, vintage clothes and jewels, farm-fresh produce, and crafts, there's nothing especially earth-shattering at this market, but the homemade lemonade is really good.

Hours: Saturday

INDEX TO ATTRACTIONS/ACTIVITIES BY NEIGHBORHOOD

Participatory Sports
Chelsea Piers (p. 269)

EAST VILLAGE

Flea Markets
NoHo Flea Market (p. 277)

FINANCIAL DISTRICT

City Sights
★ Brooklyn Bridge (p. 172)
★ Ellis Island (p. 174)
New York Stock Exchange (p. 177)
South Street Seaport (p. 181)
★ Statue of Liberty (p. 182)

Museums
Museum of Jewish Heritage—A Living Memorial to the Holocaust (p. 207)
National Museum of the American Indian (p. 220)
New York City Police Museum (p. 210)

Parks
Battery Park (p. 251)

GRAMERCY PARK/FLATIRON

City Sights
Flatiron Building (p. 176)
★ Theodore Roosevelt Birthplace (p. 183)

Comedy Clubs
Gotham Comedy Club (p. 273)

Theaters for Families
★ Tada! Youth Ensemble Theater (p. 258)

GREENWICH VILLAGE

Comedy Clubs
Comedy Cellar (p. 272)

Museums
Forbes Magazine Galleries (p. 216)

Parks
Washington Square Park (p. 254)

LITTLE ITALY

Museums
Children's Museum of the Arts (p. 214)

LOWER EAST SIDE

Museum
★ Lower East Side Tenement Museum (p. 205)

MIDTOWN

City Sights
Madison Square Garden, The New York Knicks, etc. (p. 274)
Rockefeller Center (p. 179)

Comedy Clubs
Caroline's Comedy Club (p. 271)

Museums
Whitney Museum of American Art at Philip Morris (p. 213)

Music
Radio City Music Hall (p. 261)

Museums
Museum for African Art
(p. 219)
★ New York City Fire Museum (p. 209)

STATEN ISLAND
Parks
Snug Harbor Cultural Center (p. 253)

THEATER DISTRICT
Theaters for Families
★ New Victory Theater
(p. 258)

TIMES SQUARE
City Sights
Times Square (p. 184)

UNION SQUARE
Parks
Union Square Park (p. 253)

UPPER EAST SIDE
City Sights
Temple Emanu-El (p. 183)
Comedy Clubs
Chicago City Limits (p. 272)
Comic Strip Live (p. 272)
Dangerfield's (p. 272)
Crafts
The Craft Studio (p. 265)
★ Little Shop of Plaster
(p. 265)
Our Name Is Mud (p. 265)

Makeup Makeovers
Barney's (p. 266)
Bloomingdale's (p. 267)
Face, Stockholm (p. 267)
Laura Geller Make-Up Studios (p. 268)
Museums
Asia Society (p. 214)
Cooper-Hewitt National
Design Museum (p. 215)
The Frick Collection
(p. 216)
International Center of
Photography (p. 217)
The Jewish Museum
(p. 217)
★ Metropolitan Museum of
Art (p. 192)
El Museo del Barrio
(p. 219)
Museum of the City of New
York (p. 206)
★ Solomon R. Guggenheim Museum (p. 211)
Whitney Museum of American Art (p. 212)
Theaters for Families
Kay Playhouse at Hunter
College (p. 258)

UPPER MANHATTAN
Museums
The Cloisters (p. 215)
Music
92nd Street Y (p. 260)
Parks
Riverside Park (p. 252)
Puppetry
Lenny Suib Puppet Playhouse (p. 263)

UPPER WEST SIDE

City Sights
> ★ Cathedral of Saint John the Divine (p. 173)
> Shearith Israel Spanish and Portuguese Synagogue (p. 180)
> Temple Emanu-El (p. 183)

Crafts
> Our Name Is Mud (p. 265)

Dance
> American Ballet Theater (p. 261)
> New York City Ballet (p. 262)

Film
> IMAX Theater at the American Museum of Natural History (p. 263)
> ★ Sony IMAX Theater (p. 263)

Flea Markets
> West 76th Street Flea Market (p. 278)

Makeup Makeovers
> Face, Stockholm (p. 267)

Museums
> ★ American Museum of Natural History and Rose Center for Earth and Space (p. 186)
> ★ Children's Museum of Manhattan (p. 200)
> Museum of American Folk Art (p. 220)
> The New-York Historical Society (p. 222)

Music
> Lincoln Center (p. 260)

Parks
> Riverside Park (p. 252)

Participatory Sports
> Claremont Riding Academy (p. 270)

Theaters for Families
> Theatreworks USA (p. 258)

WEST VILLAGE

Crafts
> Our Name Is Mud (p. 265)

For Circuses, see the listing on p. 264.
For Galleries, see the listing by neighborhood on pp. 224–229.
For information on Professional Sports, see pp. 273–276.

CHAPTER 6

Dining

Dining

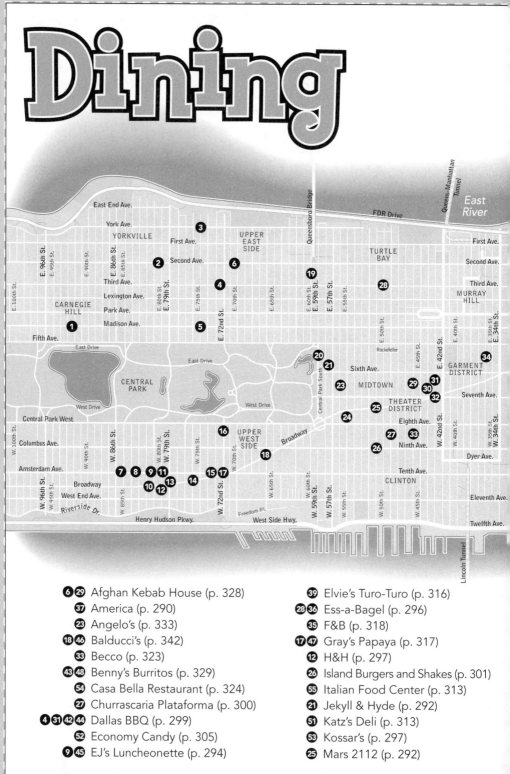

Map shows highlights only. See chapter text for more listings.

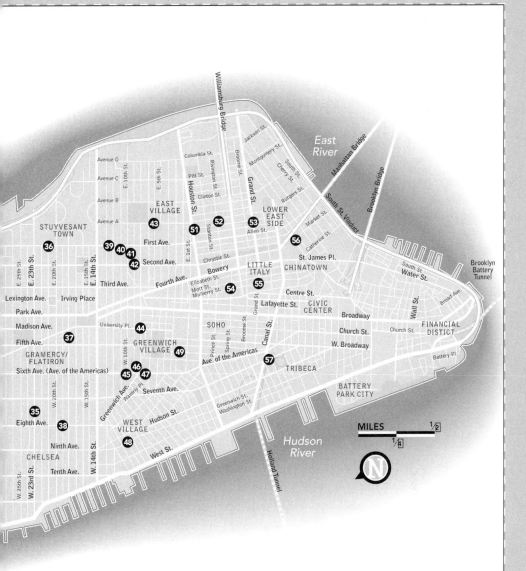

Williamsburg Bridge

East River

Jackson St.
Columbia St.
Broome St.
Montgomery St.
Cherry St.
South St.
Rutgers St.

Manhattan Bridge

Brooklyn Bridge

Avenue D
Avenue C
E. 10th St.
Avenue B
E. 5th St.
Pitt St.
Houston St.
Clinton St.

EAST VILLAGE

Avenue A

43

51 **52** **53**

Market St.

South St. Viaduct

STUYVESANT TOWN

36

First Ave.

39 **40** **61**

Second Ave.

42

Chrystie St.

Bowery

Elizabeth St.

54

Stanton St.
Allen St.

56

LOWER EAST SIDE

St. James Pl.

Catherine St.

South St.
Water St.

Brooklyn Battery Tunnel

E. 25th St.
E. 23rd St.
E. 20th St.
E. 15th St.
E. 14th St.

Third Ave.

Fourth Ave.

Mott St.
Mulberry St.

55

LITTLE ITALY

CHINATOWN

Centre St.

Lexington Ave.

Irving Place

Park Ave.

Madison Ave.

37

University Pl.

44

Fifth Ave.

GRAMERCY/ FLATIRON

Sixth Ave. (Ave. of the Americas)

W. 20th St.
W. 15th St.

45 **46** **47**

Greenwich Ave.

Waverly Pl.

GREENWICH VILLAGE

49

Prince St.
Spring St.
Broome St.

SOHO

Grand St.

Lafayette St.

CIVIC CENTER

Broadway

Church St.

W. Broadway

Wall St.
Church St.
Broad Ave.

FINANCIAL DISTRICT

Canal St.

Ave. of the Americas

57

TRIBECA

Battery Pl.

35

Eighth Ave.

38

W. 10th St.

Seventh Ave.

WEST VILLAGE

Hudson St.

48

Greenwich St.
Washington St.

BATTERY PARK CITY

Ninth Ave.

W. 14th St.

CHELSEA

W. 25th St.
W. 23rd St.

Tenth Ave.

West St.

Holland Tunnel

Hudson River

MILES   1/2
         1/4

N

In New York City, every meal is an adventure, which can be a mixed blessing. The pioneering spirit that so many children otherwise display often disappears when it comes to trying unfamiliar foods. Sometimes, kids just want to eat pizza, burgers, or hot dogs. Luckily, New York offers some of the world's finest examples of each of these items.

But if you can push your kids a little farther than usual and get them wrapped up in the culinary adventure of New York City, a world of ethnic food—some of it available nowhere else in America—awaits them. Like Korean barbecue, where you cook your own meat on tabletop grills. Or Brazilian *rodizio*, where waiters carve unlimited portions of more than twenty meats tableside off gigantic metal skewers. Have you ever been to a real, old-fashioned Romanian Jewish steakhouse, or a Tibetan restaurant, or a Filipino *turo-turo* buffet? You could easily spend a month in New York and eat the cuisine of a different nation every single day.

Of course, the more familiar ethnic cuisines, like Chinese and Italian, are also well represented, but even these come with some unusual twists. One of the greatest activities for kids is Sunday dim sum brunch in Chinatown, where busy waiters wheel steaming carts around the dining room, from which you select your meal, one little dish at a time. And several of New York's Italian restaurants offer family-style dining, where all dishes are meant to be shared.

I recoil at the notion of a "kids' restaurant," and I find most listings of such places to be patronizing and dull. You didn't come all the way to New York City to eat at TGI Friday's or McDonald's (though the flagship McDonald's establishment, in the Financial District, is a must-visit). So I've tried to list restaurants that kids will love but that are also delicious in their own right. But you should know, if the kids absolutely, positively refuse to eat anything but Burger King, that all the major national fast-food chains are well represented in every neighborhood of Manhattan. They're as easy to find as on any suburban strip.

I've organized the restaurant listings in this chapter alphabetically by cuisine (Burgers, Chinese, Indian, Pizza). After the main restaurant listings, look for special sections on ice cream, candy, bakeries, and "grownup" restaurants.

Helpful Hint
Eat at off-hours (late lunch; early dinner) to beat the crowds and avoid being rushed through your meal.

I have not, for the most part, included in this chapter the dozens of restaurants in museums and at other popular attractions. Typically, you can't even enter these restaurants unless you've paid admission to the site in question. Thus, where attractions have restaurants attached, they are discussed separately in chapter 5.

But what about the "theme restaurants," like Hard Rock Café and the new WWF restaurant? I've visited all of them—

with kids in tow—and I'll tell you my picks and pans in the "Quick Guide to Theme Restaurants."

Finally, remember, you don't have to eat every meal in a restaurant. New York has a wealth of gourmet markets, where you can buy nutritious cheese, fruit, bread, and prepared salads. I've included a list of the City's best markets, so, armed with a sharp knife and a few paper plates and plastic forks, you can feed your family healthy, economical breakfasts and lunches— and you'll only have to cope with and pay for one restaurant meal per day.

Note: Nothing changes more quickly than the New York restaurant scene. The information here was accurate at press time, but definitely call ahead before you make a special journey to any restaurant.

What the $ Ratings Mean

$ cheap; less than $10 per person
$$ moderate; $10–$25 per person
$$$ expensive; $25–$50 per person
$$$$ luxury; $50 and up per person

The $ ratings represent averages, based on what the typical customer eats at a particular restaurant. You can always spend more, and sometimes less, if you're an atypical consumer.

I've also indicated the neighborhood, using the following abbreviations:

BR: Brooklyn	BX: Bronx
CH: Chelsea	CT: Chinatown
EV: East Village	FD: Financial District
GD: Garment District	GP: Gramercy Park/Flatiron
GV: Greenwich Village	LES: Lower East Side
LI: Little Italy	MT: Midtown
MTE: Midtown East	MTW: Midtown West
Q: Queens	SH: SoHo
SI: Staten Island	TBC: TriBeCa

Top Ten "Grownup" Restaurants that Welcome Kids

1. Union Square Café (p. 295)

2. Gramercy Tavern (p. 294)

3. Mesa Grill (p. 330)

4. Calle Ocho (p. 330)

5. Ruby Foo's (p. 311)

6. Blue Water Grill (p. 291)

7. Café Luxembourg (p. 314)

8. Peter Luger (p. 339)

9. Sparks (p. 339)

10. Oyster Bar (p. 295)

TD: Theater District   TS: Times Square
UES: Upper East Side   US: Union Square
UWS: Upper West Side   WV: West Village

Payment: It's safe to assume that most restaurants where the check is more than $10 per person will accept major credit cards, and that most of the less expensive restaurants will not. However, it's always good to call ahead because restaurants occasionally change their policies, and some noteworthy moderate-to-expensive restaurants (such as the Carnegie Deli and Peter Luger Steakhouse) do operate on a cash-only basis. Where this was the case at press time, I have noted it.

Reservations: It always helps to call ahead, even where reservations are not available. You can at least assess the wait and find out whether special menu items are available, hours of operation, and the like.

DINING

A ★ indicates a particularly noteworthy restaurant for its price range or type, either because of the excellence of its food or its appeal to kids.

Insider's Tip

"When it comes to eating at places that don't accept reservations, always have a backup plan so your night doesn't turn into a nightmare. Be aware of at least one other restaurant in the area that you can visit if the wait is too long at your first choice." —*Andrew, father of two*

American

These restaurants serve the food that's most familiar to most American kids, and lots of it. They can be a godsend for parents of picky eaters because the food is simple and the choices numerous. Inspired by the roadside diner menus of old, and very often called "coffee shops" in the local New York City dialect (even though coffee is only a minor part of their business), each of these restaurants has added its own twists to this slice of Americana. *See also the entries on Burgers, Frankfurters, and French Fries.*

★ *America*	$$
9 East 18th Street (between	**212-505-2110**
Broadway and Fifth Ave.), GP	

This mega-eatery offers one of the most extensive menus you've ever seen, including the venerable Fluffernutter (a sandwich made with peanut butter and marshmallow Fluff). The place is loud and rambunctious, and even the loudest kids will blend in here.

City Fact
The apple strudel on the menu at Planet Hollywood is made from Arnold Schwarzenegger's mother's recipe.

Barking Dog Luncheonette $$
1678 Third Avenue (at 94th St.), UES   212-831-1800

A more refined version of a diner, with strong seafood selections in addition to the expected items.

Bendix Diner $
167 First Avenue (between   212-260-4220
10th and 11th Sts.), EV

High-quality diner food, and the price is right.

Blue Water Grill $$$
31 Union Square West, US   212-675-9500

Impeccable seafood. **Although this is a rather grownup restaurant, they do welcome children.**

Bubby's $$
120 Hudson Street (at North Moore), TBC   212-219-0666

A New York institution, this place is frequented by everybody who's anybody downtown.

Chat 'n' Chew $$
10 East 16th Street (between Fifth   212-243-1616
Ave. and Union Square West), GP

You can't help but love the BLTs and pink-frosted chocolate cake at this contemporary take on the greasy spoon.

Quick Guide to

The restaurants kids ask for most when they come to New York are, overwhelmingly, the nationally publicized and promoted theme restaurants. Just because they're popular, however, doesn't mean they're good—or worth the effort you have to expend to get in. Although some of the theme

Restaurant	Address	Phone Number
TOP THEME RESTAURANT PICKS		
★The World (World Wrestling Entertainment)	43rd St. and Broadway, TS	212-398-2563
Jekyll & Hyde	1409 Sixth Ave. (between 57th and 58th Sts.), MTW	212-541-9505
★Mars 2112	1633 Broadway (at 51st St.) downstairs, MTW	212-582-2112
Mickey Mantle's	42 Central Park South (between Fifth and Sixth Aves.), MTW	212-688-7777
THEME RESTAURANTS YOU CAN SAFELY SKIP		
ESPN Zone	1472 Broadway (at 42nd St.), TS	212-921-3776
Hard Rock Café	221 West 57th St. (between Broadway and Seventh Ave.), MTW	212-489-6565
Planet Hollywood	1540 Broadway (at 45th St.), TS	212-333-7827

Theme Restaurants

restaurants can be a lot of fun, many are just mediocre restaurants with a few thematic pictures on the walls—a total waste of time and a big disappointment for many young visitors. I've tried to separate the wheat from the chaff, so you can make informed decisions about whether or not to visit these restaurants.

Price Rating	Comments
$$	Great for wrestling fans. TVs run nonstop wrestling bios and matches. Wrestlers stop in when they're in town.
$$	Not for the faint of heart, this is nevertheless another winner. The horror theme is consistent throughout, and highly interactive.
$$	Get a full-length amusement-park-like ride when you gain entry to this sci-fi restaurant. When you exit, you're in what looks and feels like a cave.
$$	A worthwhile, understated restaurant for the avid baseball fan who not only follows the game but has studied baseball history, too.
$$	Offers almost nothing special for kids. A lot of TVs feature sporting events, but most viewing areas are in the bars.
$$	If you've seen one Hard Rock, you've seen them all.
$$	The same rules apply to Planet Hollywood as to Hard Rock, only Planet Hollywood is a copycat with not much in the way of originality or décor.

Comfort Diner $$
142 East 86th Street (at   212-426-8600
   Lexington Ave.), UES
214 East 45th Street (between   212-867-4555
   Second and Third Aves.), MTE

A retro look and modern menu make this one of the best diner-style restaurants in town.

★ **EJ's Luncheonette** $
1271 Third Avenue (at 73rd St.), UES   212-472-0600
447 Amsterdam Avenue (between   212-873-3444
   81st and 82nd Sts.), UWS
432 Sixth Avenue (between 9th   212-473-5555
   and 10th Sts.), WV

One of the most popular diners among native New Yorkers; just about everything is good.

Googie's $$
1491 Second Avenue (at 78th St.), UES   212-717-1122

This great neighborhood diner also has a slight Italian twist to the menu.

Gramercy Tavern $$$$
42 East 20th Street, GP   212-477-0777

The more upscale of Danny Meyer's dynamic duo (see also Union Square Café), Gramercy Tavern will serve you a meal that will be a memory the whole family will cherish. Call far, far in advance for reservations. **Be aware, this is mainly a restaurant for grownups, although it does welcome kids.**

Junior's $$
386 Flatbush Avenue (at DeKalb Ave.), BR   718-852-5257

The definitive Brooklyn diner, with orange vinyl banquettes, and some of the world's best cheesecake.

There is a smaller location in the Grand Central Station dining concourse (MTE, 212-692-9800).

Oyster Bar $$$
Grand Central Station,   **212-490-6650**
Dining Concourse, MTE

A soaring, tiled, arched ceiling and the finest fresh oysters make this one of America's greatest traditional seafood restaurants. Don't miss the made-to-order chowders.

★ Peanut Butter & Co. $
240 Sullivan Street (between   **212-677-3995**
Bleecker and West 3rd Sts.), WV

Kids love this menu, which contains, among other things, no less than fourteen variations of the peanut-butter sandwich.

★ Screening Room $$$
54 Varick Street (between   **212-334-2100**
Canal and Laight Sts.), TBC

Yes, you can eat a meal while watching a movie. The schedule varies, and most of the movies are classics. Prices are high, but this place is great, especially for teens who love cinema.

Union Square Café $$$$
21 East 16th Street, US   **212-243-4020**

Danny Meyer, who also owns Gramercy Tavern, is committed to welcoming kids no matter how popular his restaurants become with adults (they are numbers one and two in the *Zagat* Survey).

Bagels

Bagels are the signature bread product of New York, and New York bagels will simply blow you away if you've never had the real thing. They're also a great snack—or even a meal—for kids. Of all the foods in the world, I've found that bagels are the ones least likely to be rejected by kids, especially when bagels are fresh out of the oven and particularly when you get them at a real old-fashioned bagel bakery where you can watch the bagels first being boiled (to give them their unique crust) and then baked. The following are my favorite bagel bakeries in New York. Most of these shops will make bagel sandwiches, which make convenient, portable, and filling lunches.

Absolute Bagels
2788 Broadway (between 107th and 108th Sts.), UWS
212-932-2052

Bagelry
1380 Madison Avenue (at 96th St.), UES
212-423-9590
1324 Lexington Avenue (between 88th and 89th Sts.), UES
212-996-0567
1228 Lexington Avenue (at 83rd St.), UES
212-717-2080

★ Columbia Hot Bagels
2836 Broadway (between 110th and 111th Sts.), UWS
212-222-3200

David's Bagels
1651 Second Avenue (between 85th and 86th Sts.), UES
212-439-7887
228 First Avenue (between 13th and 14th Sts.), UES
212-533-8766

★ Ess-a-Bagel
359 First Avenue (at 21st St.), GP
212-260-2252

831 Third Avenue (between 50th and 51st Sts.), MTW
212-980-1010

Learning Tip

Ess-a-Bagel means "eat a bagel" in Yiddish (a mix of German, Russian, and Hebrew), the language that used to be spoken by Eastern European Jews. Term paper idea: Discuss the history of the Yiddish language, where it came from, and how many of its words and expressions (*schlep, oy vay!*) have come into common English usage.

★ H&H
2239 Broadway (at 80th St.), UWS
212-595-8003

★ Kossar's
367 Grand Street (between Essex and Norfolk Sts.), LES
212-473-4810

Kossar's bialys are the best I have ever tasted. You can watch them being made and eat them straight out of the oven at this Lower East Side bakery.

Pick-a-Bagel
1101 Lexington Avenue (at 77th St.), UES
212-517-6590
200 West 57th Street (at Seventh Ave.), MTW
212-957-5151
1475 Second Avenue (between 76th and 77th Sts.), UES
212-717-4662
601 Avenue of the Americas (between 17th and 18th Sts.), CH
212-924-4999
297 Third Avenue (between 22nd and 23rd Sts.), GP
212-686-1414

Learning Tip

Although you can find a bagel—albeit not always the best—in virtually any part of the United States, its near relative, the bialy, is still largely unknown outside New York. A bialy is a softer, more perishable bread with an indentation instead of a hole in the middle. The indentation is filled with an onion or garlic mixture. Once you've tried a hot bialy, you'll wonder if it isn't perhaps even better than a bagel.

Tal Bagels
333 East 86th Street (between First and Second Aves.), UES
212-427-6811
977 First Avenue (between 53rd and 54th Sts.), MTE
212-753-9080

Barbecue and Southern

If you're coming to New York from the South, I can't honestly recommend that you eat barbecue here. But for everybody else, you'll find New York's barbecue restaurants to be great allies in feeding your kids. Prices are a little higher than in Lexington, North Carolina, but then again they don't have to pay New York rents down there.

Cowgirl Hall of Fame	$$
519 Hudson Street (at Tenth Ave.), WV	**212-633-1133**

A slice of the South in Manhattan, this palace of barbecue and corn dogs lures kids with its wild décor.

★ *Dallas BBQ* $
1265 Third Avenue (between   212-772-9393
**   72nd and 73rd Sts.), UES**
27 West 72nd Street (between   212-873-2004
**   Columbus Ave. and Central Park West), UWS**
132 West 43rd Street (between   212-221-9000
**   Broadway and Sixth Ave.), TS**
21 University Place (at 8th St.), EV   212-674-4450
132 Second Avenue (at Saint Marks), EV   212-777-5574

Not particularly authentic, but kids love the sweet baby back ribs
and tender rotisserie chicken; and parents appreciate the incredibly reasonable prices.

Tennessee Mountain $
121 West 45th Street (between   212-398-6585
**   Broadway and Sixth Ave.), TS**
143 Spring Street (at Wooster St.), SH   212-431-3993

Good ribs, even better prices.

★ *Virgil's Real BBQ* $$
152 West 44th Street (between   212-921-9494
Broadway and Sixth Ave.), TS

Perhaps the best and most legitimate barbecue in Manhattan;
prices are a little steep, but the atmosphere is perfect for kids—lots
of nice Southern touches in a gigantic, roaring Midtown space.

City Fact

New York City has more than 20,000 restaurants today. If
you ate at a different restaurant every day, you couldn't
even keep pace with all the new openings, much less make
a dent in the 20,000!

Brazilian

The Brazilian tradition of *rodizio* is ideal for families. Waiters circle the restaurant with meat (more than twenty varieties, ranging from simple steak to more adventurous choices) on gigantic metal skewers, stopping at your table and carving it right on to your plate. One price covers unlimited meat and trips to the salad bar, though drinks are extra.

★ *Churrascaria Plataforma* $$
316 West 49th Street (between   212-245-0505
Eighth and Ninth Aves.) MTW

Burgers

If your kids like burgers, they'll have no trouble eating in New York. You'll find fantastic, gigantic burgers of every variety (grilled, fried, and steamed; beef, turkey, and tuna) all over town. These are a few of the best and most reliable, authentic, local burger joints.

Big Nick's $
2175 Broadway (between   212-362-9238
  76th and 77th Sts.), UWS
70 West 71st Street (at   212-799-4444
  Columbus Ave.), UWS

Great grilled burgers and an extensive menu of American, Greek, and Italian specialties, including very good pizza.

Burger Heaven $
9 East 53rd Street (between   212-752-0340
  Fifth and Madison Aves.), MTE
20 East 49th Street (between   212-755-2166
  Fifth and Madison Aves.), MTE

291 Madison Avenue (between   212-685-6250
40th and 41st Sts.), MTE
536 Madison Avenue (between   212-753-4214
54th and 55th Sts.), MTE

A consistently reliable local chain. Businesspeople with short lunch breaks crowd these places midday, but at all other times they're quite pleasant.

Fanelli   **$$**
94 Prince Street (at Mercer St.), SH   212-226-9412

Fanelli is one of SoHo's only remaining authentic institutions (not that I have anything against SoHo's many wonderful, new, inauthentic restaurants and shops). It has been around since 1847. Up front, you can grab a flier that explains the history of the place in exhaustive (and exhausting) detail. In addition to burgers, Fanelli has a full menu of simple, straightforward fare.

★ *Island Burgers and Shakes*   **$**
766 Ninth Avenue (between   212-307-7934
51st and 52nd Sts.), MTW

A very casual spot for a quick burger with an incredible selection of toppings. The chicken sandwiches are also excellent, as are the shakes.

Jackson Hole   **$**
1270 Madison Avenue (at 91st St.), UES   212-427-2820
1611 Second Avenue (between   212-737-8788
   83rd and 84th Sts.), UES
232 East 64th Street (between   212-371-7187
   Second and Third Aves.), UES
517 Columbus Avenue   212-362-5177
   (at 85th St.), UWS

Quick Guide to

Weekend brunch is a religion in New York, and at many restaurants it's the busiest time of the week. To beat the crowds, go early—New Yorkers tend to sleep in on weekends, and brunch business doesn't really pick up until late morning. Still, you

Restaurant	Address	Phone Number
Friend of a Farmer	77 Irving Pl. (between 18th and 19th Sts.), GP	212-477-2188
Good Enough to Eat	483 Amsterdam Ave. (between 83rd and 84th Sts.), UWS	212-496-0163
Isabella's	359 Columbus Ave. (at 77th St.), UWS	212-724-2100
NoHo Star	330 Lafayette (at Bleecker St.), EV	212-925-0070
★Popover Café	551 Amsterdam Ave. (between 86th and 87th Sts.), UWS	212-595-8555
★Sarabeth's	1295 Madison Ave. (between 92nd and 93rd Sts.), UES	212-410-7335
	945 Madison Ave. (between 75th and the Whitney Museum), UES	212-570-3670
	423 Amsterdam Ave. (between 80th and 81st Sts.), UWS	212-496-6280
Time Café	2330 Broadway (at 85th St.), UWS	212-579-5100
	380 Lafayette St. (at Great Jones), EV	212-533-7000

Brunch

should always be prepared to wait a few minutes (and sometimes more) for a brunch table in New York City. *Note:* All of these restaurants are also excellent for other meals. See also Dim Sum, under Chinese, for another interesting brunch option.

Price Rating	Comments
$$	A slice of New England in Manhattan, with excellent baked goods.
$$	Comfort food and cozy decor make this a likely family-pleaser.
$$	Huge portions distinguish this neighborhood favorite.
$$	A classic New York downtown crowd makes people-watching the activity of choice at this NoHo favorite.
$$	The popovers are great—and there are teddy bears everywhere for the kids. Very, very popular; go early.
$$	Tourists and New Yorkers alike line up outside Sarabeth's for incredible omelets, porridges, and pastries.
$$	Very reliable, this place is also often not as crowded as some of the others.

| 521 Third Avenue (at 35th St.), MTE | 212-679-3264 |
| 69-35 Astoria Boulevard (at 70th St., near LaGuardia Airport), Q | 718-204-7070 |

Jackson Hole serves a big, juicy burger that practically falls apart if you pick it up. Kids love to watch the frenzied griddle activity, where the burgers are steamed/fried under little metal domes. The menu is full of dozens of interesting topping combinations, with names like the Baldouni Burger.

| *Sassy's Sliders* | $ |
| 1530 Third Avenue (between 86th and 87th Sts.), UES | 212-828-6900 |

Like White Castle (tiny burgers on tiny buns) but better.

City Fact
Thought all McDonald's were the same? Wrong! The one at 160 Broadway in the Financial District (212-227-3828, $) is the flagship McDonald's. It has live music on a grand piano, a doorman in topcoat and tails, hostesses, marble tables, a digital stock ticker, a gift shop, flowers, and a dessert menu (including cappuccino and espresso).

Candy and Nuts

Your kids will not have experienced these stores before, but you'll be transported back to your own childhood when you wander into some of these marvelous New York candy and nut shops.

| *Bazzini* | |
| 339 Greenwich Street (at Jay St.), LES | 212-227-6241 |

One of the best nut shops in the world. If you've only ever tasted grocery store peanuts, cashews, and pistachios, you're in for a treat. And don't overlook their homemade nut brittles, either.

★ *Economy Candy*
108 Rivington Street (between   **212-254-1832**
Essex and Ludlow Sts.), LES

Arguably my favorite candy store in the world, Economy Candy is every child's (and candy-loving adult's) dream come true. With a selection of everything from candy buttons to hand-dipped chocolates, and prices ranging from a mere ninety-nine cents for large, Easter-sized jelly beans to $3 per pound for gummy candies, every child will bounce off the walls with mere anticipation (and that's before they eat the candy).

Elk Candy Co.
1628 Second Avenue (between   **212-650-1177**
84th and 85th Sts.), UES

Art-quality marzipan and molded chocolates as well as some of the regulars like gummy bears and European candy bars.

Li-Lac Chocolates
120 Christopher Street (between   **212-242-7374**
Hudson and Bleecker Sts.), WV

The selection is like that of a real old-fashioned penny-candy shop, though nothing costs a penny.

Mondel's Chocolates
2913 Broadway (at 114th St.), UWS   **212-864-2111**

Another favorite old-fashioned candy store.

Quick Guide to

These gourmet (read: expensive) chocolatiers ostensibly target an adult audience, but I've known many kids, myself as a child included, who absolutely love the display cases packed full of jewel-like European chocolates (for a price, of course).

Restaurant	Address	Phone Number
Fifth Avenue Chocolatiere	510 Madison Ave. (between 52nd and 53rd Sts.), MTE	212-935-5454
	120 Park Ave. (at 42nd St.), MTE	212-370-5355
La Maison du Chocolat	1018 Madison Ave. (between 78th and 79th Sts.), UES	212-744-7117
Neuchatel	2 West 59th St. (at Central Park South), MTW	212-751-7742
	60 Wall St. (between William and Pearl Sts.), FD	212-480-3766
Richart	7 East 55th St. (between Fifth and Madison Ave.), MTE	212-371-9369
Teuscher Chocolates of Switzerland	Rockefeller Center, 620 Fifth Ave. (between 49th and 50th Sts.), MTW	212-246-4416
	25 East 61st St. (at Madison Ave.), UES	212-751-8482

Grownup Candy Stores

Comments

The be all and end all of specialized chocolates. With two weeks notice, anything your child can conceive of, from baseball bats to ballerinas, can be sculpted in chocolate. Their caramels are to die for.

By far my favorite. All chocolates are imported from Paris, with shipments arriving several times a week. The macaroons, though very expensive, are among the finest in the world.

Another fine European chocolatier, with beautiful stores. The caramels are particularly noteworthy.

This French chocolate boutique sells incredibly detailed, hand-decorated chocolates. It's almost more of an art gallery than a candy store.

World-renowned for its intense truffles as well as other fine chocolate candies.

Nut City
1585 Second Avenue (between   **212-772-0659**
82nd and 83rd Sts.), UES

These nut, ice cream, and frozen yogurt stores are a dime a dozen around the City. But this one especially has an extremely nice staff, all happy to give samples of yogurt and ice cream to any curious customer—even if they don't ask. Be sure to tell Mafoz (the owner) I sent you.

Philip's Candy
1237 Surf Avenue (near Stillwell,   **718-372-8783**
next door to the original Nathan's), BR

The candy apples in Philip's are the crowning touch to every visit to Coney Island. Even the most mature child will revert to being a fun-loving kid. Don't forget the wet naps!

The Sweet Life
63 Hester Street (at Ludlow St.), LES   **212-598-0092**

Specializing in candy, nuts, and dried fruit, a Lower East Side institution.

Chicken

William's Bar-B-Que $
2350 Broadway (between   **212-877-5384**
85th and 86th Sts.), UWS

One of the best rotisserie chickens on the planet, but it has nothing to do with barbecue.

Money-Saving Tip

Set a limit on the number of drinks your children can order in restaurants and encourage them to take the healthier option of New York City's excellent tap water. Soft drinks in New York are very expensive (sometimes upwards of $2), and refills are not free, so the addition of a few extra drinks for each person can easily double your bill.

Chinese

New York is swimming in Chinese food, and many New Yorkers eat Chinese takeout more often than they eat at home. But a lot of New York Chinese food, especially in Chinatown, can be disappointing, expensive, and (often unpleasantly) surprising. Here are a few of the more predictable, consistent, midpriced options, all of which have extensive menus of the familiar Cantonese, Hunan, and Szechuan specialties, plus some with which you might not be as familiar.

China Fun	$$
1221 Second Avenue (at 65th St.), UES	**212-752-0810**
246 Columbus Avenue (between 71st and 72nd Sts.), UWS	**212-580-1516**
1653 Broadway (at 51st St.), MTW	**212-333-2622**

HSF	$$
46 Bowery (between Bayard and Canal Sts.), CT	**212-374-1319**

Most Chinatown restaurants serve dim sum only on weekends, but HSF does so daily.

Helpful Hint

Dim sum palaces fascinate kids. Waiters roam the dining room pushing metal carts piled high with dozens of little Chinese dishes. The choices seem infinite, so there's nearly always something for even the pickiest kid to eat. Prices tend to be very reasonable (you pay by the dish, and most are only a couple of dollars).

Jing Fong	$$
20 Elizabeth Street (between	212-964-5256
Bayard and Canal Sts.), CT	

The largest of the dim sum restaurants, and one of the best.

Mee	$
219 First Avenue (at 13th St.), EV	212-995-0333
547 Second Avenue (between	212-779-1596
30th and 31st Sts.), GP	
922 Second Avenue (at 49th St.), MTE	212-888-0027
795 Ninth Avenue (at 53rd St.), MTW	212-765-2929

★ *New York Noodletown*	$$
28½ Bowery (at Bayard St.), CT	212-349-0923

Ollie's	$$
2957 Broadway (at 116th St.), UWS	212-932-3300
2315 Broadway (at 84th St.), UWS	212-362-3111
1991 Broadway (at 67th St.), UWS	212-595-8181
200B West 44th Street (between	212-921-5988
Broadway and Eighth Ave.), TS	

★ *Pig Heaven* $$
1540 Second Avenue (between 212-744-4333
80th and 81st Sts.), UES

Learning Tip

How do dim sum restaurants know what to charge at the end of a meal? At some restaurants, they use plates with different designs for each dish; at the end of the meal, they count the plates. At other places, you get a little card and each waiter stamps it to indicate what you ate.

Ruby Foo's $$$
2182 Broadway, UWS 212-724-6700
1626 Broadway, TS 212-489-5600

A pan-Asian dim sum and sushi fantasy. **A family-friendly restaurant, although mainly for adults.**

★ *Triple Eight Palace* $$
88 East Broadway (between 212-941-8886
Division and Market Sts.), CT

My favorite dim sum restaurant, with terrific food at low prices.

Wu Liang Ye $$
215 East 86th Street (between 212-534-8899
 Second and Third Aves.), UES
36 West 48th Street (at Fifth 212-398-2308
 and Sixth Aves.), MTW
338 Lexington Avenue (between 212-370-9647
 39th and 40th Sts.), MTE

Learning Tip

Did you know that Cuba traditionally had a large Chinese community? Paper topic idea: Trace the history of Chinese immigrants in Cuba and the unique challenges they faced. And while you're at it, sample the inexpensive, delicious food at La Caridad (2199 Broadway at 78th Street, UWS, 212-874-2780, $).

Deli and Sandwiches

If you're new to the City's great delis, you'll likely find the sandwiches shocking. Many are impossible to pick up due to their sheer bulk, which in part explains why they can cost in the $10 neighborhood (most adults, much less kids, cannot eat more than a half). But these are also the best sandwiches in the world, and you'll love the uniquely New York atmosphere at our old-time delis.

Artie's New York Delicatessen	**$$**
2290 Broadway (between 82nd and 83rd Sts.), UWS	**212-579-5959**

The first good, new New York deli to come along in years, this is a faithful retro reproduction of an old-time Jewish deli. Plus it's brand new and impeccably clean.

Carnegie Deli	**$$**
854 Seventh Avenue (at 55th St.), MTW	**212-757-2245**

The second-best pastrami after Katz's Deli, and good renditions of Jewish standbys like matzoh ball soup and potato pancakes. Cash only.

Learning Tip

Though it is today a Jewish deli mainstay, pastrami was invented by the American Indians. Did you know that pastrami, corned beef, and brisket are all made from the same piece of meat: the beef brisket? The only difference is in the cooking. Pastrami is dry-cured and smoked. Corned beef is cured in brine. Brisket is simply boiled.

★ *Italian Food Center* $
186 Grand Street (at Mulberry St.), LI   212-925-2954

The Italian answer to the Jewish deli, with first-rate cold cuts (salami, prosciutto, sopresatta, etc.) served on crusty Italian bread. Friendly staff completes the experience.

★ *Katz's Deli* $$
205 East Houston Street (at Ludlow St.), LES   212-254-2246

"Send a Salami to Your Boy in the Army," reads the World War II–era sign up front, but you go to Katz's for the best pastrami available, and also for delicious hot dogs and knishes. Cash only.

Second Avenue Deli $$
156 Second Avenue (at 10th St.), EV   212-677-0606

A real neighborhood deli, with fewer tourists in evidence than at the others. The hot entrees are wonderful. Cash or AmEx only.

Stage Deli   **$$**
834 Seventh Avenue (between   212-245-7850
53rd and 54th Sts.), MTW

The menu is full of sandwiches evocatively named after celebrities, and the portions are gigantic. Not as good as the neighboring Carnegie, in my opinion, but less cramped and crowded.

Eclectic

Café Luxembourg   **$$$**
200 West 70th Street, UWS   212-873-7411

Gorgeous Art Deco French bistro with some of the best food in the neighborhood. **For adults, but welcomes kids.**

Dojo   **$**
14 West 4th Street (between   212-505-8934
    Broadway and Mercer St.), WV
24-26 St. Marks Place (between   212-674-9821
    Second and Third Aves.), EV

Asian-influenced, healthy food at excellent prices.

Shopsin's   **$$**
54 Carmine Street, WV   212-924-5160

A really unusual New York institution, with interesting ex-hippie owners and a diverse international menu.

Money-Saving Tip

Plan ahead for your meals—coordinate them with other activities—so you aren't forced to eat mediocre, overpriced food in your hotel restaurant or at expensive Midtown tourist traps.

Quick Guide to Department Store Dining

The restaurants in New York's better department stores—many of which serve excellent food—are some of New York's best-kept secrets. Most New Yorkers won't actually bother to go through the maze of a department store to get lunch, so these restaurants tend to be nice little urban enclaves. And they're all used to handling families with children. So next time you're wandering the stores, consider staying for a meal.

Restaurant	Address	Phone Number	Price Rating
Cafe American Style at Lord & Taylor	424 Fifth Ave., MTE	212-391-3344	$$
59th & Lexington at Bloomingdale's	1000 Third Ave., UES	212-705-2000	$$
Fred's at Barney's	10 East 61st St., UES	212-833-2200	$$
Nicole's at Nicole Farhi	10 East 60th St., UES	212-223-2288	$$
SFA Cafe at Saks Fifth Avenue	611 Fifth Ave., MTE	212-940-4080	$$
The Tea Box at Takashimaya	693 Fifth Ave., MTE	212-350-0180	$$

> *Yaffa Cafe* $
> 97 St. Marks Place (between 212-674-9302
> 1st St. and A Ave.), EV

Eclectic, Middle Eastern–inspired menu with great salads served twenty-four hours a day, seven days a week.

Filipino

> ★ *Elvie's Turo-Turo* $
> 214 First Avenue (between 212-473-7785
> 12th and 13th Sts.), EV

Turo-turo means "point-point," and that's exactly what you do at this Filipino buffet. Just point to what you want, and it's yours.

Insider's Tip

"Encourage kids to be open-minded about eating and trying new things; explain to them that it's all about the adventure."
—*Penny, grandmother of two*

Frankfurters

It may sound strange, but the official way to eat a frankfurter in New York City is to wash it down with a glass of papaya juice. It's one of those amazing food combinations you just have to try for yourself, and many kids love the sweetness of the tropical fruit. I urge you to avoid street-vendor frankfurters—they're usually boiled and bland—and seek out one of these places instead. See also Katz's Deli (under Deli and Sandwiches) and F&B (under French Fries).

★ Gray's Papaya $
2090 Broadway (at 72nd St.), UWS   212-799-0243
402 Sixth Avenue (at 8th St.), WV   212-260-3532

One of the great dining bargains in the history of humanity: Two delicious grilled hot dogs with all the fixings and a fourteen-ounce fruit juice (papaya, banana, or coconut—it costs extra for pineapple and fresh-squeezed orange or grapefruit) for $1.95.

The Original Nathan's $
Coney Island, BR

Opened in 1916 by Polish immigrant Nathan Handwerker, Nathan's is the classic New York hot dog stand. Nathan's is now a chain, but the Coney Island branch is the original.

★ Papaya King $
179 East 86th Street (at Third Ave.), UES   212-369-0648

The hot dogs at Papaya King are similar to those at Gray's (Mr. Gray used to work here). They may even be a little meatier, but they should be—they cost more than twice as much.

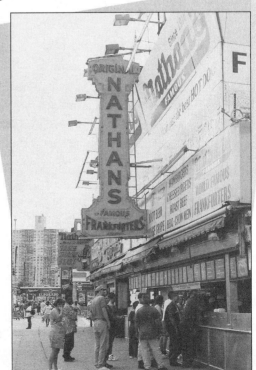

The Original Nathan's, Coney Island

French Fries

★ *F&B*	$
269 West 23rd Street (between Seventh and Eighth Aves.), CH	**646-486-4441**

Delicious Belgian-style twice-fried fries and unusual hot dog combinations. Plus, for the parents, there are little soda pop–sized bottles of Champagne.

Pommes Frites	$
123 Second Avenue (7th St. and St. Marks Pl.), EV	**212-674-1234**

Hot, crispy fries served in a paper cone. You have a choice of dozens of toppings (some of which are included in the price of the fries and some of which cost fifty cents). I recommend (as does the staff) a combination of ketchup, mayonnaise-based "frites sauce" and chopped onions—all of which are free.

German

Hallo Berlin	$$
402 West 51st Street (between Ninth and Tenth Aves.), MTW	**212-541-6248**

A great spot for wurst-loving families.

Greek

Aegean $$
221 Columbus Ave (at 70th St.), UWS   212-873-5057

Moderately priced Greek in a typically overpriced neighborhood.

Learning Tip

Haloumi—A salty, mozzarella-like cheese, usually broiled or
  fried.

Kafteri—Spicy feta cheese spread.

Melitzanosalata—Eggplant spread, usually with a liberal application of garlic. Virtually identical to the Middle Eastern *babaganouj.*

Saganaki—Most Greek-American menus translate it as
  "flaming cheese," but it need not be served flaming. The
  term actually refers to the metal plate on which the
  cheese is cooked. In many Greek restaurants, the dish
  will be finished with brandy and served flaming.

Skordalia—Mashed potato and garlic spread, served cold.

Taramosalata—Fish roe spread. Even though this spread looks
  as though it must be dairy-based, the main ingredients are
  simply oil and fish roe (*tarama*). When whipped, the oil be-
  comes emulsified through the incorporation of air (much as
  with mayonnaise), accounting for the spread's creaminess.

Tzatziki—Yogurt/garlic/cucumber spread, often with a little
  mint. Although garlic is a standard ingredient, *tzatziki*
  provides a cooling effect.

Delphi $$
109 West Broadway (at Reade St.), TBC   212-227-6322

Delicious grilled meats.

Elias Corner $$
2402 31st Street (at 24th Ave.), Q   **718-932-1510**

Astoria, Queens, is New York's major Greek neighborhood, and Elias Corner is the best restaurant in the area. Emphasis on fresh seafood.

★ Niko's Mediterranean Grill $$
2161 Broadway (at 76th St.), UWS   **212-873-7000**

Exceptional food given the low- to-midrange prices. The menu is gigantic, but nothing seems to suffer. Portions are generous, and ingredients are top-notch. Several dishes are identified by their region of origin within Greece, making for an educational and enlightened menu.

Uncle Nick's $$
747 Ninth Avenue (between   **212-245-7992**
50th and 51st St.), MTW

A traditional Greek grilled-fish restaurant, with plenty of other choices for those who don't like seafood.

Ice Cream

Although old-fashioned ice-cream parlors and soda fountains have gone the way of the buffalo in many parts of America—and New York has lost its fair share as well—a few are still going strong in the City.

Chinatown Ice Cream Factory $
65 Bayard Street (between   **212-608-4170**
Mott and Elizabeth Sts.), CT

Exotic, fun flavors, like ginger, lychee, mango, almond cookie, and taro.

*The Original Chinatown
Ice Cream Factory*

Ciao Bella $
27 East 92nd Street
(at Madison Ave.), UES
  212-831-5555
285 Mott Street
(between Prince and
Houston Sts.), LI
  212-431-3591

Ciao Bella ice cream is only 20 percent air and 10 percent butter-fat, making it denser, creamier, and tastier than most.

Emack & Bolio's $
56 Seventh Avenue (between   212-727-1198
  13th and 14th Sts.), WV
389 Amsterdam Avenue   212-362-2747
  (between 78th and 79th Sts.), UWS
151 West 34th Street (in Macy's,   212-494-5853
  4th floor), MTW

Made in a small Massachusetts dairy, this is incredibly good ice cream. The chocolate peanut butter cup, vanilla bean speck, and grasshopper pie are all great, and perhaps your family will be large enough to tackle the Emack Attack, a bowl packed with forty scoops (for $40).

Peter's Homemade $
185 Atlantic Avenue (at Court St.), BR   718-852-3835

Delicious, stabilizer-free ice cream in 140 unusual flavors like ginger, pecan pie, Campari-grapefruit sorbet, Vienna fingers, chunky cappuccino brownie, carrot cake, and molasses-ginger snap.

★ Serendipity $
225 East 60th Street (between   212-838-3531
Second and Third Aves.), UES

Charming Victorian decor—Tiffany lamps, wire chairs, and an all-white interior—and old-fashioned ice-cream sundaes drowned in gobs of hot fudge.

Indian

You'll find dozens of Indian restaurants clustered around East 6th Street between First and Second Avenues (Manhattan's "Little India"). You'll also find a smaller group on Lexington Avenue in the 20s and 30s. These places tend to be cheap and the food plentiful, making them ideal for families. These are a few of the better ones.

Curry in a Hurry $
119 Lexington Avenue (at 28th St.), GP   212-683-0900

Helpful Hint
Bring entertainment with you. If you have a game, project, or topic of discussion at the ready in the event of delays, your kids won't mind the wait (for a table or for food) quite so much.

Raj Mahal $
322 East 6th Street (between   212-982-3632
First and Second Aves.), EV

Indonesian

This cuisine, rarely seen on our shores, features interesting, often spicy food. Kids who already like Chinese food will find plenty of approachable dishes.

Bali Nusa Indah $
651 Ninth Avenue (between   212-765-6500
45th and 46th Sts.), MTW

Italian

Italian food is America's favorite food, and New York has the best Italian food in America. *Buon appetito!*

★ *Becco* $$
355 West 46th Street (between   212-397-7597
Eighth and Ninth Aves.), MTW

Three varieties of amazing homemade pasta daily, all you can eat. Plus a full Italian menu including excellent fish.

Lunchtime in Little Italy

Bella Luna $$
584 Columbus Avenue   212-877-2267
(between 88th and 89th Sts.), UWS

Particularly family-friendly neighborhood Italian.

Carmine's $$
200 West 44th Street (between   212-221-3800
    Broadway and Eighth Ave.), TS
2450 Broadway (between   212-362-2200
    90th and 91st Sts.), UWS

The original family-style Italian, Carmine's is always noisy and
crowded, but happily so.

★ **Casa Bella Restaurant** $$
127 Mulberry (at Hester St.), LI   212-431-4080

My favorite Italian in Little Italy, where restaurants are often dis-
appointing tourist traps. But not Casa Bella!

★ **Sambuca** $$
20 West 72nd Street (between Columbus   212-787-5656
Ave. and Central Park West), UWS

With the best food of the family-style Italian restaurants, Sam-
buca is a little more upscale than the others, but you'll see plenty
of kids having a great time.

Helpful Hint

The larger your group, the more fun it is to eat at New
York's family-style Italian restaurants. Everybody can share
the large platters of salads, pastas, and meats, which provide variety for the kids and interest for the folks. Lines
tend to be long, but these places will take reservations
for parties of six or more.

Tony's $$
1606 Second Avenue (between   212-861-8686
83rd and 84th Sts.), UES

Not as popular or crowded as the other family-style Italian restaurants—perhaps because of its East Side location—Tony's is a good bet for weekends and other busy times.

Money-Saving Tip

If you're traveling in a large group, eat at family-style Italian restaurants and at Asian restaurants where it's common to share food. That way, children aren't forced to order entire entrees they won't be able to finish (and you're not forced to pay for them!).

Japanese

Kids often either like Japanese food, or they don't—or so they think. New York has an embarrassment of riches when it comes to this wonderful cuisine, and we're not just talking sushi. These are a few of the more casual, family-appropriate spots. Also look for the Daikichi Sushi and Teriyaki Boy Japanese fast-food chains; they're not fabulous, but they're cheap and nourishing.

Haru $$
433 Amsterdam Avenue   212-579-5655
   (at 81st St.), UWS
1329 Third Avenue (at 76th St.), UES   212-452-2230

From the same folks who brought us Carmine's, Artie's Deli, and Polistina's Pizza comes this extremely competent interpretation of a classic American Japanese restaurant, with an emphasis on sushi. Very popular, with friendly service.

Menchanko-Tei	$
131 East 45th Street (between Third and Lexington Aves.), MTE	212-986-6805
43-45 West 55th Street (between Fifth and Sixth Aves.), MTW	212-247-1585

Hot, steaming, fresh Japanese noodle soups. Perfect for a winter meal on the run.

★ *Shabu-Tatsu*	$$
1414 York Avenue (at 75th St.), UES	212-472-3322
216 East 10th Street (between First and Second Aves.), EV	212-477-2972

You cook your own food by dunking strips of meat into a pot of boiling broth. A great participatory eating experience for kids.

Tsunami	$$
70 West 3rd Street (between La Guardia and Thompson Sts.), WV	212-475-7770

New York's only floating sushi bar—the chefs put the food in little "boats," which then float around the bar where you pick them up.

Jewish

Sammy's Roumanian Jewish Steakhouse	$$$
157 Chrystie Street at Delancey St.), LES	212-673-0330

Sammy's is a not-to-be-missed, only-in-New-York, rollicking good time. If this is how they eat every day in Romania, I'm moving there!

Quick Guide to Kosher Restaurants

Though New York has many Jewish restaurants and kosher-style delis, not all are strictly kosher according to traditional Jewish dietary laws. Thus, if your beliefs require a higher level of observance, these restaurants all have Orthodox supervision.

Restaurant	Address	Phone Number	Price Rating
China Shalom	686 Columbus Ave. (between 93rd and 94th Sts.), UWS	212-662-9676	$$
★Dimple Indian	11 West 30th St. (between Fifth and Sixth Aves.), MTW	212-643-9464	$
Dougie's BBQ & Grill	222 West 72nd St. (between Broadway and West End Ave.), UWS	212-724-2222	$$
Great American Health Bar	35 West 57th St. (between Fifth and Sixth Aves.), MTW	212-355-5177	$
Kosher Delight	1365 Broadway (at 36th St.), MTW	212-563-3366	$
	1156 Sixth Ave. (at 45th St.), MTW	212-869-6699	

Kebabs

The ideal cheap, filling sustenance for families on the move, these skewers of marinated meat really hit the spot.

★ *Afghan Kebab House*	$
764 Ninth Avenue (between 51st and 52nd Sts.), MTW	212-307-1612
155 West 46th Street (between Sixth and Seventh Aves.), TS	212-768-3875
1345 Second Avenue (between 70th and 71st Sts.), UES	212-517-2776

Korean

In the "Little Korea" neighborhood, right in the shadow of the Empire State Building, you'll find a whole bunch of restaurants where you can cook your own meat on tabletop grills. Communicating with the largely non-English-speaking waiters can be a little challenging, but as long as you can smile and point, you'll be okay. Of the restaurants, Won Jo and Woo Chon are two of my favorites.

Dok Suni's	$$
119 First Avenue (between 7th St. and St. Marks Pl.), EV	212-477-9506

A more Americanized, hip, downtown version of a Korean restaurant, with spare ribs to die for.

Won Jo	$$
23 West 32nd Street (between Broadway and Fifth Ave.), MTW	212-695-5815

★ *Woo Chon*	$$
8 West 36th Street (between Fifth and Sixth Aves.), MTW	212-695-0676

Mexican and Tex-Mex

Mexican food is cheap and familiar, and there's no shortage of it in New York. These places will fill your family's bellies for just a few dollars.

★ *Benny's Burritos*	$
93 Avenue A (at 6th St.), EV	212-254-2054
113 Greenwich Avenue (at Jane St.), WV	212-727-3560

Economical, filling burritos in a great downtown setting.

Burritoville	$
451 Amsterdam Avenue (between 81st and 82nd Sts.), UWS	212-787-8181
141 Second Avenue (between 8th and 9th Sts.), EV	212-260-3300
1489 Second Avenue (between 77th and 78th Sts.), UES	212-472-8800
144 Chambers Street (between West Broadway and Greenwich), TBC	212-571-1144
166 West 72nd Street (between Columbus and Amsterdam Aves.), UWS	212-580-7700
36 Water Street (at Broad St.), FD	212-747-1100
1606 Third Avenue (between 90th and 91st Sts.), UES	212-410-2255

Top-notch burritos filled with brown rice and mostly natural ingredients.

Calle Ocho   **$$$**
446 Columbus Avenue, UWS   **212-873-5025**

Creative Nuevo Latino cuisine in a slick Upper West Side setting. **This chic restaurant is mainly for adults, although it does welcome kids.**

Gabriela's   **$$**
685 Amsterdam Avenue (at 93rd St.), UWS   **212-961-0574**

A little more upscale than the others, Gabriela's serves more complex, nuanced Mexican cuisine. A real treat.

Manhattan Chili Company   **$$**
1697 Broadway (between   **212-246-6555**
53rd and 54th Sts.), MTW

A real favorite of families, it's one of the best deals in the Theater District.

Mary Ann's   **$$**
1503 Second Avenue (between   **212-249-6165**
** 78th and 79th Sts.), UES**
2452 Broadway (between   **212-877-0132**
** 90th and 91st Sts.), UWS**
116 Eighth Avenue (at 16th St.), CH   **212-633-0877**
300 East 5th Street (at Second Ave.), EV   **212-475-5939**

A good Mexican mini-chain with a pro-kids attitude.

Mesa Grill   **$$$**
102 Fifth Avenue, CH   **212-807-7400**

TV Food Network star chef Bobby Flay's Southwestern cuisine never fails to dazzle. **A "grownup" restaurant that welcomes kids.**

★ *Rocking Horse Cafe Mexicano* $$
182 Eighth Avenue (at 19th St.), CH   212-463-9771

Excellent sit-down Mexican. Among the best in town, but not overpriced.

Taco Taco $
1726 Second Avenue (between   212-289-8226
89th and 90th Sts.), UES

My favorite taco spot, with amazing soft-shell tacos.

Pastries

If you're looking for a snack or dessert, rather than a meal, stop into one of these world-famous pastry shops.

Bonte Patisserie $
1316 Third Avenue (between   212-535-2360
75th and 76th Sts.), UES

Traditional European patisserie.

Cupcake Café $
522 Ninth Avenue (at 39th St.), MTW   212-465-1530

Cupcake specialist.

De Robertis $
176 First Avenue (between   212-674-7137
10th and 11th Sts.), EV

Old-fashioned Italian pastries.

Ferrara	$
195 Grand Street (between Mulberry and Mott Sts.), LI	**212-226-6150**

Italian pastries in a grand historic restaurant.

Sant Ambroeus	$
1000 Madison Avenue (between 77th and 78th Sts.), UES	**212-570-2211**

Fabulous European desserts.

Soutine	$
104 West 70th Street (between Columbus Ave. and Broadway), UWS	**212-496-1450**

Handmade, delicious pastries of all kinds.

★ *Veniero's*	$
342 East 11th Street (between First and Second Aves.), EV	**212-674-4415**

My favorite Italian pastry shop. The miniature pastries, aside from being very inexpensive, are totally addictive.

Pizza

The New York slice is synonymous with great pizza, and it seems there's a pizzeria on every block in the City. For purposes of planning a meal, there are really two categories of pizzeria: ones where you can grab a slice on the go, and ones where you sit down and order whole pies (you can get a whole pie at a by-the-slice place, but not vice versa). The by-the-slice places tend to offer a thicker, cheesier slice, whereas the sit-down pizzerias usually bake a thinner-crusted, more gourmet pie, often in a traditional high-temperature brick oven. No matter, though—both are great!

★ *Angelo's* $
117 West 57th Street (between   212-333-4333
Sixth and Seventh Aves.), MTW

Superb thin-crust pizza (whole pies only) baked in a coal oven.

Freddie & Pepper's $
303 Amsterdam Avenue   212-799-2378
(between 74th and 75th Sts.), UWS

This pizza-by-the-slice joint has a superlative, subtly flavored sauce, and the guys in the store are very friendly.

John's $$
278 Bleecker Street (between   212-243-1680
    Sixth and Seventh Aves.), WV
498 East 64th Street (between   212-935-2895
    First and York Aves.), UES
260 West 44th Street (between   212-391-7560
    Broadway and Eighth Ave.), TS

John's has expanded lately, building Barnes & Noble-sized pizza superstores in the major uptown neighborhoods, and quality has slipped a little, but it's one of the more useful pizzerias because of its convenient locations and efficient service. The Bleecker Street original is better than the others. Whole pies only.

Marco Polo $
1289 Madison Avenue   212-427-3777
(between 91st and 92nd Sts.), UES

Marco Polo serves the Classic New York Slice, and the hordes of local private school students lined up at the door for slices every weekday at lunchtime are a testament to consistently good output. Marco Polo may not be the best pizza in New York, but it is the best slice in the neighborhood.

Naples 45 $
200 Park Avenue (at 45th St.), MTE   212-972-7001

Some of the best thin-crust, whole-pie-only pizza around. *Hint:* Order at the counter and take it to go or eat it at the little tables up front—you'll pay half as much as you would if you sit in the main dining room.

Patsy's $$
2287-2291 First Avenue   212-534-9783
  (between 117th and 118th Sts.), UES
1312 Second Avenue (at 69th St.), UES   212-639-1000
61 West 74th Street (between   212-579-3000
  Central Park West and Columbus Ave.), UWS
509 Third Avenue (between   212-689-7500
  34th and 35th Sts.), MTE
67 University Place (between   212-533-3500
  10th and 11th Sts.), EV

Another great old pizzeria that didn't reproduce as well as it should have. The 117th Street location is by far the best, but it's in a marginal neighborhood. The others are on par with John's. Whole pies only, and also very good pastas and salads.

★ *Polistina's* $$
2275 Broadway (between   212-579-2828
81st and 82nd Sts.), UWS

Polistina's pies are beautiful to behold, the mozzarella cheese is excellent, the toppings are first-rate—especially the mushrooms—and the pizzas all have a little fresh basil sprinkled over them. Whole pies only.

Insider's Tip

"New Yorkers are used to getting what they want in restaurants, and within reason your kids' needs should be accommodated. Ask for what you want at the time of your order and be specific: If your child wants no sauce on the pizza, make sure to say so up front and most places will happily oblige." —*Jennifer, mother of two*

Sal & Carmine's	$
2671 Broadway (between	212-663-7651
101st and 102nd Sts.), UWS	

Sal & Carmine's serves a very nice classic New York slice with a thin coating of high-quality mozzarella and a well-spiced sauce. Plus, the guys behind the counter are a real hoot. For some unknown reason, the small seating area in the back is decorated with Wallase Ting posters and French fashion advertisements.

Stromboli	$
112 University Place (between	212-255-0812
12th and 13th Sts.), EV	

A good place to grab a slice in the Village.

Totonno's	$$
1524 Neptune Avenue (between	718-372-8606
15th and 16th Sts.), BR	
1544 Second Avenue (between	212-327-2800
80th and 81st Sts.), UES	

Totonno's mozzarella cheese is truly a cut above the rest. On a good day, Totonno's may very well serve the best pizza in New York. But it can be inconsistent, and the Manhattan branch isn't nearly as good as the Coney Island original. Whole pies only.

V&T $
1024 Amsterdam Avenue 212-663-1708
(between 110th and 111th Sts.), UWS

An old-fashioned, red-checkered-tablecloth pizzeria. Whole pies only. Very popular with the students at Columbia University.

★ **Vinnie's** $
285 Amsterdam Avenue 212-874-4382
(between 73rd and 74th Sts.), UWS

If there is an award for nicest pizza guys, it has to go to the men behind the counter at Vinnie's. And the pizza at Vinnie's is just about the best classic New York slice available today.

Polish

The Polish American restaurants in the East Village offer large menus that mix American diner staples with Polish and Eastern European classics like pierogies (little meat or cheese dumplings) and blintzes (cheese or fruit rolled in a thin crepe-like dough). Wander up First Avenue and look for other East European restaurants and stores.

Christine's $
208 First Avenue (between 212-254-2474
12th and 13th Sts.), EV

Soup

Soup has always been a popular New York quick bite, but there has been a veritable explosion of soup sales in the wake of *Seinfeld*'s popularization of Soup Kitchen International on West 55th Street. Now, you'll also see stores like Hale & Hearty Soup, Daily

Top Ten Unique and Unusual New York Restaurants

1. Sammy's Roumanian Jewish Steakhouse (p. 326)

2. Screening Room (p. 295)

3. Churrascaria Plataforma (p. 300)

4. Woo Chon (p. 329)

5. Katz's Deli (p. 313)

6. Tsunami (p. 326)

7. Shabu-Tatsu (p. 326)

8. Tibet Shambhala (p. 340)

9. Elvie's Turo-Turo (p. 316)

10. Gray's Papaya (p. 317)

Soup, Mr. Soup, and Soup Nutsy, but none are as good (or as rude) as the original. A must-visit for kids who are old enough not to mind getting screamed at.

★ *Soup Kitchen International*   **$**
**259-A West 55th Street (between   212-757-7730
Eighth Ave. and Broadway), MTW**

Southeast Asian and Pan-Asian

The cuisines of Southeast Asia are complex and varied, but for the most part kids who already like Chinese food can adapt to the new flavors. For the less adventurous eaters, look for the dishes that are pretty similar to familiar Chinese staples, particularly the noodle and fried rice preparations.

Holy Basil	**$$**
149 Second Avenue (between	**212-460-5557**
9th and 10th Sts.), EV	

One of the best Thai restaurants in town, with exceedingly friendly service.

Kelley & Ping	**$$**
127 Greene Street (between	**212-228-1212**
Houston and Prince Sts.), SH	

Interesting pan-Asian food and an offbeat, downtown setting make this place popular with teens.

Penang	**$$**
109 Spring Street (between	**212-274-8883**
Greene and Mercer Sts.), SH	
240 Columbus Avenue	**212-769-3988**
(at 71st St.), UWS	
1596 Second Avenue (at 83rd St.), UES	**212-585-3838**
64 Third Avenue (at 11th St.), EV	**212-228-7888**

A reliable Malaysian chain, good for families.

Thailand Restaurant	**$$**
106 Bayard Street (between	**212-349-3132**
Baxter and Mulberry Sts.), CT	

Very popular with employees of the New York court system by day and with families by night.

Steak

Steak at the top New York steakhouses can be expensive—$30 and up for the basic steak, without any appetizers or sides—and the portions are too large for most kids other than football-playing teens. Listed here are a few steakhouses that combine quality and value, and also happen to be especially kid-friendly—plus a couple of the more expensive classics.

Chimichurri Grill	$$
606 Ninth Avenue (between 43rd and 44th Sts.), MTW	212-586-8655

An Argentinean steakhouse, which means a festive atmosphere and quality steaks at reasonable prices. The chimichurri steak sauce (garlic, parsley, olive oil, and spices) is out of this world.

Christos Hasapo-Taverna	$$$
41-08 23rd Avenue (at 41st St.), Q	718-726-5195

A Greek steakhouse and butcher shop in Astoria, Queens. Great dry-aged steaks at much lower prices than you'd pay in Manhattan.

Peter Luger	$$$$
178 Broadway, Williamsburg, BR	718-387-7400

Considered by many to be the finest steakhouse in America. **Although it does welcome kids, this is definitely a "grownup" restaurant.**

Sparks	$$$$
210 East 46th Street, MTE	212-687-4855

If you can't make it to Peter Luger in Brooklyn, Sparks, in Manhattan, is almost as good. **It welcomes kids, although it is definitely a "grownup" restaurant.** World-class wine list.

Tibetan

Tibet is pretty much sandwiched between India and China, so, as you might imagine, Tibetan cuisine is a bit like a cross between Indian and Chinese. You'll recognize dishes from both cultures (Indian curry, Chinese dumplings), but the food has its own charms as well. Many kids find it less "scary" than either Chinese or Indian, because the preparations tend to be simpler. These three restaurants (yes, New York has multiple Tibetan restaurants) are my top picks:

Lhasa $$
96 Second Avenue (between   212-674-5870
5th and 6th Sts.), EV

Dopka $$
136 West Houston Street (between   212-995-5884
MacDougal and Sullivan Sts.), WV

★ *Tibet Shambhala* $$
488 Amsterdam Avenue   212-721-1270
(between 83rd and 84th Sts.), UWS

Dining Without Restaurants

New York has an ample supply of chain supermarkets (Food Emporium, Gristede's, Sloan's, Pioneer, and more) and mini-marts (all over town and often open twenty-four hours a day), but the best groceries come from the City's many gourmet mega-stores. These hybrids of a gourmet store and a supermarket are a unique urban phenomenon, and New York has many wonderful examples of them from which to choose.

Agata & Valentina
1505 First Avenue (at 79th St.), UES   212-452-0690

A relative newcomer with a bright future. Open daily 8 A.M.–9 P.M.

Quick Guide to Food Courts

The glory of a food court is that each family member can choose from a variety of foods, and everybody can still dine together at one of the communal tables. Check out these food courts for painless family dining.

Food Court	Address	Comments
Grand Central Station	42nd St. and Park Ave., MTE	The newly renovated dining concourse is truly something to behold, with a great variety of foods, all from local establishments (no national chains allowed).
Manhattan Mall	33rd St. and Sixth Ave., MTW	A good assemblage of fast food and a few more healthful options, plus a view of the Empire State Building.
Pier 17	At the South Street Seaport, FD	The top floor's food court resembles those in many suburban shopping malls, but you're right on New York's East River.

★ *Balducci's*
424 Avenue of the Americas   **212-673-2600**
(at Ninth St.), WV
155 West 66th Street (Broadway), UWS

One of the best gourmet stores for the money in New York. Open daily 7:00 A.M.–8:30 P.M.

Chelsea Market
75 Ninth Avenue (between   **212-243-6005**
15th and 16th Sts.), CH

Top-notch marketplace, with many vendors, in Chelsea. Open Monday through Friday 7 A.M.–8 P.M., Sunday 10 A.M.–6 P.M.

Citarella
2135 Broadway (at 75th St.), UWS   **212-874-0383**
1313 Third Avenue (at 75th St.), UES

Originally one of New York's premier fish markets, now also offering first-rate meat, produce, and everything else. Open Monday through Saturday 7 A.M.–9 P.M., Sunday 9 A.M.–7 P.M.

Dean & DeLuca
560 Broadway (at Prince St.), SH   **212-431-1691**

Tony, overpriced, gorgeous. Open Monday through Saturday 9 A.M.–8 P.M., Sunday 9 A.M.–7 P.M.

Eli's
1411 Third Avenue (between   **212-717-8100**
80th and 81st Sts.), UES

Similar inventory to Vinegar Factory (see p. 345), but in more luxurious surroundings. Open daily 7 A.M.–9 P.M.

City Fact

The stone that was used to construct Eli's was imported from Jerusalem by the owner.

Fairway Downtown
2127 Broadway (at 74th St.), UWS   212-595-1888

The best for the price/quality equation. Open daily, 6 A.M.–1 A.M.

Fairway Uptown
2328 Twelfth Avenue (at 126th St.), UWS   212-234-3883

Like Fairway Downtown, but larger, better, less crowded, and with free parking (a really big deal for New Yorkers). Because of its inaccessibility (too far to walk; not particularly close to public transportation), you really need a car to shop here. Open daily 8 A.M.–11 P.M.

Snack time

Gourmet Garage

453 Broome Street (at Mercer St.), SH	212-941-5850
301 East 64th Street (between First and Second Aves.), UES	212-535-6271
2567 Broadway (between 96th and 97th Sts.), UWS	212-663-0656

A mini-chain of warehouse-style gourmet stores. Some great stuff, but hit-or-miss overall. Open daily; hours vary according to location.

Grace's Marketplace

1237 Third Avenue (at 71st St.), UES	212-737-0600

Lovely Upper East Side store owned by a Balducci family faction. Open Monday through Saturday 7:00 A.M.–8:30 P.M., Sunday 8:00 A.M.–7:00 P.M.

Grand Central Marketplace

On the Grand Central Station Main Concourse, MTE
Each purveyor/stall has its own telephone number

Elegant new marketplace with dozens of gourmet food stalls. Open Monday through Friday 7 A.M.–9 P.M., Saturday 9 A.M.–7 P.M., Sunday 9 A.M.–5 P.M.

Union Square Greenmarket

Union Square Park (along Broadway and East 17th St.), US

New York's premier farmers market. Go very early for the best selection. Open Monday, Wednesday, Friday, Saturday, early morning until midafternoon.

For other area greenmarkets, see the Council on the Environment of NYC's Web site: www.users.interport.net/~conyc/.

> *Vinegar Factory*
> **431 East 91st Street (between**   **212-987-0885**
> **First and York Aves.), UES**

Same owner as Eli's. Warehouse-style gourmet store; expensive with beautiful produce. Open daily 7 A.M.–9 P.M.

> ★ *Zabar's*
> **2245 Broadway (at 80th St.), UWS**   **212-787-2000**

A classic (a temple to some, a homecoming to others, or just a really good place to shop to the rest), and still one of the best. Open Monday through Friday 8:00 A.M.–7:30 P.M (Saturday until 8:00 P.M.)., Sunday 9:00 A.M.–6:00 P.M.

INDEX TO DINING BY NEIGHBORHOOD AND CUISINE

*Southeast Asian and
Pan-Asian*
Kelley & Ping (p. 338)
Penang (p. 338)

TIMES SQUARE

Barbecue and Southern
★ Dallas BBQ (p. 299)
Tennessee Mountain
(p. 299)
★ Virgil's Real BBQ (p. 299)

Chinese
Ollie's (p. 310)
Ruby Foo's (p. 311)

Italian
Carmine's (p. 324)

Kebabs
★ Afghan Kebab House
(p. 328)

Pizza
John's (p. 333)

Theme Restaurants
ESPN Zone (p. 292)
★The World (WWE)
(p. 292)

TRIBECA

American
Bubby's (p. 291)
★ Screening Room (p. 295)

Greek
Delphi (p. 319)

Mexican and Tex-Mex
Burritoville (p. 329)

UNION SQUARE

American
Blue Water Grill (p. 291)
Union Square Café (p. 295)

Grocery Stores/Markets
Union Square Greenmarket
(p. 344)

UPPER EAST SIDE

American
Barking Dog Luncheonette
(p. 291)
Comfort Diner (p. 294)
★ EJ's Luncheonette
(p. 294)
Googie's (p. 294)

Bagels
Bagelry (p. 296)
David's Bagels (p. 296)
Pick-a-Bagel (p. 297)
Tal Bagels (p. 298)

Barbecue and Southern
★ Dallas BBQ (p. 299)

Brunch
★ Sarabeth's (p. 302)

Burgers
Jackson Hole (p. 301)
Sassy's Sliders (p. 304)

Candy and Nuts
Elk Candy Co. (p. 305)
Nut City (p. 308)
La Maison du Chocolat
(p. 306)
Teuscher Chocolates of
Switzerland (p. 306)

Chinese
China Fun (p. 309)
★ Pig Heaven (p. 311)
Wu Liang Ye (p. 311)

Department Store Dining
59th & Lexington at
Bloomingdale's (p. 315)

CHAPTER 7

Shopping

Shopping

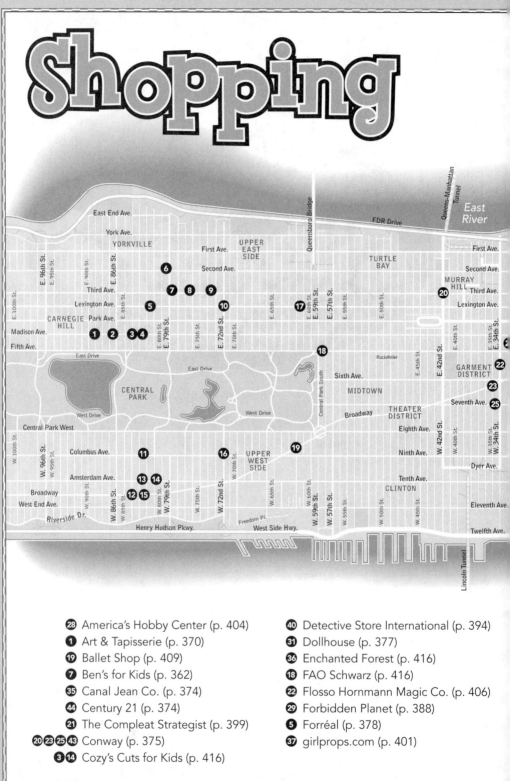

Map shows highlights only. See chapter text for more listings.

East
River

Williamsburg Bridge

Jackson St.
Columbia St.
Pitt St.
Clinton St.
Broome St.
Montgomery St.
Cherry St.
South St.
Manhattan Bridge
Brooklyn Bridge
South St. Viaduct

Avenue D
Avenue C
Avenue B
Avenue A

STUYVESANT
TOWN

Houston St.

EAST
VILLAGE

First Ave.
Second Ave.

Stanton St.
Rivington St.
Grand St.
Market St.
Catherine St.

LOWER
EAST
SIDE

Allen St.

South St.
Water St.

Brooklyn
Battery
Tunnel

E. 10th St.
E. 15th St.
E. 14th St.
E. 5th St.
E. 1st St.

Chrystie St.
St. James Pl.

CHINATOWN

E. 25th St.
E. 23rd St.
E. 20th St.

Third Ave.

Fourth Ave.

Bowery
Elizabeth St.
Mott St.
Mulberry St.

LITTLE
ITALY

Centre St.

CIVIC
CENTER

Wall St.
Broad Ave.

FINANCIAL
DISTICT

Irving Place
Park Ave.

㉚

㉛

Lafayette St.

㊸ Broadway

㊹ Church St.

Church St.

㉖

㉙

University Pl.

㉝

㉞ ㉟

㊱

Grand St.

Spring St.

㊸

㊺

Madison Ave.

Fifth Ave.

GREENWICH
VILLAGE

Prince St.

㊲

㊳

Broome St.

㊴

Broadway

Church St.

W. Broadway

GRAMERCY/
FLATIRON

㉗

Sixth Ave. (Ave. of the Americas)

㉜

W. 10th St.

Ave. of the Americas

SOHO

㊶

Canal St.

TRIBECA

Battery Pl.

㉘

W. 20th St.
W. 15th St.

Greenwich Ave.
Waverly Pl.
Seventh Ave.

Greenwich St.
Washington St.

BATTERY
PARK CITY

MILES   ½
        ¼

Eighth Ave.

WEST
VILLAGE

Hudson St.

㊵

Hudson Tunnel

Ninth Ave.
CHELSEA
Tenth Ave.

W. 25th St.
W. 23rd St.
W. 14th St.

West St.

Hudson
River

Ⓝ

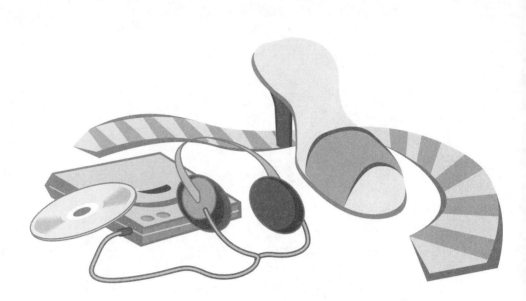

"**W**e didn't come all the way to New York just to shop!" you say. But shopping in New York City isn't just about buying things; it's an activity and attraction unto itself. Shopping doesn't have to mean spending money and wasting time like the characters of the movie *Clueless*. New York City shopping can be just as entertaining (Tannen's Magic Store), culturally enlightening (Chinatown), and educational (Maxilla & Mandible) as seeing a show, going to a museum (indeed, most of the museums have interesting shops within), or reading a book (and that's not to mention all of New York's wonderful independent booksellers!).

It's getting harder and harder to find unique, interesting, independent stores in most of America. Just about every mall in every town has exactly the same stores. But New York City, which isn't a mall town, is the last bastion of the independents. Department stores, specialty shops, boutiques, street vendors, and kiosks all offer original New York-esque products that you'll be hard-pressed to find anywhere else. Even if you do end up in a chain store in New York City, you may very well be visiting the original—like Saks Fifth Avenue or Barnes & Noble—or the flagship.

Shopping is deeply embedded in the culture of New York. We're a varied bunch, and each of us is accustomed to being able to find anything, whenever we want it, and for whatever price we want to pay ("Never pay retail!" is the battle cry of many a New York shopper). You're in a city with more than 40,000 retail outlets. If you can't find it here, it probably doesn't exist—though you will probably want to look elsewhere for farm equipment. Whether your children are partial to street fairs (which abound in the City throughout the temperate months), the hip world of secondhand stores in Greenwich Village, or the high-falutin' boutiques on the Upper East Side, even the pickiest, most specialized, most budget-conscious shoppers will find something.

Although rents and sales taxes (8.25 percent, except for shoes and clothes under $110 per item) are high, the enormous volume of sales in many New York stores means there's still plenty of money to be saved by shopping in the City. Then again, though I don't advise it, you can also easily spend more money shopping for your kids in New York City than a full year at Yale or Harvard would cost.

A word to the wise: As with all things, kids—and even the most devoted teenage shoppers—will have limited attention spans for dragging around the City's stores. So set priories for their shopping time (and yours) and save your visits to the Gap and Footlocker for home.

Store hours: Most of the larger stores are open 10 A.M. to 6 P.M. Monday through Saturday (with extended hours until 8 P.M. on Thursday) and Sunday 12 P.M. to 5 P.M. But it's always best to call ahead to make sure a particular store will be open (some of the smaller boutiques, especially, change their hours often).

The following abbreviations are used to indicate the age-appropriateness of each store.

PK   Toddlers and pre-kindergarten; birth–4 years

K   Kids; 5–8 years

PT   Pre-teens; 9–12 years

T   Teenagers; 13 years and older

I've also indicated the neighborhood, using the following abbreviations:

BR: Brooklyn	BX: Bronx
CH: Chelsea	CT: Chinatown
EV: East Village	FD: Financial District
GD: Garment District	GP: Gramercy Park/Flatiron
GV: Greenwich Village	LES: Lower East Side
LI: Little Italy	MT: Midtown
MTE: Midtown East	MTW: Midtown West
Q: Queens	SH: SoHo
SI: Staten Island	TBC: TriBeCa
TD: Theater District	TS: Times Square
UES: Upper East Side	US: Union Square
UWS: Upper West Side	WV: West Village

Major Shopping Districts

In New York, no matter where you walk, stores abound. But there are some major shopping districts that every dedicated shopper loves to hit when visiting the City, whether for the first time or the fiftieth. Most of the stores mentioned here are described in more detail in the sections that follow; these neighborhood overviews are intended as a taste of things to come.

Fifth Avenue: Starting at FAO Schwarz at 58th Street and down to Saks Fifth Avenue at 49th Street, Fifth Avenue is a main thoroughfare. On this strip you'll find Trump Plaza (worth a look), Tiffany, Disney, NikeTown (around the corner on 57th St.), Coca-Cola, H&M, and Rockefeller Plaza. Farther along, at 40th Street, you'll hit Lord & Taylor.

Madison Avenue: The whole of Madison Avenue from 58th Street up to 94th Street consists of one high-end boutique after another, many of them flagship stores for designers (which many girls find fascinating). As you stroll up Madison, you'll pass the back entrance to FAO Schwarz, plus Barney's, TSE, BéBé, Jacadi, Polo, Oilily, Tartine et Chocolat, Olive & Bette's, Catimini, and Wicker Garden's Children. **Columbus Avenue:** Full of small boutiques, the avenue will have your children wandering happily along Columbus from the Capezio store at 66th Street, to Betsey Johnson, Z'Baby, and the weekend flea market at 77th Street, to Maxilla and Mandible near the Museum of Natural History.

SoHo: The streets of SoHo are rife with excellent shopping opportunities, enough to make any young girl squeal with delight—and any parent clutch the credit cards tightly. The main drags are along Spring Street, Prince Street, and West Broadway, though there are plenty of other crisscrossing smaller streets to browse. This is an excellent people-watching neighborhood.

The Village: 8th Street in the West Village and St. Marks Place in the East Village, this is the stuff that Hollywood movies are made of. Along 8th Street, between Fifth and Sixth Avenues especially, shoe stores abound, as do secondhand stores (like Andy's Chee-Pees), punk shops, and leather-goods shops. On the other side of Astor Place, between Third and Second Avenues, is where the real show is—tattoo parlors and piercing shops, lots of angry (harmless) youths in black (usually torn) clothing, street vendors with silver jewelry, punk shops selling leather and studs, rock posters—you get the idea. Most kids get a big kick out of this neighborhood, primarily because it's different from what they're accustomed to seeing. This strip is more for the show than anything else.

South Street Seaport and Pier 17: This is a great area for a picnic, lunch at the food court, a browse, a break, or all four. South Street Seaport includes different shops, most of which, like Brookstone, Abercrombie & Fitch, and Laura Ashley, you probably have back home. But the setting is lovely (the old cobblestone streets are the originals), there's a worthwhile museum, and, if you wander over to Pier 17 (the Seaport's central fixture), you can check out the sailboats, get a great view of the Brooklyn Bridge, and grab a fresh-squeezed lemonade. It's a great stop to coordinate with a visit to Liberty Island or Wall Street, or a ride on the Staten Island Ferry.

Lower Manhattan and the Financial District: Though mostly an office and professional area, there are some real gems in the neighborhood surrounding the former World Trade towers, such as the Century 21 department store. And money spent in the neighborhood is especially helpful to, and appreciated by, New York's businesses that are trying to rebuild downtown. For a comprehensive listing of stores in the area, visit the Web site of the New York Downtown Alliance at www.downtownny.com.

Manhattan Mall: The Manhattan Mall is not as much a great shopping destination (most of the stores are chains) as it is a great place to have lunch (there's an extensive food court on the top floor, with some more healthful options beyond the regular fast-food scene—salads, Greek food, deli sandwiches), take an indoor break, and get a great (free) view of the Empire State Building. It's also the ideal jumping-off point for a trip to Macy's and a walk down Broadway toward Union Square.

Commissioning a work of art outside the Met

A Note About Gift Shops

Nearly every museum and attraction in the City has an extensive and elaborate gift shop where you can browse through a well-chosen selection of everything from books to jewelry, clothes, house gifts, and art. If you are visiting any of the City's zoos, they are also good destinations for gift- and treat-buying for the children. So is, surprisingly enough, the main branch of the New York Public Library at 42nd Street and Fifth Avenue. I have not listed those shops here—they are discussed in chapter 5.

A ★ indicates a particularly noteworthy store for its price range, type, or appeal to kids.

Clothing

Of the literally hundreds of clothing and shoe stores in New York City, these are my favorites.

Au Chat Botté	*PK*
1192 Madison Avenue (at 87th St.), UES	**212-722-6474**

Very expensive, high-end European infant and toddler clothing—lots of pinks and blues—and baby furniture.

Baby Gap	*PK*
341 Columbus Avenue (at 76th St.), UWS	**212-875-9196**

Although there are more Gap stores around than you can shake a stick at, Baby Gaps are rare. This is a particularly nice and well-stocked one.

Bambini	**PK/K**
1367 Third Avenue (at 78th St.), UES	**212-717-6742**

Excellent selection of shoes and casual and dress clothes for children 3 months to 8 years. European imports are big here.

BéBé Thompson   PK/K/PT/T
1216 Lexington Avenue   212-249-4740
(between 82nd and 83rd Sts.), UES

Cute, sweet clothes—nothing but the best for the jet-setters. De-signer labels available; prices are high. Infant to 14 years.

★ Ben's for Kids   PK
1380 Third Avenue   212-794-2330
(between 78th and 79th Sts.), UES

One-stop shopping for your infant or toddler (up to 3 years), in-cluding not only clothes, but also furniture, strollers, clothing, and toys. A Manhattan favorite.

Bloomers   PK/K/PT
1042 Lexington Avenue   212-570-9529
(between 74th and 75th Sts.), UES

Designer clothes for infants 3 months to size 6x, plus children's sleepwear so exquisite it's a shame to use it just for sleeping—the owner prefers to think of it as playwear, too (up to size 12).

Bombalulu's   PK/K/PT
101 West 10th Street (between   212-463-0897
Seventh Ave. and Greenwich), WV

Hip, downtown clothing and toys.

Calypso Enfant   PK/K/PT
426 Broome St. (between   212-965-8910
Houston and Prince Sts.), EV

The downtown crowd has designer labels, too. There's even a line of baby bath products and clothes for mothers at the adult Ca-lypso store, located around the corner. Infant to 12 years.

Catimini	PK/K/PT
1284 Madison Avenue (between	212-987-0688
91st and 92nd Sts.), UES	

Very expensive and beautiful children's clothing. Catimini is the be-all and end-all in children's fashion, and the clothes are exceptionally comfortable. Infant to size 12 girls; up to size 10 boys.

East Side Kids	PK/K/PT/T
1298 Madison Avenue (between	212-360-5000
92nd and 93rd Sts.), UES	

Extensive selection of shoes and sneakers up to adult size 10.

G.C. William	PK/K/PT/T
1137 Madison Avenue (between	212-396-3400
84th and 85th Sts.), UES	

Casual to formalwear for boys to size 20 and girls to size 16. Also a good selection of girly knick-knacks—funky pads, pens, jewelry, and the like.

Good-Byes Children's Resale Shop	PK/K
230 East 78th Street (between	212-794-2301
Second and Third Aves.), UES	

Baby and children's gently used clothing, books, toys, and equipment. Newborn to 5 years.

Granny Made	PK/K
381 Amsterdam Avenue (between	212-496-1222
78th and 79th Sts.), UWS	

The merchandise has a handmade feel to it. Full line of layette plus unique, beautiful, classy sweaters and clothes for infant to age 7.

Great Feet (by Stride Rite)	PK/K/PT/T
1241 Lexington Avenue	212-249-0551
(at 84th St.), UES	

An excellent selection of dressy and casual shoes for children of all ages, featuring Sam & Libby, Nine West, Adidas, Nike, Kenneth Cole, Sperry, and, of course, Stride Rite.

★ *Greenstones & CIE*	PK/K/PT
1184 Madison Avenue (between	212-427-1665
86th and 87th Sts.), UES	
442 Columbus Avenue	212-580-4322
(at 81st St.), UWS	

A terrific, reasonably priced clothing destination for infants and boys and girls up to size 12. Hats, shoes, and slippers for infants, too. This store is new and bustling with customers.

★ *Harry's Shoes*	PK/K/PT/T
2299 Broadway (at 83rd St.), UWS	212-874-2035

You'd think they were giving something away at Harry's by the hordes of people who fill the store during operating hours. That certainly isn't the reason (nor is it the brusque service). Rather, the crowds come for the incredible selection of fine shoes for the entire family.

★ *Infinity*	PK/K/PT/T
1116 Madison Avenue (at 83rd St.), UES	212-517-4232

Infinity specializes in preteen clothing, but also sells for ages 4 to adult. The stock includes casual and dressy and novelty accessories. The store does a lot of mail order (20 percent of its business comes from mail order customers).

Jacadi   PK/K
1296 Madison Avenue (at 92nd St.), UES   212-369-1616
787 Madison Avenue (between   212-535-3200
66th and 67th Sts.), UES

Upscale French infants' clothing in muted and pastel colors.

Jane's Exchange   PK/K/PT
207 Avenue A (between 12th and   212-674-6268
13th Sts.), EV

Children's consignment store (up to size 12), plus maternity clothes.

La Layette   PK
170 East 61st Street (between   212-688-7072
Lexington and Third Aves.), UES

Extremely high-end frilly clothing for infants to children's size 2. Also a worthwhile stop for layettes, gifts, hand-painted furniture, and fine European linens.

La Petite Etoile   PK/K/PT/T
746 Madison Avenue (between   212-744-0975
64th and 65th Sts.), UES

French and Italian clothing lines for newborn to 14 years. Stock includes mostly casual clothes, but there are also some selections for dress up (including christening gowns).

★ *Lester's*   PK/K/PT/T
1534 Second Avenue (at 79th St.), UES   212-734-9292

A real New York institution, Lester's has been selling to New York parents since 1948. Still a family-run business (with plenty of third-generation customers coming through), Lester's caters to children from newborn up to size 16 girls, size 20 boys. The stock includes top clothing brands—imported and domestic—plus sneakers, dress, and casual shoes. Lester's also has a full layette department—everything the mother needs for her infant, birth to 3 months. They'll even hold onto the merchandise for you if you're superstitious about bringing it home before the baby is born. A good place to stock up for your daughter on accessories, jewelry, hair bits and bobs, and for kids going to camp with care packages, bunk junk, and camp labels.

★ *Little Eric*	**PK/K/PT/T**
1331 Third Avenue (between	**212-288-8987**
76th and 77th Sts.), UES	
1118 Madison Avenue (between	**212-717-1513**
83rd and 84th Sts.), UES	

An incredible selection of children's dress and casual shoes, all with the Little Eric label. Also name-brand sneakers. Sizes to men's 8 and women's 9.

Littlestars New York City	**PK/K**
968 Third Avenue (at 58th St.), MTE	**212-826-7159**

Clothes for children up to 8 years old, plus furniture.

Magic Windows and Magic Windows Baby	**PK/K/PT/T**
1186 Madison Avenue (between	**212-289-0028**
86th and 87th Sts.), UES	

Everything from casual everyday wear to clothes dressy enough for weddings. Also a good place to pick up baby blankets and stuffed animals. Newborn to size 16.

★ *Morris Brothers*   **K/PT/T**
2322 Broadway (at 84th St.), UWS   212-724-9000

You can outfit the whole family, kindergartners through teens, at Morris Brothers, a favorite destination of New York mothers for casual clothing and summer camp stock.

Nursery Lines   **PK**
1034 Lexington Avenue (at 74th St.), UES   212-396-4445

Emphasis on Italian imports, hand-knit sweaters and hand-embroidered clothes for children up to age 4. Also custom-designed nursery furniture.

Oilily   **PK/K/PT**
870 Madison Avenue   212-628-0100
(between 70th and 71st Sts.), UES

Brightly colored, soup-to-nuts clothing (reminiscent of Provençal-style fabrics) and accessories for ages newborn to 12.

Once Upon a Time   **PK/K/PT/T**
171 East 92nd Street (between   212-831-7619
Lexington and Third Aves.), UES

You can outfit your child from infant to size 14 at this UES store, which sells gently used (if used at all) clothing in season.

Second Act Children's Wear   **PK/K/PT/T**
1046 Madison Avenue (between   212-988-2440
79th and 80th Sts.), UES

Barely used clothing for infants, boys, and girls up to age 13, as well as toys, dolls, a great selection of books, and sometimes ice skates and inline skates. The range of quality is from very expensive clothing down to Gap and Levis.

★ *Shoofly*	**PK/K/PT**
465 Amsterdam Avenue (between	**212-580-4390**
82nd and 83rd Sts.), UWS	
42 Hudson Street (between	**212-406-3270**
Duane and Thomas Sts.), TBC	

If I had to choose one store for kids' shoes, I'd have to say that Shoofly is right up there. The best selection in town (includes the largest selection of imported children's shoes in the country). Also good for children's accessories and accoutrements like hats, belts, and socks.

Small Change	**PK/K/PT/T**
964 Lexington Avenue (at 70th St.), UES	**212-772-6455**

Beautiful, classy floral dresses for girls and babies. Clothes for newborns to size 12 boys and size 14 girls. Also a small selection of shoes and accessories.

Spring Flowers	**PK/K/PT**
1050 Third Avenue (at 62nd St.), UES	**212-758-2669**
905 Madison Avenue (at 72nd St.), UES	**212-717-8182**

Strictly high-end (with branches in Beverly Hills and Palm Beach), this boutique outfits infants and boys to size 8, girls to preteen (approximately size 14 girls). Casual, dressy, and formal wear, plus a selection of shoes for kids.

Tartine et Chocolat	**PK/K**
1047 Madison Avenue (at 80th St.), UES	**212-717-2112**

A tremendous selection of high-end French import clothing for infants through children's size 10. Tartine also carries a full line of layette accoutrements and baby equipment plus a limited number of furniture items, including cribs, dressers, armoires, nursery items, linens, and accessories.

Wicker Garden's Children	**PK**
1327 Madison Avenue	**212-410-7001**
(between 93rd and 94th Sts.), UES	

Very expensive boutique with mostly white and dress-up clothes. Children's furniture is also a big part of the inventory. Newborn to size 4.

★ ***Z'Baby and Company***	**PK/K/PT/T**
100 West 72nd Street	**212-579-BABY (2229)**
(at Columbus), UWS	
996 Lexington Avenue	**212-472-BABY (2229)**
(at 72nd St.), UES	

High-end, too-cute designer clothes. Infant to age 15.

Zitomer	**PK/K/PT/T**
969 Madison Avenue	**212-737-5560**
(between 75th and 76th Sts.), UES	

This amazing store—nearly a department store—started out as a pharmacy. Over the years, as other tenants moved from the building, Zitomer expanded to include a full selection of mostly

Money-Saving Tip

A few months before you leave home, stop buying the kids things that can wait, like clothes and shoes, and save some of the purchasing for the trip. When kids ask for things, say, "Let's buy that in New York." This will build anticipation and add to the shopping budget, even though it's money you would have spent at home anyway.

European clothing, for children newborn to age 14, with everything from casual to formalwear. Head for the third floor for the toy (and game) department, and don't overlook the bath and hair accessories—and school uniforms, too.

Extras

★ *Art & Tapisserie*	PK/K/PT/T
1242 Madison Avenue (at 89th St.), UES	**212-722-3222**

A delightful selection of wooden toys and puzzles, original furnishings (step stools, tables and chairs, toy chests), hooded towels (the cutest you've ever seen), blankets, and clothes (newborn to 14 years). A great place to buy gifts.

Little Extras	PK/K/PT
676 Amsterdam Avenue (at 93rd St.), UWS	**212-721-6161**

The selection of infant mobiles alone is worth the trip to this store, but they also stock children's furniture, stuffed animals, infant toys and supplies, and a great selection of birth announcements.

Teen Clothing

Teen clothing is a totally different proposition from kids' clothing. For today's hip teens, the downtown scene is where it's at. Although the uptown stores like Barney's, Bendels, and Bloomies carry the latest high-end fashions, and many children's clothing stores market to teens, it's in the Village, SoHo, and even Chinatown—at the grownup stores—where you'll find the funkier clothes most teens really want. Secondhand clothing stores abound in these neighborhoods, as do outdoor markets, up-to-the-minute celebrity status shops, and make-up boutiques. These are some of the best for teens.

Top Ten Unique or Very Unusual Stores

Alice Underground	PT/T
481 Broadway (between	212-431-9067
Grand and Broome Sts.), SH	

A New York City classic. The stock consists mostly of vintage clothes with a smaller selection of new originals (including imports from around the world).

Amsterdam Boutique	T
454 Broadway (between	212-925-0422
Grand and Howard Sts.), SH	

Subtlety is not the name of the game here. Teen girls happily shop for fitted clothes, leather pants, sequins, and anything brightly colored.

372

SHOPPING

Andy's Chee-Pees	PT/T
691 Broadway (between	212-420-5980
Third and Fourth Aves.), EV	

An all-time favorite (albeit somewhat overpriced) for cool vintage and secondhand clothes. About one-fourth of the stock is new clothing.

Anik	PT/T
1355 Third Avenue (between	212-861-9840
77th and 78th Sts.), UES	
1122 Madison Avenue (between	212-249-2417
83rd and 84th Sts.), UES	

Attractive fashion-forward clothes for teen girls.

Anthropologie	K/PT/T
375 West Broadway (between	212-343-7070
Spring and Broome Sts.), SH	

A fabulous selection of eclectic, expensive clothes for teens. Expect to find $39 T-shirts and the like. A great place for browsing, and there are tons of gadgets, gift items, and housewares, too.

Antique Boutique	PT/T
712 Broadway (between	212-460-8830
4th St. and Astor Pl.), EV	

A great place to shop for vintage clothing and mass-market, trendy, fashion-forward styles. Downstairs, look for designer labels.

Avirex	**PT/T**
652 Broadway (between	**212-254-4000**
Houston and Prince Sts.), SH	

Avirex is especially good on casual clothes for boys, particularly T-shirts, pants, bomber jackets, and other sporty wear.

Betsey Johnson	**PT/T**
138 Wooster Street (between	**212-995-5048**
Prince and Houston Sts.), SH	
248 Columbus Avenue (between	**212-362-3364**
71st and 72nd Sts.), UWS	
251 East 60th Street (between	**212-319-7699**
Second and Third Aves.), UES	
1060 Madison Avenue (at 80th St.), UES	**212-734-1257**

Full line of the famous Betsey Johnson clothing for girls, teens, and women.

Big Drop	**PT/T**
174 Spring Street (between	**212-966-4299**
West Broadway and Thompson), SH	
1321 Third Avenue (between	**212-988-3344**
75th and 76th Sts.), UES	

Fashionable, trendy girls' clothes that are sure to delight.

Buffalo Chips	**PK/K/PT/T**
355 West Broadway (between	**212-625-8400**
Broome and Grand Sts.), SH	

This is what we call chic Western wear. Huge selection of cowboy boots (including some that have been previously worn), belts, and hats. Who doesn't know somebody that could use a pink cowgirl hat? Also suede cowboy and cowgirl outfits for kids.

★ *Canal Jean Co.*   **K/PT/T**
504 Broadway (between   **212-226-1130**
Spring and Broome Sts.), SH

As a teen, this classic store was always a stop on my New York City walking circuit, and it remains so for most in-the-know kids with offbeat tastes. With a large selection of jeans, shirts, and casual wear, this store demands a visit, if only for a browse. Also check out the vintage and surplus sections.

★ *Century 21 Department Store*   **PK/K/PT/T**
22 Cortland Street (at Broadway), FD   **212-227-9092**
www.c21stores.com

New York's "best kept secret"—this department store is a New York favorite, and you'll find something here you won't find at other department stores—bargains. Century 21 is a discount department store. European and American fashions, including designer labels, are discounted up to 70 percent off retail prices.

Cheap Jack's   **PT/T**
841 Broadway (between   **212-777-9564**
13th and 14th Sts.), US

Though nothing at Cheap Jack's is actually cheap, the store does have a great selection of vintage clothes.

Chill on Broadway   **PT/T**
427 Broadway (at Howard St.), SH   **212-343-2709**

A fashionable selection of clothes and shoes at affordable prices with a wide range, from baggy linen trousers to colorful dresses, floral prints, and snakeskin-textured red leather shoes.

*Want to go
for a ride?*

★ *Conway*	PK/K/PT/T
1333 Broadway (at 35th St.), FD (largest store, including shoes)	212-967-3460
151 William Street (between Fulton and Nassau Sts.), FD	212-374-1072
45 Broad Street (Exchange-Beaver), FD	212-943-8900
201 East 42nd Street (at Third Ave.), MTE	212-922-5030
11 West 34th Street (between Fifth and Sixth Aves.), MTW	212-967-1370
450 Seventh Avenue (between 34th and 35th Sts.), MTW	212-967-1371
225 West 34th Street (between Seventh and Eighth Aves.), MTW	212-967-7390

Conway is a great stop for children from early childhood through the teenage years. Up-to-date fashion knockoffs at extremely good prices should satisfy not-too-picky children and parents. Don't expect to find the highest quality workmanship on these clothes, but they'll last until your child outgrows them or the fashion changes.

Daffy's	K/PT/T
335 Madison Avenue (at 44th St.), MTE	212-557-4422
1311 Broadway (at 34th St.), MTW	212-736-4477
111 Fifth Avenue (at 18th St.), GP	212-529-4477
125 East 57th Street (between Lexington and Park Aves.), MTE	212-376-4477

Name-brand clothing for the family, at discounted prices.

Danskin	K/PT/T
159 Columbus Avenue (between 67th and 68th Sts.), UWS	212-724-2992

Minimalist clothing, tank tops, workout clothes, leotards, and the like.

Da'Vinci	PT/T
37 West 8th Street (between Sixth Ave. and MacDougal St.), WV	212-674-4746

A vast selection of Italian imported shoes, belts, and bags.

Detour	PT/T
Women's: 154 Prince Street (at West Broadway), SH	212-966-3635
Men's: 425 West Broadway (between Prince and Houston Sts.), SH	212-219-2692

A strong selection of reasonably priced (very hard to find in SoHo), trendy clothes.

Diesel	K/PT/T
770 Lexington Avenue (across from Bloomingdale's), UES	212-308-0055

A huge example of this chain store (lots of jeans and such), Manhattan's Diesel even has a theme-style restaurant that's fun for the kids.

★ *Dollhouse*	PT/T
400 Lafayette Street (at East 4th St.), EV	212-539-1800

French and American styles of very chic clothing.

8th Street Lab	PT/T
69 East 8th Street (between Mercer St. and Broadway), EV	212-228-9657

A gold mine of trendy Village-wear. With loud music pounding all around, your teen will be thrilled to go through the racks of hip downtown clothing, plus sunglasses and funky accoutrements.

Energywear	PT/T
140 East 63rd Street (at Lexington Ave.), UES	212-752-5360

Predictably skimpy clothes. This fitness-oriented store (most items relate to sports and fitness) is part of the Equinox gym. There's a selection of clothes for working out (and some for going out), and equipment as well.

Flying A	PK/PT/T
169 Spring Street (at West Broadway), SH	212-965-9090

Half the stock in this store is shoes (including fur clogs), and the other half is clothes and accessories, like tiny T-shirts, socks, fun purses, and even a small selection of baby/toddler shirts, too.

★ *Forréal*	PT/T
1369 Third Avenue (between 78th and 79th Sts.),UES	212-396-0563
1200 Lexington Avenue (between 81st and 82nd Sts.), UES	212-717-0493

Forréal Basics	PT/T
1335 Third Avenue (between 76th and 77th Sts.), UES	212-734-2105

Extremely popular at this moment with teen girls around town, Basics and the dressier uptown stores have racks of something for every occasion. Basics has jeans and T-shirts and casual wear. Often mothers end up shopping for themselves while they wait for their extremely choosy daughters.

Galo	K/PT/T
825 Lexington Avenue (between 63rd and 64th Sts.), UES	212-832-3922

European imported shoes for boys and girls up to size 38 (approximately size 7, American, for men; 8 for women).

H&M	PK/K/PT/T
640 Fifth Avenue (at 51st St.), MTE	212-489-0390

All the rage since it hit Fifth Avenue (they can't manage to keep the shelves stocked), H&M is a huge Swedish department store with great styles and a lot of variety—and the price is ever so right!

Intermix	PT/T
1003 Madison Avenue (between 77th and 78th Sts.), UES	212-249-7858

| 125 Fifth Avenue (between 19th and 20th Sts.), CH | 212-533-9720 |

Trendy contemporary clothing that most every girl seems to want to have.

| *Lord of the Fleas* | PT/T |
| 2142 Broadway (at 75th St.), UWS | 212-875-8815 |

Hip, fun clothing—ideal for the girl who likes to be original (and that doesn't have to mean weird).

| *Know Style* | PT/T |
| 44 West 8th Street (between Sixth Ave. and MacDougal St.), WV | 212-529-7655 |

A large selection of clothes for guys and girls, at reasonable prices.

| *Lucky Brand* | PT/T |
| 38 Greene Street (at Grand St.), SH | 212-625-0707 |

Lucky Brand retail store for jeans.

| *Marsha D.D.* | PK/K/PT/T |
| 1574 Third Avenue (between 88th and 89th Sts.), UES | 212-831-2422 |

A favorite destination for Upper East Side kids, D.D. is jam-packed (though slightly less so now that the store has been relocated to its new, more spacious digs on Third Avenue) with casual clothes (including bathing suits) for kids' sizes 4 to 16 for girls, 4 to 20 for boys. Also good for trinkets, gadgets, and summer-camp packages.

Medici   **PT/T**
420 Columbus Avenue (at 80th St.), UWS   212-712-9342

Up-to-the-minute shoe fashions, primarily featuring the Medici brand.

M.W. Teen   **K/PT/T**
1188 Madison Avenue (at 87th St.), UES   212-289-0181

Next door to Magic Windows, Teen provides upscale clothing to fashion-conscious teens (boys to size 12, girls to teen sizes—approximately age 16) as well as jewelry and accessories.

Necessary Clothing   **PT/T**
470 Broadway (between   212-966-9011
Grand and Broome Sts.), SH

One of the many giant stores that line Broadway. Full of affordable, trendy, brightly colored, mostly skimpy clothes for girls.

Nelly M.   **PT/T**
1309 Lexington Avenue (at 88th St.), UES   212-996-4410

Fashionable, skimpy clothing is the stock and trade at this UES boutique.

Nicole Miller   **PT/T**
780 Madison Avenue (at 66th St.), UES   212-288-9779
134 Prince Street (between   212-343-1362
**   West Broadway and Wooster St.), SH**

The place to shop if you're a fan of Nicole Miller's funky style.

Old Navy Clothing   **PK/K/PT/T**
610 Avenue of the Americas   212-645-0663
**   (at 18th St.), CH**

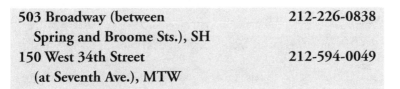
503 Broadway (between	212-226-0838
Spring and Broome Sts.), SH	
150 West 34th Street	212-594-0049
(at Seventh Ave.), MTW	

This chain hasn't been around all that long, and many towns still don't have one. For fashionable, affordable casual clothes by the same people who own the Gap and Banana Republic, this is a good stop if you don't have a local branch.

Olive & Bette's	PT/T
1070 Madison Avenue (at 81st St.), UES	212-717-9655
252 Columbus Avenue (at 72nd St.), UWS	212-579-2178

Expect to pay more than $100 for jeans at this superhip women's clothing store. Featured in the likes of *Mademoiselle* and *Marie Claire,* O & B belongs to the scantily clad club.

| *Phat Farm* | PK/K/PT/T |
| 129 Prince Street (at Wooster St.), SH | 212-533-PHAT |

Especially good for boys, the store features Phat Farm brand casual clothes, jeans, jackets, and shoes for the whole family.

| *Polo-Ralph Lauren* | PK/K/PT/T |
| 867 Madison Avenue (at 72nd St.), UES | 212-606-2100 |

You won't find a more beautiful place to stock up on Polo clothing. Although the help can be a bit stiff, the gorgeous surroundings more than make up for the staff's snootiness.

Learning Tip

Have a peek into the Polo Store at 72nd Street and Madison Avenue. Gertrude Rhinelander Waldo commissioned this beautiful mansion as a personal residence, but she never moved in.

Rampage	PK/K/PT/T
127 Prince Street (at Wooster St.), SH	212-995-9569

Casual clothes like jeans, tank tops, T-shirts and lots of knitwear.

Reminiscence	PT/T
50 West 23rd Street (between Fifth and Sixth Aves.), CH	212-243-2292

A great selection of vintage clothing for trendy teens who are out to make a statement. A good place to stock up on funky gift items, too.

Replay Store	PK/K/PT/T
109 Prince Street (at Greene St.), SH	212-673-6300

Especially good for jeans for the whole family—you'll never see a more varied selection of fades anywhere.

Rugged Sole	PT/T
7 West 8th Street (between Fifth Ave. and MacDougal St.), WV	212-477-7555

A truly vast selection of sneakers.

Sacco	PT/T
2355 Broadway (at 86th St.), UWS	212-874-8362
324 Columbus Avenue (at 75th St.), UWS	212-799-5229
111 Thompson Street (between Prince and Spring Sts.), SH	212-925-8010
94 Seventh Avenue (at 16th St.), CH	212-675-5180

Whatever shoe styles are hot, they've got them at Sacco, with their own label to boot.

★ *Scoop*   **PT/T**
1275 Third Avenue   **212-535-5577**
  (between 73rd and 74th Sts.), UES
532 Broadway (between   **212-925-2886**
  Spring and Prince Sts.), SH

Teen girls go crazy over this place, as do the aspiring teens (they struggle for a find, just so they can purchase anything with the Scoop label) who are trying so hard to be with it. The best selection is at the uptown branch, where there are three Scoop stores in a row, all interconnected. Prices are steep, fashions are fleeting, and styles are far too risqué for my taste, but I'm sure these girls don't want my opinion on this one, anyway.

Screaming Mimi's   **PT/T**
382 Lafayette Street (between   **212-677-6464**
East 4th St. and Great Jones), EV

A mix of vintage clothes, sportswear, shoes, and trinkets from the 1950s through the 1970s, as well as newer, more current items.

Shoe Closet   **PT/T**
9 West 8th Street (between   **212-529-0840**
MacDougal St. and Fifth Ave.), WV

A large selection of not-too-crazy shoes.

Shoe Plaza   **PT/T**
60 West 8th Street (at Sixth Ave.), WV **212-420-8832**

Another 8th Street shoe emporium with a giant inventory.

Sofia   PT/T
828 Lexington Avenue (between   212-207-4370
63rd and 64th Sts.), UES

Retro styles of skimpy, trendy clothes for mature teens with brave—or indifferent—parents.

Stella Dallas   PT/T
218 Thompson Street (between   212-674-0447
Bleecker and West 3rd Sts.), WV

A small, somewhat dingy store packed with a good vintage selection; I almost bought my wedding dress at this old Village gem.

Tani   PT/T
2020 Broadway (between   212-873-4361
69th and 70th Sts.), UWS

An excellent selection of high-quality and fashionable shoes and boots.

Trash and Vaudeville   PT/T
4 St. Mark's Place (between   212-982-3590
Second and Third Aves.), EV

Clothing and shoes best described as punk and rocker styles. It's a great stop for a peek at the current European fashions.

Urban Outfitters   K/PT/T
162 Second Avenue (between   212-375-1277
    10th and 11th Sts.), EV
374 Avenue of the Americas   212-677-9350
    (between Waverly St. and Washington Sq.), WV
628 Broadway (between   212-475-0009
    Bleecker and Houston Sts.), SH

There's no shortage of hip and trendy clothes, gifts, furniture, and trinkets at this homegrown New York City fave (now a national chain).

★ *Venus*   K/PT/T
382 West Broadway (between   **212-966-4066**
Broome and Spring Sts.), SH

The stock in this downstairs store is sure to bring a smile to everyone's face. Half crazy-clothes (the Bruce Lee button-down shirt is amongst my favorites) and half gadgets and accoutrements (boas, wigs, etc.), Venus is definitely good for a visit. The staff is a real hoot, too.

Village Designer Shoes   PT/T
1186 Madison Avenue (between   **212-534-4807**
86th and 87th Sts.), UES

Very fashionable (and expensive) shoes for girls wearing adult sizes 5½ and up. Just because the shoes are nice, don't assume the staff will also be nice; but don't be too put off—they mean no harm.

Village Leather   PT/T
355 Sixth Avenue (between   **212-352-3105**
West and 4th Sts.), WV

Whether you decide to let your daughter buy the high-heeled boots with glitter is up to you, but rest assured, they do have them here. They also have a tamer selection of shoes, leather pants, and jackets, for those not quite up to the red spiked numbers.

Warehouse   PT/T
581 Broadway (between   **212-941-0910**
Houston and Prince Sts.), SH

On the fringe of SoHo, here's a wide selection of fashionable clothes at reasonable prices.

| *What Goes Around Comes Around* | **PT/T** |
| 351 West Broadway (between Broome and Grand Sts.), SH | **212-343-9303** |

This store's stock is based on the premise that fashion repeats itself. It is also a high-end boutique vintage clothing store (with SoHo rent to pay). Don't expect to find many bargains.

| *Yellow Rat Bastard New York City* | **PT/T** |
| 478 Broadway (between Broome and Grand Sts.), SH | **212-219-8569** |

Good for boys especially, don't let the name scare you at this very downtown store. Jeans and other casual clothes are the hits here.

| *Zara* | **PK/K/PT/T** |
| 580 Broadway (between Prince and Houston Sts.), SH | **212-343-1725** |

This Spanish department store carries clothes with flair—good for the whole family.

Insider's Tip
"Visit SoHo on a weekend, when it's most crowded, for the ultimate in people-watching." —*Billy, father of two*

Bookstores

We have Barnes & Noble and Borders all over town (including the original Barnes & Noble, and the largest one). But, because you've come all the way to New York City, you'll surely prefer to take advantage of our unique local (often family-run) bookstores.

Top Ten Favorite Stores for Parents to Stock Up for Kids

1. Lester's (p. 365)

2. Ben's for Kids (p. 362)

3. Harry's Shoes (p. 364)

4. Z'Baby and Company (p. 369)

5. Shoofly (p. 368)

6. Century 21 (p. 374)

7. Morris Brothers (p. 367)

8. Art & Tapisserie (p. 370)

9. Little Eric (p. 366)

10. Conway (p. 375)

Bank Street Books   PK/K/PT
610 West 112th Street (at Broadway), UWS   212-678-1654

Catering to children and teachers, this one is worth the trip uptown.

Bookberries   PK/K/PT
983 Lexington Avenue (at 71st St.), UES   212-794-9400

A good selection of picture books. One nice feature is that they'll put together gift baskets with a selection of your favorite books.

Books of Wonder   PK/K/PT/T
16 West 18th Street (between   212-989-3270
Fifth and Sixth Aves.), GP

Specialty bookstore focusing on hard-to-find and collectors' titles. Children are welcome, and story hour at 11:45 A.M. on

Sundays is an especially popular time at this neighborhood store. The selection is appropriate for infants to midteens.

Choices—The Recovery Bookshop	**PK/K**
220 East 78th Street (between	**212-794-3858**
Second and Third Aves.), UES	

This store is of the self-help variety, but they also have a very good selection of children's books.

Drama Book Shop	**K/PT/T**
250 West 40th Street, MTW	**212-944-0595**

A limited selection of drama and theater books geared toward children, including books on children in theater, paper doll books, and paper theater cutouts.

Forbidden Planet	**K/PT/T**
840 Broadway (at 13th St.), US	**212-473-1576**

Science fiction and fantasy books, with a good selection of children's comic books, trading cards, and games, too.

Gryphon Bookshop	**PK/K/PT/T**
2246 Broadway (between	**212-362-0706**
80th and 81st Sts.), UWS	

Used books with extensive children's section.

J. Levine Books & Judaica	**PK/K/PT/T**
5 West 30th Street, (between	**212-695-6888**
Park and Madison Aves.), MTE	

A large selection of Jewish books for all ages of children.

The Julliard School Bookstore   PT/T
60 Lincoln Center Plaza, UWS   212-799-5000, ext. 237

An extensive selection of music, recordings, and books about music—it's Julliard, what do you expect?

Librairie de France   PK/K/PT/T
610 Fifth Avenue, Rockefeller   212-581-8810
Center Promenade, MTE

A full complement of books in French for all ages of children, as well as adults.

Logos Bookstore   PK/K/PT/T
1575 York Avenue (between   212-517-7292
83rd and 84th Sts.), UES

Specializing in religious titles—but not exclusively—Logos carries an extensive selection of Christian, Jewish, and secular books for children and adults. There's even a small outdoor garden, perfect for a quiet break.

Rand McNally Map & Travel Store   PK/K/PT/T
150 East 52nd Street (between   212-758-7488
Lexington and Third Aves.), MTE

In addition to the great map selection, this store also carries games, puzzles, activities for the car, globes, and other interesting travel-related items.

Rubys Book Sale   PK/K/PT/T
119 Chambers Street (between   212-732-8676
Church St. and West Broadway), FD

Large selection of children's books, all ages.

Shakespeare & Company Booksellers	PK/K/PT/T
716 Broadway (at East 4th St.), EV	212-529-1330
939 Lexington Avenue (at 69th St.), UES	212-570-0201
137 East 23rd Street (at Gramercy St.), GP	212-505-2021
1 Whitehall Street (between	212-742-7025
Broadway and Bowling Green), FD	

A New York institution, be prepared for brusque service (old New York style), but they carry a good selection.

Strand Bookstore	PK/K/PT/T
828 Broadway (at 12th), US	212-473-1452
Strand Annex	PK/K/PT/T
95 Fulton Street (three	212-732-6070
blocks east of Broadway), FD	

This is New York's favorite place to browse for secondhand, scarce, and out-of-print books. A New York establishment of long standing, with a slogan that says it all: "Home of 8 miles of books."

Teachers College Bookstore	PK/K
1224 Amsterdam Avenue	212-678-3920
(at 120th St.), UWS	

The huge selection of educational and children's books is why people are willing to make the trip so far uptown. Offers two floors of children's books in addition to educational toys and extensive teacher's sections.

West Side Judaica & Bookstore	PK/K/PT/T
2412 Broadway (between	212-362-7846
88th and 89th Sts.), UWS	

Jewish books for adults and children.

> ## Charlie's Pick of New York City's Top Comic Book Stores*
>
> Cosmic Comics (p. 391)
>
> Gotham City Comics (p. 391)
>
> Midtown Comic (p. 392)
>
> Roger's Time Machine (p. 391)
>
> *Charlie is my 11-year-old-nephew.*

Collectibles, Cards, and Comics

★ *Cosmic Comics*	PT/T
36 East 23rd Street, 2nd floor (at Madison Ave.), GP	212-460-5322

Cosmic is the cleanest of the lot, and the comics are the most physically accessible, even to younger kids—comics are displayed in low-level bins. And perhaps best of all, if you're lucky enough to be here on a Sunday, the special (from noon to 6 P.M.) is half-price on new comics for kids under 16.

★ *Gotham City Comics*	PT/T
800 Lexington Avenue, 2nd floor (at 62nd St.), UES	212-980-0009

Gotham City offers very good service and a big selection of new and used comics.

It's "A"nother Hit   K/PT/T
131 West 33rd Street (between   **212-564-4111**
Sixth and Seventh Aves.), MTW

This is a favorite stop of city boys because they carry everything: Comics, toys, collector's cards, memorabilia, and sports cards (baseball, basketball, hockey, football, soccer, and racing).

Jim Hanley's Universe   PT/T
4 West 33rd Street (between   **212-268-7088**
Fifth Ave. and Broadway), MTW

Expect to find a wide selection of comics at this friendly store.

★ Midtown Comic   PT/T
200 West 40th Street (at 7th Ave.), TD   **212-302-8192**

This second- and third-floor store (comics on second, toys and trading cards on third) has a very good selection of new and used comics. And if you get hungry, there are lots of good restaurants just downstairs.

MVP Cards   PT/T
256 East 89th Street (between   **212-831-2273**
Second and Third Aves.), UES

A good selection of sports cards: baseball, basketball, football . . .

Roger's Time Machine   PT/T
207 West 14th Street (2nd fl.; between   **212-691-0380**
Seventh and Eighth Aves.), CH

These guys are serious about comics. They carry a broad selection from current to collectibles, underground and alternative.

Great atmosphere, and the best pricing on used comics. The staff is super-friendly, and, best of all, there are chairs for the weary parents (and kids).

★ *The Sleep of Reason* 47 West 8th Street (between MacDougal St. and 6th St.), WV	K/PT/T 212-982-7901

It's well worth the trip up the flight of stairs (second floor) to get to this crowded, friendly comic book store. The selection is vast, everyone is welcome, and the staff couldn't be nicer. If they don't have what you're looking for, they can tell you who does.

St. Marks Comics 11 St. Marks Place (between Second and Third Aves.), EV 150 Chambers (between West Broadway and Greenwich), FD	K/PT/T 212-598-9439 212-385-4108

Don't expect handholding at this Saint Marks Place comic book mecca. They have a tremendous selection, though they don't take very good care of their stock, perhaps because the store occupies such a small space (comics are piled on the floor). Be up on your pricing, too, because the prices are somewhat random and often out of line with reality.

In addition to the comic book stores listed, walk along Saint Marks Place, between Second and Third Avenues, for a handful of other shops.

Consumer Electronics

I've found that kids, especially boys, absolutely love to spend hours upon hours in the gigantic electronics stores of New York City.

B & H Photo-Video   **K/PT/T**
420 Ninth Avenue (between   **212-444-6615**
33rd and 34th Sts.), MTW

An extensive selection of camera, audio, and video equipment. Prices are as good as you'll find.

★ *Detective Store International*   **K/PT/T**
173 Christopher Street   **212-366-6466**
(at West Side Hwy.), WV

Sells all sorts of high-tech gadgets like you see in the movies: Surveillance equipment, body armor, special alarm systems, metal detectors . . . a real hit with the boys.

Hammacher Schlemmer   **K/PT/T**
147 East 57th Street (between   **212-421-9000**
Lexington and Third Aves.), MTE

High-end, high-tech gadgets for the person who has everything, or who just wants to play with toys.

★ *J&R*   **K/PT/T**
Addresses all along Park Row, FD   **800-426-6027**

Ten related stores on Park Row between Beekman and Anne Streets carrying every conceivable type of electronic equipment, from computers to cameras.

The Sony Store   **K/PT/T**
550 Madison Avenue (between   **212-833-8830**
55th and 56th Sts.), MTE

You can see and play with all of the latest Sony gadgets at this welcoming, high-tech emporium. Perfect to coordinate with a visit to Sony World of Wonder.

Spectra	**K/PT/T**
903 Madison Avenue (between	**212-744-2255**
72nd and 73rd Sts.), UES	

Home theater electronics store.

Insider's Tip

"When visiting a department store, it helps to have a plan of attack. Know what you're looking for, or you'll waste all your time wandering. If you separate from your kids, which you might want to do if they're old enough, pick a place and time to meet at regular intervals." —*Addie, mother of two*

Department Stores

Department stores in New York are an entire culture unto themselves, and each one has a distinctive personality.

Barneys	**PK/K/PT/T**
660 Madison Avenue (at 61st St.), UES	**212-826-8900**

Popular with the Hollywood set, Barneys is a status symbol all its own.

Bloomingdale's	**PK/K/PT/T**
1000 Third Avenue (between	**212-355-5900**
59th and 60th Sts.), UES	

This remains a favorite stop for preteen and teenage girls, from the Bloomies undies to the multitudes of make-up counters.

| *Henri Bendel* | PK/K/PT/T |
| 712 Fifth Avenue (at 55th St.), MTE | 212-247-1100 |

A high-end boutique-ish department store with a great make-up department.

Lord & Taylor	PK/K/PT/T
424 Fifth Avenue (between	212-391-3344
38th and 39th Sts.), MTE	

A very extensive children's department is only one of the draws at this New York City classic.

City Fact

Even in this age of mega-malls and superstores, Macy's remains the world's largest department store: An entire New York City block.

| *Macy's* | PK/K/PT/T |
| 34th Street (at Broadway), MTW | 212-695-4400 |

You could spend an entire day walking the many floors at Macy's, and many people do. If you happen to be in New York City during Thanksgiving, be sure to watch the Macy's parade,

Learning Tip

Macy's wasn't always the largest department store in the world. Term paper idea: Where was the first Macy's and how did it get its start? How did Macy's differ from any other store of its time? (Example: Did any store offer a money-back guarantee before Macy's?)

or, at holiday time, you can check out the extensive Christmas windows.

Saks Fifth Avenue	PK/K/PT/T
611 Fifth Avenue (between	212-753-4000
49th and 50th Sts.), MTE	

A good destination for the entire family to shop or browse, SFA also has a very good restaurant with a worthwhile view.

Dolls and Dollhouses

Manhattan Doll House	K/PT/T
236 Third Avenue (between	212-253-9549
19th and 20th Sts.), GP	

Miniatures, dollhouses, and dolls for play and collectors.

★ *New York Doll Hospital*	K/PT/T
787 Lexington Avenue (2nd fl.;	212-838-7527
between 61st and 62nd Sts.), UES	

This hundred-year-old business (opened in 1900) is a real New York institution. A tiny space that can hold only three to four people at any given time, it is as much a museum as a store. Here they buy and sell antique dolls and restore animals (of the stuffed variety), toys, dolls, and mechanical toys. They can also outfit your doll in made-to-order clothes, shoes, and socks. "We can repair it if was made today, yesterday, or thirty years ago, it's just a matter of mechanics," say the owners. Don't mind the piles of heads and headless doll bodies lying on the floor—it's all part of this place's charm.

Kids' Top Ten Favorite Stores

1. girlprops.com (p. 401)

2. Scoop (p. 383)

3. Infinity (p. 364)

4. Forréal (p. 378)

5. J&R (p. 394)

6. Dollhouse (p. 377)

7. Enchanted Forest (p. 416)

8. The Sleep of Reason (p. 393)

9. America's Hobby Center (p. 404)

10. H&M (p. 378)

Tiny Doll House	K/PT/T
1179 Lexington Avenue (between	212-744-3719
79th and 80th Sts.), UES	

TDH sells dollhouses, furniture, and accessories. They can outfit you with everything you need for your house (starting at about age 5 and up), but it's not a store for unruly tots because there are lots of collectibles, too.

Games

Chess Forum	K/PT/T
219 Thompson Street (between	212-475-2369
3rd and Bleecker Sts.), WV	

Just across the street from the Chess Shop, Chess Forum carries a similar stock with an equal number of enthusiasts.

Chess Shop   K/PT/T
230 Thompson Street (between   212-475-9580
3rd and Bleecker Sts.), WV

A wide range of chess boards, pieces, and instructional information on display, with devotees playing inside.

The Compleat Strategist   K/PT/T
11 East 33rd Street (between   212-685-3880
Fifth and Madison Aves.), MTE

This is a popular destination for older boys in search of board
games, strategy games, and role-playing games (like Dungeons
and Dragons).

★ *Forbidden Planet*   K/PT/T
840 Broadway (at 13th St.), US   212-473-1576

An enormous store selling a variety of strategy, board, and video
games, books, videos, and T-shirts.

Game Quest   K/PT/T
1596 Third Avenue (between   212-423-0697
89th and 90th Sts.), UES

Video games are the specialty of the house, but don't expect to
find demos out for play.

Game Show   K/PT/T
1240 Lexington Avenue   212-472-8011
   (at 84th St.), UES
474 Sixth Avenue (at 12th St.), WV   212-633-6328

Primarily games and puzzles geared toward teens and adults
(though they do carry some toys and gadgets that are appropriate

for younger kids, especially in the summer, when New York parents are planning packages for sleep-away camp).

Games Workshop	**K/PT/T**
54 East 8th Street (between	**212-982-6314**
Broadway and Mercer St.), WV	

A full complement of tabletop strategy and war games. The friendly staff will be more than happy to tell you all about this hobby if you let them.

Video Gamesters	**K/PT/T**
244 West 14th Street (between	**212-929-3366**
Seventh and Eighth Aves.), CH	

A wide selection of video games, with a few on display for play—but mostly a buying destination.

Gifts and Goodies

Alphabets	**K/PT/T**
2284 Broadway (between	**212-579-5702**
82nd and 83rd Sts.), UWS	
115 Avenue A (at 7th St.), EV	**212-475-7250**
47 Greenwich Avenue (between	**212-229-2966**
Sixth and Seventh Aves.), WV	

Teen-appropriate gifts and gadgets. Look for insightful T-shirts, hip messenger-type bags, and other retro cool gift items. Also lunch boxes and stuffed animals.

E.A.T. Gifts   PK/K/PT/T
1062 Madison Avenue (between   212-861-2544
80th and 81st Sts.), UES

This store is packed with original gift items. Look for tasteful piñatas, T-shirts, dolls, umbrellas, mini dollhouse accessories, jewelry, and books. You'll be able to find something for everyone on your list here.

★ *girlprops.com*   PK/K/PT/T
153 Prince Street (downstairs,   212-505-7615
West Broadway), SH

This store is an absolute bonanza for every girl! There are thousands of items to choose from, which is difficult to believe, considering how small the space is. Despite the pricey location, the motto is "Inexpensive . . . we never say cheap." One step inside and you'll see it's true: Power bracelets are a mere $0.99, bead bracelets are twelve for $1.99, and real feather boas (something every family should have) are only $7.99. Whatever a girl's budget, she'll be able to spend it here.

It's a Mod, Mod World   K/PT/T
85 First Avenue (between   212-460-8004
Fifth and Sixth Aves.), EV

A hip Village gift store where they make lots of their own products and also carry some of the usuals, like candles, journals, CDs, salt and pepper shakers, and ashtrays.

La Brea	K/PT/T
1321 Second Avenue (between 69th and 70th Sts.), UES	212-879-4065
1575 Second Avenue (between 81st and 82nd Sts.), UES	212-772-2640
2130 Broadway (between 74th and 75th Sts.), UWS	212-873-7850
2440 Broadway (at 90th St.), UWS	212-724-2777

Unique and funny gifts and gadgets: T-shirts, cards, candles, bath crystals, glow-in-the-dark finger paints, and other nifty bric-a-brac.

★ *New York Firefighter's Friend*	K/PT/T
263 Lafayette Street (between Prince and Spring Sts.), LI	212-226-3142
	www.nyfirestore.com

This is a great stop for any firefighting enthusiast in the family. They carry all sorts of firefighter stuff: fire trucks (the toy kind), T-shirts, caps, teddy bears, books, pajamas, raincoats, and, of course, boots. It's not primarily a toy store, though, but rather a store for people seriously interested in firefighting.

One Shubert Alley	PK/K/PT/T
1 Shubert Alley (between 44th and 45th Sts. at Broadway and Eighth Ave.), MTW	212-944-4133

A good stop for those looking to buy Broadway souvenirs. T-shirts, buttons, and posters are at the top of the list for New York City gifts.

Popover's Plums	PK/K/PT/T
555 Amsterdam Avenue (at 87th St.), UWS	212-496-9648

A wide selection of gift items and trinkets ranging from stuffed animals to jewelry and candles.

P.S. I Love You	K/PT/T
1242 Madison Avenue (between	212-722-6272
89th and 90th Sts.), UES	

Best for girls, this store specializes in gifts and trinkets. Look for campy T-shirts (good for the boys too), silver jewelry, purses, candles, boxer shorts, pens, cards, and other gifty items.

Ricky's New York City	K/PT/T
590 Broadway (between	212-226-5552
Prince and Houston Sts.), SH	

If the wide selection of boas doesn't draw you into this store, perhaps the strobe lights and pulsing, youthful crowd will. Originally more of a cosmetics-type store, Ricky's still carries a wide range of hair care products, along with the newer additions (key chains, jewelry, kitschy lunch boxes, brightly colored wigs, and other fun stuff).

United Nations	K/PT/T
First Avenue (between 45th	212-963-4465
and 46th Sts.), MTE	

Stop in here after your UN visit because this is a great place to buy meaningful gifts and souvenirs. The complex has multiple shops within it, but

Chinatown is gift central

Helpful Hint

Visit busy areas like Times Square and the South Street Seaport first thing in the morning and midweek to avoid unpleasant crowds.

the most promising for kids are the post office (for stamp collecting), bookshop, and the main gift shop, on the lower level. Many children find the postcards featuring flags of all of the participating UN countries a good purchase, as well as calendars, dolls, and books.

Hobbies and Crafts

★ *America's Hobby Center* 146 West 22nd Street (between Sixth and Seventh Aves.), CH	K/PT/T 212-675-8922

An excellent destination for an extremely extensive (they do a huge mail order and even an export business) selection of models, including model rockets, boats, trains, cars, airplanes, and even the equipment to upgrade models to remote control.

Gampel Supply 39 West 37th Street, MTW	K/PT/T 212-398-9222

This neighborhood is rife with accoutrements for every creative child: Beads, feathers, patches, you name it, they've got it. Wander up and down 37th and 38th Streets and along Sixth Avenue to see the selection and pick your favorite shop.

Jan's Hobby Shop 1557 York Avenue (between 82nd and 83rd Sts.), UES	K/PT/T 212-861-5075

Everything the aspiring or expert model builder needs, including paints, books, brushes, and the models themselves. If your child is a real enthusiast, be sure to spend a minute talking to Fred, the proprietor who has turned his love for building models into a very successful career.

Lee's	K/PT/T
220 West 57th Street (between	**212-247-0110**
Seventh Ave. and Broadway), MTW	

Lee's sells an enormous collection of supplies for the professional artist and draftsman.

★ *New York Central Art Supply*	K/PT/T
62 Third Avenue (between	**212-473-7705**
10th and 11th Sts.), EV	

A top pick for art supplies, especially paper—both homemade and commercial. Some fans say they have the best selection in the United States, others say it's the best in the world. There's only one way to find out . . .

★ *Pearl Paint*	K/PT/T
308 Canal Street (between	**212-431-7932**
Church St. and Broadway), CT	**www.pearlpaint.com**

Pearl Paint is a New York classic. It offers discounted prices on all tools that any artist, budding or professional, could wish for. The store has grown over the years and now not only occupies the entire building at 308 Canal, but also has offshoots (framing, paint, office accoutrements) out the back door and down the block.

Red Caboose	PK/K/PT/T
23 West 45th Street (downstairs,	**212-575-0155**
between Fifth and Sixth Aves.), MTW	

Everything the young train enthusiast could ever hope for and more. Complete train sets and accessories for the beginner, and

collectibles for older kids (and adults). The selection is great, and
the prices won't leave you short of breath.

Learning Tip

Pier 17 and much of the South Street Seaport are built on
"reclaimed land." It used to be under water. Term paper
idea: Where was the original shorefront road near the
South Street Seaport? What is/was its name? How many
extra streets were added by reclaiming land during the
eighteenth and nineteenth centuries? When was the South
Street Seaport turned into a shopping district and how
many years later was Pier 17 added?

Magic

Abracadabra	**K/PT/T**
19 West 21st Street (between	**212-627-5194**
Fifth and Sixth Aves.), CH	

Look for everything from make-up and costumes to props, wigs,
gags, magic, and hats.

★ *Flosso Hornmann Magic Co.*	**K/PT/T**
45 West 34th Street (6th fl., rm. 606;	**212-279-6079**
between Fifth and Sixth Aves.,), GD	

This shop has been around since 1869, and if that isn't enough
to impress you, perhaps this will: It's the oldest magic shop in
the world. Amateurs and professionals alike flock to this well-
stocked magic museum, and the kind staff puts on little shows
for the kids.

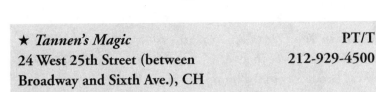

★ *Tannen's Magic*   PT/T
24 West 25th Street (between   212-929-4500
Broadway and Sixth Ave.), CH

You're just as welcome to stop in for a browse as for a shop at Tannen's, and chances are pretty good that you'll catch a spontaneous show if you hang around. Another of New York's favorite establishments, Tannen's is a perfect stop for magic lovers, whether they're beginners or advanced.

Music

Colony Record & Tape Center   T
1619 Broadway (at 49th St.), MTW/TS   212-265-2050

Specializing in hard-to-find titles, of interest mostly to collectors.

Generation Records   PT/T
210 Thompson Street (between   212-254-1100
Bleecker and West 3rd Sts.), WV

Specializing in new and used rock, alternative, gothic, industrial, punk, and hardcore music; available on compact disc, vinyl, cassette, and 7-inch singles.

Other Music   PT/T
15 East 4th Street (at Lafayette), EV   212-477-8150

Experimental and independent labels are the attraction at OM. If it's out there, OM is likely to have it, and the staff is extremely friendly so don't be afraid to ask.

Rocks in Your Head	PT/T
157 Prince Street (between	212-475-6729
West Broadway and Thompson St.), SH	

They could be friendlier in this well-stocked shop, but they won't bite, and the selection of new and used CDs and LPs is worth the effort. They also carry videos, books, and T-shirts.

Second Coming Records	PT/T
235 Sullivan Street (between	212-228-1313
3rd and Bleecker Sts.), WV	

New and used CDs, LPs, and cassettes—don't expect to find the Spice Girls here.

Tower Records	K/PT/T
692 Broadway (at West 4th St.), GV	212-505-1500

Tower Outlet	K/PT/T
20 East 4th Street (at Lafayette), GV	212-228-7317

The largest Tower in the City, the Outlet is a New York City original.

In addition to the record stores listed above, others are along St. Marks Place between Second and Third Avenues. Good for a browse, but know your prices because some of the spots along this street are a bit out of line.

Out of This World, Science-Related Stuff

★ *Maxilla & Mandible*	K/PT/T
451 Columbus Avenue (between	212-724-6173
81st and 82nd Sts.), UWS	

More like a museum than a store, M&M never fails to make an impression on those who enter this small shop. The stock ranges from boxed tropical insects (yes, they're dead and they're real) to seashells and skeletons. They even have a "want list" so you can make requests, and they'll see if they can find what you're looking for.

Star Magic	**K/PT/T**
745 Broadway (at Eighth Ave), EV	**212-228-7770**
1256 Lexington Avenue	**212-988-0300**
(at 85th St.), UES	

All kinds of books, toys, rocks and minerals, plastic dinosaur figures, holograms, stars and sparkles, music, planetarium kits, rockets, and dragon figurines. "Space age gifts," they say.

Helpful Hint

If shopping is becoming too time-consuming, set a time limit per store or per day so that the entire visit to New York City isn't spent inside stores.

Sports

★ *Ballet Shop*	**K/PT/T**
1887 Broadway (between	**212-581-7990**
62nd and 63rd Sts.), UWS	

As a young girl, this store was my absolute favorite stop on trips into the City to see the New York City Ballet and American Ballet Theater. Full of T-shirts, books, collector's items (signed toe shoes), music, and ballet trinkets. Any aspiring dancer will be in heaven in this one-of-a-kind store.

Blades Board & Skate	K/PT/T
120 West 72nd Street (between Broadway and Columbus Ave.), UWS	212-787-3911
659 Broadway (between Bond and Bleecker Sts.), EV	212-477-7350
Chelsea Piers, Pier 62, West 23rd Street (at West Side Hwy.), CH	212-336-6299
160 East 86th Street (between Lexington and Third Aves.), UES	212-996-1644
1414 Second Avenue (between 73rd and 74th Sts.), UES	212-249-3178

The name says it all.

Capezio	PK/K/PT/T
1650 Broadway (2nd fl.; at 51st St.), MTW	212-245-2130

There are a handful of Capezio stores throughout the City, but this one is the largest and stocks dancewear of all kinds.

Eastern Mountain Sports	K/PT/T
20 West 61st Street (between Broadway and Columbus Ave.), UWS	212-397-4860
591 Broadway (at Houston St.), EV	212-966-8730

A regional chain, EMS carries a full line of outdoor gear and equipment.

Learning Tip

Before there were cars, people got around New York City by horse. There are still stables in Manhattan and, amazing as it may sound, they're vertical—just like apartment buildings, but for horses. Term paper idea: Discuss the history, importance, and decline of the horse in the development of New York City.

★ *Miller's*	K/PT/T
117 East 24th Street (between Park and Lexington Aves.), GP	212-673-1400

Every time my husband's teenage niece visits the City from Seattle, Miller's is the first place she wants to go to check out the full line of equestrian equipment.

Modell's	K/PT/T
1535 Third Avenue (between 86th and 87th Sts.), UES	212-996-3800
200 Broadway (between Fulton and John Sts.), FD	212-964-4007
51 East 42nd Street (between Vanderbilt and Madison Aves.), MTE	212-661-4242

The reasonable prices at this sporting goods store should leave you with enough left over to take the kids on that tour of Madison Square Garden. Modell's, or Mo's as it is known locally, is reputed to be the oldest family-owned and operated sporting goods chain store in the country.

Paragon Sports	K/PT/T
867 Broadway (at 18th St.), US	212-255-8036

Paragon started out as a small-time sporting goods store and has expanded to include everything from hiking and camping gear to equipment for tennis, skiing, and in-line skates. Certainly not the cheapest (expect to pay retail), but it's the most extensive selection of so many items in any given place in the City.

Peck and Goodie	**K/PT/T**
917 Eighth Avenue (between	212-246-6123
54th and 55th Sts.), MTW	

A New York institution for skaters, Peck and Goodie stocks ice skates, inline skates, and even skateboards.

Soccer Sport Supply Company	**K/PT/T**
1745 First Avenue (between	212-427-6050
90th and 91st Sts.), UES	800-223-1010

The best (highest quality and best selection) soccer and rugby gear around. This store does a tremendous amount of mail-order business both nationally and internationally.

Tent & Trails	**K/PT/T**
21 Park Place (between	212-227-1760
Broadway and Church St.), FD	

By far the best camping store in the City. I have outfitted myself for many weekend camping outings as well as intense Himalayan treks and backpacking trips here. They have everything you need, a knowledgeable if somewhat ornery staff, and amazingly low prices. They pack into three floors what suburban stores would display in twenty. If you don't see it, ask for it because it's probably hidden behind three other items.

Yankees Clubhouse Shop	**K/PT/T**
393 Fifth Avenue (between	212-685-4693
36th and 37th Sts.), MTE	
110 East 59th Street (between	212-758-7844
Park and Lexington Aves), UES	
8 Fulton Street (at South	212-514-7182
Street Seaport), FD	

This is the place to outfit yourself for a ball game or to buy souvenirs.

Money-Saving Tip

Set an allowance for children in advance—and tell them about it—so that they know they can make a finite number of New York City purchases on the trip, and they can plan accordingly. This will save you money and stress; it will save your children from raised expectations and tantrums.

Theme Stores

Coca-Cola Fifth Avenue	PK/K/PT/T
711 Fifth Avenue (between	212-418-9260
55th and 56th Sts.), MT	

Fully stocked with Coca-Cola wear and gifts.

The Disney Store	PK/K/PT/T
711 Fifth Avenue (at 55th St.), MTE	212-702-0702
141 Columbus Avenue (at 66th St.), UWS	212-362-2386

It speaks for itself—the largest store is on Fifth Avenue.

NBA Store	K/PT/T
666 Fifth Avenue (at 52nd St.), MTE	212-515-6221

A full complement of National Basketball Association clothing and accessories.

Nike Town	K/PT/T
6 East 57th Street (between	212-891-6453
Fifth and Madison Aves.), MTE	

This is more of a Nike museum than a store, though everything is for sale, including all the most recent styles.

Pokémon Center NY	PK/K/PT/T
10 Rockefeller Plaza (at 48th St.,	212-307-0900
between 5th and 6th Aves.), MTW	

The new Pokémon Center, located in Rockefeller Center, is a must for Pokémon aficionados. It's chock full of new and exclusive merchandise as well as unique Pokémon attractions, such as the Ultra Pokédex, the Gotta Catch 'em All! Station, animatronic characters throughout the store, a sound and light show, the PoKéBaLL, and the Pokémon Trainer Gym.

Warner Bros. Studio Store	PK/K/PT/T
1 Times Square (at Broadway	212-840-4040
and 42nd St.), TS	

See the Quick Guide to Theme Restaurants in chapter 6 for related theme stores.

Toys

A Bear's Place	PK/K
789 Lexington Avenue (between	212-826-6465
61st and 62nd Sts.), UES	

A good selection of wooden toys and puzzles, unique puppets, games, and furniture. The emphasis here is on toys that are unique or very distinctive.

Big City Kite Co.	K/PT/T
1210 Lexington Avenue	212-472-2623
(at 82nd St.), UES	

A small store with a big inventory of kites and every kite-flying accessory imaginable: Books, videos, and other simple flying objects.

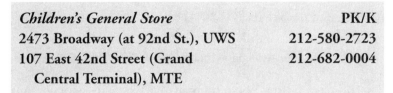

Children's General Store	PK/K
2473 Broadway (at 92nd St.), UWS	212-580-2723
107 East 42nd Street (Grand Central Terminal), MTE	212-682-0004

A nice selection of children's toys that you won't find everywhere else.

| **Chimera** | PK/K/PT/T |
| 77 Mercer Street (between Spring and Broome Sts.), SH | 212-334-4730 |

Chimera is full of nifty novelties of all sizes and shapes. The merchandise is mainly geared toward older children and adults, but there's a good inventory of stuffed animals for younger kids.

| **Classic Toys** | PK/K/PT/T |
| 218 Sullivan Street (between Bleecker and West 3rd Sts.), WV | 212-674-4434 |

Great for children who are into vehicles, this store specializes in toy soldiers, cars, and airplanes for play and for collecting. Also stuffed animals.

Union Square Greenmarket

★ *Cozy's Cuts for Kids*   **PK/K**
1125 Madison Avenue (at 84th St.), UES   212-744-1716
448 Amsterdam Avenue (at 81st St.), UWS 212-579-2600

The primary purpose of most visits to Cozy's is haircuts, but there's also a nifty selection of toys, bath toys and products, hair care items and accessories, puzzles, bubbles, dolls, and books.

Dinosaur Hill   **PK/K**
306 East 9th Street (between   212-473-5850
First and Second Aves.), EV

Dinosaur toys, stuffed animals, and puppets are the theme of the house, but don't be discouraged if your child isn't in the dinosaur craze—plenty of other enchanting options are available, with an especially quirky appeal. The store is particularly hospitable to browsers.

★ *Enchanted Forest*   **PK/K**
85 Mercer Street (between   212-925-6677
Spring and Broome Sts.), SH

When your children walk into the Enchanted Forest, it's as if they're walking into a fantasy land. There are tin toys and stuffed toys, toys that evoke past eras, and toys straight out of the imagination. Don't expect to find things that you'd see in chain toy stores; everything about this store is unique, especially the toys. A good place to stop for a break from the City.

★ *FAO Schwarz*   **PK/K/PT/T**
767 Fifth Avenue (between 58th and   212-644-9400
59th Sts.), MT

This is more of a destination than a place to shop (though you certainly can buy plenty of incredible stuff here). People literally line up at the entrance to get in at busy times of the year, and they find it well worth the wait. Full of every kind of stuffed animal (half a floor's worth), multitudes of board games, books, infant toys and accessories, a candy department, a whole line of Barbie dolls and accessories, not to mention the $19,500 mini-Range Rover! Every child is sure to delight in a visit to this store. Allow plenty of time to explore.

Geppetto's Toybox	PK/K/PT
10 Christopher Street (between	**212-620-7511**
Greenwich and Gay Sts.), WV	

A unique selection of new (for newborn to 12) and collectible toys, including Teddy bears, dolls, party favors, rocking horses, and others.

Hornboms	PK/K
1500 First Avenue (between	**212-717-5300**
78th and 79th Sts.), UES	

Carries a wide variety of toys, including some specialty toy store items (including the entire line of Thomas the Tank toys and Brio) and some mass market (like Fisher-Price) too. The selection is primarily aimed at children 5 and under.

Mary Arnold Toys	PK/K/PT/T
1010 Lexington Avenue (between	**212-744-8510**
72nd and 73rd Sts.), UES	

Toys for all ages of children and also adults. Also a small selection of baby equipment and furniture, like rockers and chairs.

Penny Whistle Toys	PK/K/PT
448 Columbus Avenue (between 81st and 82nd Sts.), UWS	212-873-9090
1283 Madison Avenue (between 91st and 92nd Sts.), UES	212-369-3868

Very popular with neighborhood kids, Penny Whistle carries a good selection of quality toys neatly packed into tight surroundings.

★ *Toys "R" Us*	PK/K/PT/T
1514 Broadway (at 44th St.), MTW	800-869-7787
www.toysrus.com	

The Toys "R" Us flagship store is hardly "just" a toy store. At 110,000-square-feet, this glass-enclosed building is the largest toy store in the world and the largest retail store in Times Square. And with a 60-foot-tall Ferris wheel, a giant roaring dinosaur, a life-size Barbie townhouse, and three floors of toys and games, it certainly gives the New York Favorite FAO Schwarz a run for its money.

West Side Kids	PK/K
498 Amsterdam Avenue (at 84th St.), UWS	212-496-7282

A great neighborhood toy store with a promising selection of toys, games, dolls and furniture, books, book-related videos, plush animals, and other tantalizing treats.

Money-Saving Tip

Before you visit stores like FAO Schwarz, explain to your children that it's not about buying, but rather it's about the experience—sort of like an interactive museum, only better. They can play with, touch, read, and experiment with toys without buying them, which isn't possible at most other toy stores. Much of the merchandise at fancy toy stores is available elsewhere for less.

INDEX TO SHOPPING BY NEIGHBORHOOD

Index
by Neighborhood

Index

A